The Christian Missionaries in Coastal Maharashtra

The Christian Missionaries in Coastal Maharashtra

Encapsuling their Historical, Social, Educational, Medical & Literary Endeavours

Dr. Neeta M. Khandpekar, D. Litt
Department of History, University of Mumbai
Mumbai / India

CWI
Christian World Imprints(TM)

First Published in 2015 by

Christian World Imprints(TM)
Christian Publishing & Books from India
H-12 Bali Nagar, **New Delhi-110015**
info@christianworldimprints.com
www.ChristianWorldImprints.com
Phone: +91 11 25465925 Fax: +91 11 25173055

ISBN-13: 978-93-5148-034-1 (HB) ISBN-10: 93-5148-034-8 (HB)
ISBN-13: 978-93-5148-056-3 (PB) ISBN-10: 93-5148-056-9 (PB)

Cataloging in Publication Data--DK
Courtesy: D.K. Agencies (P) Ltd. <docinfo@dkagencies.com>

Khandpekar, Neeta M. author.
The Christian missionaries in coastal Maharashtra : encapsuling their historical, social, educational, medical & literary endeavours / Dr. Neeta M. Khandpekar, D. Litt (Department of History, University of Mumbai).
pages cm
Includes bibliographical references (pages) and index.
ISBN 9789351480341 (HB)
ISBN 9789351480563 (PB)

1. Missionaries--India--Maharashtra. 2. Maharashtra (India)--Church history. I. Title.

DDC 266.0095479 23

The maps used in this book are not to scale.

Printed at Chawla Offset Printers

This book is dedicated to
Dr. R. H. H. Goheen –
The Magician of the Surgical Knife

DALTON STATE

DALTON STATE COLLEGE — UNIVERSITY SYSTEM OF GEORGIA

Monday, August 18, 2014

Foreword

It is an honor to introduce Dr. Neeta M. Khandpekar's work on Christian Missions in the Coastal Maharashtra (Konkan) region of India. Readers will find that it is a valuable telling of the story of men and women who devoted themselves to the care of Indians in need and the consequences of their works.

The main focus is on the work of Catholic and Protestant Missions. The Presbyterian Mission happens to be one of the Chief Protestant Missions and many of their extant records are stored in the Presbyterian Historical Society in Philadelphia, Pennsylvania. This is a work well worth reading because it brings to light their stories with personal touches. It also shows the manner in which their story fits into the larger picture of modern Indian history.

Readers should appreciate the fact it is valuable to have the story of Christian Missions in India told by scholars from different religious traditions. Works such as this one provide readers with a different perspective than those written in British colonial times or that a Christian worldview would provide. And a book such as this one also adds to a more diverse historical understanding of India.

When Dr. Khandpekar visited the United States I was able to offer some guidance about where to go for resources and to arrange contacts to help with research. It is always a delight to see younger colleagues one aids along the way accomplish good things such as this book. So it is with an almost parental pride that I commend this book to you the reader.

Dr. Jack Waskey

Reverend Andrew J. Waskey, PCUSA, honorably retired

Pastor Emeritus, Morton Memorial Presbyterian Church

Professor of Social Science, Dalton State College, Dalton, Georgia (USA)

650 COLLEGE DRIVE *DALTON, GEORGIA *30720-3797 *Ph. 706-272-2691 *Fax 706-272-2698 *800-829-4436

AN EQUAL OPPORTUNITY/AFFIRMATIVE ACTION PROGRAM INSTITUTION www.daltonstate.edu

Preface

The coastal region of Maharashtra can be broadly classified as North Konkan and South Konkan. My M.Phil dissertation (1995) covered Seventeenth Century history of specific ports of Chaul, Dabhol, Rajapur and Vengurla. The Socio-Economic study of the entire Konkan coastline (Sixteenth and Seventeenth Century history) was undertaken as a doctoral project. My study in this region for about a decade brought forth frequent evidences of humanitarian work done by Christian Missionaries in diverse fields. The three year postdoctoral research award of UGC, New Delhi went a long way in fulfilling the motive of undertaking it as a major project. The review of reference material in this direction showed complete lack of specific Missionary works in the Konkan region while those available were of very general nature.

The present work covers a majority of Missionary stations along the coast line of Maharashtra (Konkan) with evidences of cross- links with Missionary stations of Ahmednagar as well as those as far as Madras, Gujarat, Calcutta and Agra. In this process, some of the left out stations do deserve some attention and may be taken as future projects.

The timely help rendered by the Missionaries in the field of medicine and education remains unmatched. The techniques used especially in surgery were far ahead of its times. The Missionary habit of recording the day to day events and publishing them in newspapers, weeklies and other bulletins of those days go a long way in shaping this project. The dedication of the Missionaries to various fields is noticeable. In fact the families of the Missionaries were involved in this work. While working in Vengurla, I came across St. Lukes Hospital which was established under the leadership of Dr. R. H. H. Goheen who with his family was deputed to this region. Dr. R. H. H. Goheen, a medical doctor by profession is still remembered as '*Govind Doctor*' and the St. Lukes Hospital as '*Batyacha Dawakhana*' in the Vengurla town. Goheen the medical legend established the St. Lukes Hospital and performed surgeries unmatched during those times. The hospital had patients from as far as Goa. Later, the Leprosarium and Tuberculosis Centre were added to the existing structure of the Hospital. St. Lukes Hospital is no more functional. Traces of educational work carried out by the wives of the Missionaries in support of Mission are visible. Prof. Robert Goheen was born at Vengurla had opportunity to visit his birth place as US Ambassador to India in 1977. He could provide direct information on his father through our correspondence for about 3 years just before his death in Princeton, USA in 2007. Prof. Goheen had shared the valuable family photographs and information leading to the family tree of the Goheens. In fact it calls for a special biography covering the works of his father Dr. R. H. H. Goheen. After Dr. Goheen's tenure, two more Surgeon's won the heart of local community namely late Dr. Lester Servid followed by Dr. Ronald Seaton both presently in USA who have provided data for the current project.

Systematic research methodology and fresh data inputs have been gathered and compiled in the present work. The current book is aimed at providing help to future research scholars, educationalists and social workers. It is strongly felt that the Missionary methods of recording, publishing, providing education through different channels, involvement and initiative would surely provide a platform for improvement in any education system. The impact of Missionary efforts to establish educational and medical stations with dedicated staff are even visible today. Their social contribution in the field of education for women, disabled children and aged population is of much relevance even in present times.

An attempt has been made to study the social work of Missionaries along with its progression and impact. The present work has been divided into ten chapters.

Chapter 1 tries to trace the first Missionaries who had arrived along with the foreign powers through the sea route. It introduces the word Missionary and its definition in the Christian faith and perspective. This is followed by the classification of various Missionary orders and establishment of Churches. A brief coverage of the review of the Church histories has been carried out.

Chapter 2, 3 and 4 are devoted to the major social activities which include.,

1. The Education Mission
2. The Medical Mission and
3. The Social and Religious Mission

This research aims to illustrate the process of interaction between Euro-American Missionaries and the natives. In this neo liberal era with immense socio-cultural changes occurring especially through social contact, the present work deals with the two faced formula namely the backward looking and forward looking in the context of Christian Missionaries.

An exhaustive number of primary references like the *Bombay Guardian, Western India Notes, Oriental Christian Spectator* have been used and the relevant information has been provided to bring out the efforts of the Missionaries in the field of education, medicine and others solely in the context as a social machinery.

The pioneering work of Christian Missions in the educational and medical field has been systematically brought out and presented which forms the essence of this book. Efforts are made to include the mathematical figures/data relevant to the explanation. A large number of illustrations/ pictures have been incorporated. At places the plates of original scripts of references have been added to make the work more appealing.

The educational work includes the work of various Missionaries. The starting days of their work marks this chapter. Establishment of Printing Press for bringing out the first text books in Vernacular and English language has been dealt with. The other important issues covered include the education for women, Sunday Schools, technical education, tract and book society etc.

The present premier institutions conducted under the guidance of Missionaries imparting education in the Mumbai and Kalyan regions of Maharashtra has been brought out in detail. These institutes are the real life examples of the sustained efforts of the Missionary work started centuries back. The educational institutes include St. Xaviers College, Mumbai (an autonomous institution now), Sophia College, Mumbai, Nirmala Niketan, Mumbai, Wilson College, Mumbai and The Old Lourdes School, Kalyan. An attempt has been made to present individual institution's efforts in imparting quality education to the students as well as the social activities conducted for the benefit of the society.

The founding years of the Medical Mission, its propagation and impact in the coastal areas of Maharashtra with special reference to Vengurla has been studied. The Presbyterian Mission of the Western India having head quarters at Miraj near Kolhapur (ghat region) had played a major role in Vengurla.

In context of women education, the Zenana work, the industrial work, Sunday schools for the social as well as religious purposes have been highlighted in Chapter 4. The lesser known 'Salvation Army' an organization of Missionaries is also included.

Chapter 5 includes the literary works of Christian Missionaries through their write ups in the news bulletins, magazines and books. Special efforts are made to discuss and display the channels of propagation of faith and education through the local weekly like *Bombay Guardian. The Western India Notes* was a regular news bulletins covering various aspects of Christian literature. The works were further supported by the publications in *Oriental Christian Spectator*, *Missionary Herald, Dyanodaya, International Bulletin, The Voice of India, The Examiner, The Catholic News Review* and *The Telegraph and Courier News Paper* have been studied and presented in this chapter. The plates showing the first page of original sources have been included for most of the newsletters/ bulletins.

Chapter 6 covers the Indian contribution to the Missionary work. The Indian converts (Indian Missionaries) who carried forward the work of Original Christian Missions have been dealt with. Their views and extensive writings bring out the impact of the Christian Missions in a big way. The works of Baba Padmanji, Rev.

Narayan Sheshadri, Pandita Ramabai, Rev. N. V. Tilak etc have been highlighted. A brief account of the initial years of their conversion is included to have a complete view of the social situation.

Sharada Sadan, the brain child of Pandita Ramabai and her work for the deprived class of the society has been brought out. The 'Opium Trade' and the role played by the Missionaries in its control and eradication have been dealt with.

The process of inculturation is covered in Chapter 7. The process and impact of inculturation in the Vasai region of the Maharastra has been highlighted. The Uran pocket of Maharashtra has also been included in the inculturation process. The chapter includes illustrations such as 'Christ in Yogic Mudra', Indianisation of religious literature/ prayers, Symbols of all faiths etc. The role of Jeevan Darshan Kendra, Vasai in the process of inculturation has been included. The overall efforts of the Christian community of Vasai in this direction have been highlighted in this chapter.

Chapter 8 covers the four major issues during second half of the nineteenth century which became the centre of concern for the Missionaries. This chapter highlights the interesting ways they followed to make society aware about the prime issue of concern namely drinking habit, Anglo-Asiatic opium traffic, famine and plague. Thomas Evans and Canon Wilberforce's views on alcoholic drinks had been very forceful. Interest in the opium question was revived in the 1880's and 1890's, when a large-number of Missionaries had began to participate actively in the anti-opium crusade.

Chapter 9 introduces the Christian Voluntary movements and organizations like the Bombay Tract and Book Society (BTBS), Vernacular Christian Education, Young Women's Christian Association (YWCA), Young and Men's Christian Association (YMCA). The motives of these groups and their activities are presented in detail.

Chapter 10 includes the conclusion of the above work. It tries to judge and relate the impact of Christian Missionaries work in the present context. The main focus had been to study the efforts and culture needed to improving the standards of education in vernacular medium schools. It tries to bring out the structure of these institutions in sustaining and imparting quality education.

The dedication aspect of the medical work for the poor and the deprived class of the society is dealt with. The other branches of work having direct/indirect impact on the society as a whole have been brought out.

The Appendices include the letters of private correspondences and personal interview's along with the questionnaire. This is followed by exhaustive Bibliography/Reference material used in the book. The list of abbreviations and list of maps/ illustrations has been included at the beginning and the list of libraries referred along with their contents has been placed at the end of the book.

In a nutshell the Study is both descriptive and analytical based on primary as well as secondary sources of data. Various published and un-published records, books and journals were consulted. The primary data was collected through letter correspondence and interview schedules using a set of predetermined questions.

A picture tells a story some told, some untold, some waiting to be told and hence the work contains many pictures and photographs. The book is equally supported by wide number of illustrations and references. Primary sources have been used extensively along with direct inputs from the Missionaries who worked in the region of Konkan. The research dissertations available along with the local history from scholars of discrete regions of Konkan are included. This work was presented in more than 20 national and international conferences.

Prof. P. P. Mishra's expertise went a long way in structuring the present work. His constant support and guidance during my foreign visits gave me exclusive opportunities to place my work before international scholars. From bottom of my heart I would like to thank Prof. P. P. Mishra of Sambalpur University, Odisha and his wife for her wholehearted support during the tenure of this work.

My father in law Late Shri Madhukar Ramchandra Khandpekar had accompanied me to various research conferences and field work, I owe my dedication to him for this.

The field work was made possible by funds from UGC. The University Grants Commission (UGC) postdoctoral research award (2004-2007) could make this work come to its present form. The travel assistance for my visits to Malyasia and Rome were duly sponsored by Indian Council of Historical Research (ICHR) and UGC. Late Prof. T. V. Pathy of Aurangabad had been a source of inspiration throughout this work and his blessings would always remain with me. Detailed discussions with Shri Shriram Mantri and his support in present work is duly acknowledged.

Discussions with late Dr. Robert F Goheen (Professor at Princeton and US Ambassador to India in 1977), Dr. Ron and Edith Seaton (USA) and late Dr. Lester P. Servid (USA) went a long way in shaping this project.

The support provided by Principal Dr. Harsha Mehta, Principal Dr. Vaidehi Daptardar and Principal Dr. Sudha Vyas of KJSAC helped me in the completion of this work.

The Staff of History Department at Sambalpur as well as my institution were very kind to provide timely help in this direction.

Thanks are due to Prof. M. D. David, Bishop Thomas Dabre, Fr. Aubrey Mascerenhas, Fr. Julian Saldanha, Fr Rudolph Andrades, Mr. and Mrs. Dhanawade, Sister Dhanam, Sister Ananda, Sister Gaitonde, Fr. Jose Pereira, Fr Thomas Reddy, Fr. Prasad who helped me a great deal in locating and reading the historical sources with their knowledge of local history. Dr. Ambadas Manjulkar took me to JDV library, Pune for first time and I owe my thanks to him for this help.

Thanks are due to Prof. Chittabrata Palit, Prof. Ranjan Chakrabarti (Vice Chancellor, Vidyasagar University), Prof. Rattanlal Hangloo (Vice Chancellor, Kalyani University), Dr. Somnath Rode, Prof. Deepak Gaikwad (Head, Pune University), Prof. S. P. Pati and his wife (Sambalpur), Shri H. Naik (Mumbai), Prof Shobhanan (Kerala Univ), Prof. Sathiaraj Arulappan (Kerala), Fr. Noel Seth (Pune Papal Seminary), Fr. Machardo (Lourdes School, Kalyan), Fr. Britto (Vasai), Prof. Ruby Maloni (Head, Department of History, University of Mumbai), Prof. Jack Waskey (Dalton, USA), Shalva Weil (Israel), Prof. Joseph Bara (JNU), Principal Dr. Tarun Barnabas (Ahmednagar College), Shri B. L. Shah ji (Century Rayon, HO) and Shri B. L. Malooji (ex Indophil, Philippines).

The constant support of my husband Dr. Mahendra and my affectionate children Omkar and Avani was always with me. My in-laws, parents and brother Bhavesh and his wife Namita rendered valuable support. I shall thank my student Anurag Patil who helped me to read the initial draft. I wish to thank staff of Maharashtra State Archives., Mumbai, Goa Archives, Asiatic Library (Mumbai), St. Xaviers College: Heras Institute of Indian History and Culture Library (Mumbai), Sophia Centre for Women, Nirmala Niketan Library, Baisinger Memorial Library (Miraj), St. Pius Seminary Library (Mumbai), Vasai Jeevan Kendra, University of Mumbai and various other libraries in and around Maharashtra and Goa.

I am deeply grateful to many people who helped me during this study. I would like to thank many individuals whose exchange of ideas, data and general companionship helped me in the quest for the history of the period.

Dr. Neeta M. Khandpekar
Department of History
University of Mumbai
Santacruz (E), Vidyanagari
Mumbai- 400 098, India
Email: neeta_khandpekar@yahoo.com

Prominent Abbreviations Used

Abbreviation	**Detail**
BG	Bombay Guardian
OCS	Oriental Christian Spectator
WIN	Western India Notes
BTBS	Bombay Tract and Book Society
BABS	Bombay Auxiliary Bible Society
YWCA	Young Women's Christian Association
YMCA	Young Men's Christian Association
IHS	Iesus Huminious Salvator
OUP	Oxford University Press
ZBMM	Zenana Bible and Medical Mission
CMAI	Christian Medical Association of India
APM	American Presbyterian Mission
AMM	American Marathi Mission
CMS	Church Missionary Society
IMS	Indian Museum Society
SJ	Society of Jesus
SPG	Society for the Propagation of Gospel
ME	Methodist Episcopical
SPCK	Society for Promotion of Christian Knowledge
OP	Ouday Prabha (Marathi)
CVES	Christian Vernacular Education Society

DNA	Daily News Analysis
EPW	Economic and Political Weekly
IA	Indian Antiquary
IHC	Indian History Congress
OL	Our Lady
IFNS	Indian Female Normal School
SPFEE	Society for Promoting Female Education in the East
CHAI	Church History Association of India
CMJI	Christian Medical Journal of India
CMAI	Christian Medical Association of India (formerly MMA- Medical Missionary Association)
NCERT	National Council Of Educational Research And Training
CCS	Child-Centred System
CCR	Congregation of Carmellite Religious

Maps, Figures, Pictures, Charts, Tables, Slides & Plates
(Chapter-wise)

Chapter-1

Chapter-2

Chapter-3

Chapter-4

Chapter-5

Chapter-6

Chapter-7

Chapter-8

Chapter-9

Contents

Chapter 1

Advent of Christianity in India

Chapter 1

Advent of Christianity in India

1.1 An Introduction

The work of Missions in Western India became more visible with the invasion of foreign powers in this region. The historical records prove the influence of their work on the social and cultural fabric of the country. This present work makes an endeavor to analyze Missionary programme with its diverse ramifications in coastal belt of Maharashtra.

The glamour of the East and the rich and highly lucrative spice trade of India attracted maritime nations of Europe to explore the opportunities as early as 15th Century[1]. The presence of foreign power led to a host of Missionary activities in the region. Together with evangelical activities the Christian Missionaries have established schools, dispensaries and provided amenities as books, clothing and scholarships for their converts. Nonetheless Missionaries have been often criticized for offering these benefits.

The sea route through which the foreign powers entered and settled in India gave rise to Missionary activities on the coast and their penetration in the inlands. The earlier Missionaries came from the Iberian Peninsula.

---

1 M. J. Seth, "The Second Oldest Christian Church in Bengal" in *Bengal Past and Present,* January – June 1936, p. 43

Maharashtra happens to be a geographical unit with distinct individuality as reflected from its culture and economic life. Coastal Maharashtra is synonymous with the Konkan coast extending from Daman Ganga river in the north to the Terekhol river in the south. The coast of Maharashtra ranges from Dahanu (Thane District) to Vengurla (Sindhudurg District in South Konkan). The coast line covers a distance of 500 kms from north to south as shown in the (Map 1.1.) Administratively, it includes districts of Thane, Raigad, Ratnagiri, Sindhudurg and Mumbai. The cultural and economic life in turn leans heavily on the coastal capital, Bombay (now Mumbai). No other town either on the same coast or on the eastern side of the Indian Peninsula dominates its hinterland as completely as does Mumbai. Mumbai bears the imprint of successive cultures which have thrived here from

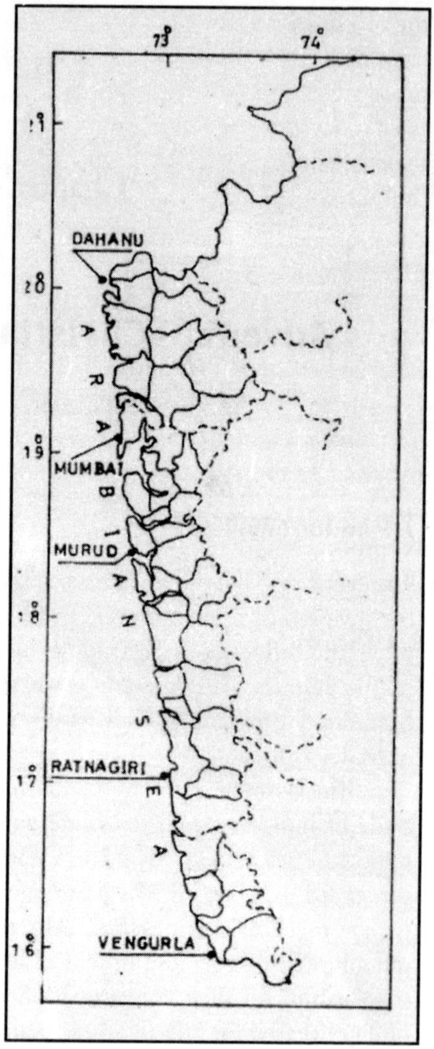

Map 1.1

Coast line of Maharashtra (Konkan belt) (Source : Shrikant Karlekar, "Geo Morphology of the Konkan Coast", in *Geography of Maharashtra* edited by J Diddee, S. R. Joag, Kale and Datye, New Delhi, 2002, p.59)

the original Koli islanders to the British empire-builders. The social transformation brought by the Missionaries namely the 'inculturation process' has shaped Mumbai right from the Pre-Portuguese period. Even today when the foreign powers are no more politically involved, their Missionary activity is on. The convent schools form one of the prominent Missionary activities. It would be fruitful to bring out a systematic account of Missionary activities on the coast of Maharashtra from past to present.

The coastal belt of Maharashtra based on its physical and cultural characteristics is divided into North Konkan, Middle Konkan and South Konkan. The North Konkan extends from Dahanu to Karanja. It includes Vasai, Mumbai, Thana and Kalyan. The middle Konkan is the coast line between Uran to Srivardhan. It coincides with Raigad district formerly known as Kolaba district. The South Konkan includes Ratnagiri and Sindhudurg coastal divisions. Kankavali, Kudal, Sawantwadi, Malvan and Vengurla[2] fall under its jurisdiction.

1.2 The Missionary and the Mission Work

Christianity is itself an Asiatic religion. In returning to Asia, she is returning to her native land. There is no reason why Asia should look askance at her or refuse her a hearing. Europe was indebted to Asia for the light of true religion, before she presumed to offer to Asia again, a participation in its blessings. The manners and customs, the scenery and the social life that present themselves in the gospels actually find their counterpart much more in the customs, and usages, and environments of the people of this country, than in those of Englishmen. In its costume it is stranger to the men of Europe and of America, than to those of Asia[3].

H. W. Fry speaking on Missionary methods mentions most important branches of Missionary work along with Zenana as depicted below (Figure 1.1)

---

2 There was British India Company's steamer 'The Vingurla' in 1880 (*BG* March 16, 1880)

3 *Bombay Guardian (BG)*, April 25, 1857, Front Page

Fry speaks on Missionary enterprise be conducted on the soundest and best principles.

The question is frequently asked as to what is the best form of Missionary work? Some people object to education and even medical work, thinking that Missionary effort should be entirely confined to Evangelism.

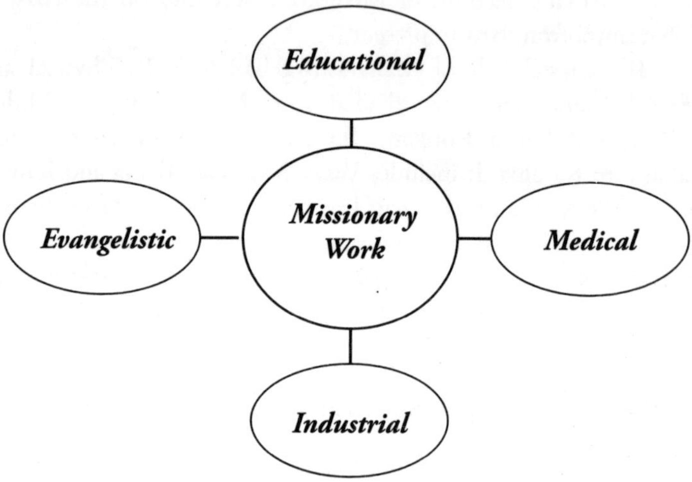

Figure 1.1: Classification of Missionary Work

Fry further says that evangelism has its place but since Missionaries and their flocks are residents of this world of pain and sorrow they should also pay attention to other branches.

Industrial Missionaries would not only be self supporting but they would help financially to support the Missions. It talks about the urgent need of Missionary helpers (self supporting industrial workers). They would be the Missionary's deacons, Sunday school teachers and general honorary assistants. They would form the rank and file of the workers and they would be just as eligible to bring forth the fruits of the spirit as the Missionary or Evangelist himself. Rev. T. Davis wrote an essay 'The Growth of Missions in Western India'[4], wherein he wrote the different Missionary societies here with their diverse methods of work were not sectarian like in west.

4 *BG* October 05, 1901, p.11

The Missionary work often concerns itself with the teaching of the Christian religion and subsequently, the organization of the Church as indigenous, national and catholic.

One of the most encouraging signs of Missionary work in the Presidency in the nineteenth century was the marked increase of the Christian agency. There were 1,946 Christian workers in 1900 of all kinds as against 1,073 in 1890. A comparative chart of Christian agencies during 1890-1900 is reproduced below (Table 1.1)

Table 1.1: Comparative chart of Christian Agencies during 1890 and 1900 (Source : *BG*, October 5, 1901, p.11)

Christian Agencies	*Year 1890*	*Year 1900*
Foreign Ordained Agents	96	116
Foreign Lady Agents	96	36
Foreign Lady Workers	69	164
Indian Ordained Agents	37	53
Indian Evangelists	231	426
Indian Teachers	349	641
Indian Female Workers	291	510
Total	**1,073**	**1,946**

Non Christian Agency	*Year 1890*	*Year 1900*
Non Christian Male Teachers	263	329
Non Christian Female Teachers	35	32
Total	**298**	**361**

The definition of the word Missionary varies. According to Rev. A Buzacott "a Missionary is necessarily a traveller and often in remote and unfamiliar countries, of which he is sometimes the discoverer and explorer"[5]. Amongst the meanings given in dictionary, the word 'Mission' comes from the Latin *missio* which means 'let go' or 'send'.

5 Rev. A. Buzacott, *Mission Life in the Islands of the Pacific*, John Snow and Co., London, 1966, p. 63

It further says 'Mission' means a series of special religious services to deepen or spread religious faith[6].

Sir Bartle Frere[7] in his work[8] defines Missionary work as to preach the Gospel message, and to put in the power of hearers fully to comprehend the scheme of redemption through Christ. Sometimes Missionaries have been called Philanthropist[9] and also Ambassador of the Cross. Christianity includes the concept of 'Missions' and Missionaries who acted as 'sacred specialists' and 'sacred intelligentsia' and served as carriers of Christian faith. They are said to be "the men sent by Christ to spread the Gospel and win souls for him"[10].

The early two stages of the History of Christian contacts with India shows the chief interest of Missions in the moral and religious transformations which they effect.

Rev. J Hudson Taylor delivered: 'Itineration far and near as an Evangelising Agency' lecture at Missionary conference in Shanghai on May 12, 1877. He further exclaims "Jesus went through all the cities and villages, teaching in their Synagogues, and preaching the Gospel of the Kingdom, and healing every sickness and every disease among the people." In this lecture he did not discuss relative merit of itinerant and localized Missionary work, and analogy has been made with merits of land and water, of mountains and plains, of animals and vegetables. He said "all exist, all are indispensable, the one does not supersede the other, but supplements it, and is its necessary complement"[11].

Of the first Indian Missionaries we have no account. There is a legend which attributes to the Apostle Thomas to the establishment of the Christian Church in India[12] (today's Syrian Christians

---

6 Readers Digest: *Universal Dictionary* (reprint), RD Association Ltd., UK, 1988, pp. 1988-89.

7 Was Governor of Bombay (1862-67).

8 Bartle Frere, *Indian Missions*, G.C.S.I & Co., London, 1873, p. 8.

9 Someone said that the man who would cause two blades of grass to grow where only one grew before is a Philanthropist.

10 As quoted in S. K. Bhattacharya, *Christian Missionaries and Indian Societies*, Mohit Publications, New Delhi, 1999, p. 4.

11 *BG*, January 19, 1878, front page.

12 John William K., *Christianity in India: A Historical Narrative*, Smith Elder and Co., London, 1859, p. 3.

especially of Kerala). On the Konkan coast the Apostle Bartholomew might have landed in Kalyan[13] in about 55 A. D. He preached by word of mouth and by example from the very beginning of his landing in Konkan. Sixth century Kalyan was visited by Cosmas Indikopleustes, who found there 'a Bishop who is appointed from Persia'. This presupposes the existence of a Christian Community at Kalyan. News of this Christianity was once more communicated to the West by the Zealous Dominican Jourdain (Jordanus) Catalani de Severac in the year 1321. He was the first Latin Missionary to arrive in North Konkan[14]. He had reached the shores of India from Persia in the Company of four Franciscan Friars, three priests, Frey Thomas of Tolentine, Frey James of Padua, Frey Peter of Sienna and one lay brother Frey Demetrius of Tiflis. These four Franciscans landed in Thana (Thane) where they were martyred a few days later. In the meantime Fr. Jourdain Baptized thirty-two Catechumens at Sopara[15], where he found many Nestorian Christians and a Church dedicated to St.Thomas, the Apostle. He also advised the Friars to come to Sopara because they would be well stationed there and would be able to live in common, and more so as this place was rich because of the fertility of the soil. Pope John XXII appointed Jordanus himself as the first Latin Bishop of this area. However, due to some adverse factors, the contact with the main Church was lost and the Christian communities in this area faded in to oblivion[16].

In the earlier periods (discussed above) Christianity was introduced by Missionaries or traders belonging to the Eastern Church who could not lay claim to any political power. The inherent power appealed to the religious sense of the people[17].

In the beginning of sixteenth century, Christianity entered upon a second stage of its history with the coming of the Portuguese

13 Kalyan refers to present day Kalyan in Thane district lying on the central railway.

14 Aiyangar S. History of The Syrian Church" in *The Quarterly Journal of the Mythic Society* Vol. 3, No.4, 1912, p.138.

15 Sopara refers to present day NalaSopara in Mumbai.

16 *Catholic Directory of the Archdiocese of Bombay*, 3rd Edition, Ahura Printing Press, Bombay, 1982, pp.1-2.

17 Oomman Philip "Christianity in India-Retrospect and Prospect" in *The Indian Review*, Vol. 46, No.2, February 1945, p. 76.

to India. Here, Christianity came with the sword of the Portuguese to parts of India, where the Portuguese had established political domination. The use of compulsion or force for attaining, what they conceived to be the highest good of those, who were outside the Church was but a part of the code of conduct of the Western Church of those days.

The Portuguese methods of coercion and persecution which they resorted to for the purpose of winning adherents to the Christian Church form one of the darkest chapters in the history of Christianity in India. But, at the same time this was a period when the Roman Church was launching its great Missionary enterprise. According to EGK Hewat, 1534-1600 was the period of great Mission founding.

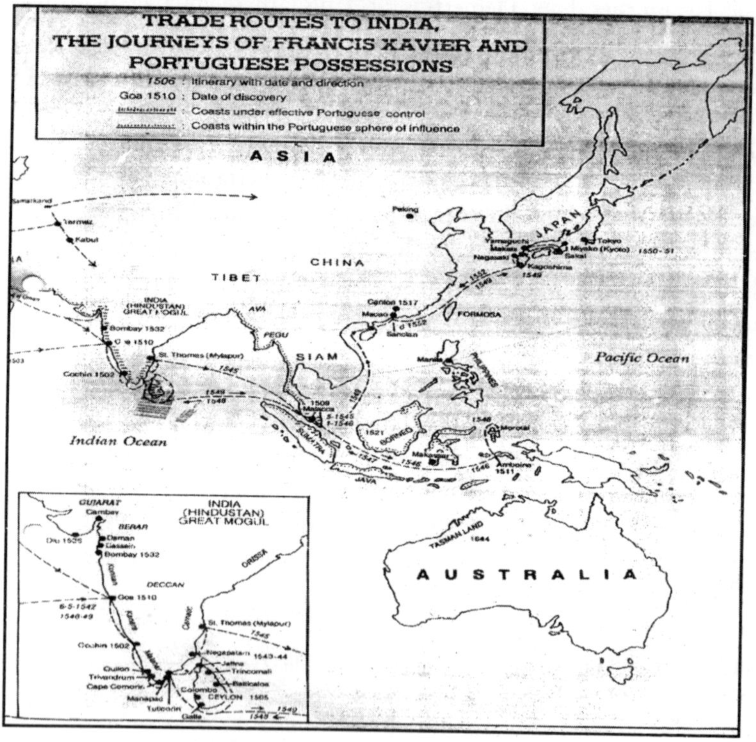

Map 1.2: Trade Routes to India
(Source: George Menechery ed. *The St. Thomas Christian Encylopedia of India,* Vol.1, Trichur, 1982, p.149)

Francis Xavier, the famous Missionary came to India (Map 1.2) at a time when Portuguese were at the zenith of political power. Printing in India owes its origin to Christian Missionaries from Portugal and the Netherlands (Holland) in Western Europe. The Jesuits brought the first printing press into India in 1550[18]. The activities of this press were restricted to print religious books, bilingual dictionaries and grammars that was essential to carry on their Missionary work[19]. The first Indian printed book 'St. Francis Xavier's Catechism of Christian Doctrine' came out in 1557. Father Stephens the first Englishman to visit India wrote '*Christian Purana*' which exercised great influence on Konkani Catholics[20].

1.3 The Missionary Orders

The four Missionary orders to carry the message of Christ were the Jesuit Order, Dominican Order, Franciscan Order and the Augustinian order.

1.3.1 The Jesuit Order

Picture 1.1:
St. Ignatius of Loyola
(Source: http://www.gonzaga.ie/home/files/032IgnatiusLoyola.jpg retrieved on 8th February 2009)

Ignatius of Loyola (1491-1556), son of a Spanish nobleman was severely wounded and crippled in the Spanish war of 1521 against France. While in hospital he read about the life of Christ and the Saints. Upon this he is said to have adopted to spend his life as a soldier for Christ. In 1534, after undergoing a spiritual conversion, he started an organization for clergy men to work wholly as

18 Chummar Choondal, *The Missionaries and Malayalam Journalism*, Minerva Books, Kerala, 1975, p. 28.

19 Piade Menezes Rodrigues, "Interactive Relationship between Goa and Bombay Journalism" in P. P. Shirodkar (ed), *Goa's External Relations*, Other India Book Store, Goa, 1992, p. 91.

20 C. S. Sreenivasa Charier "European Pioneer Studies in South Indian Languages" in *Bhartiya Vidya*, Vol. 5, Bombay, 1945, p. 72.

soldiers of Jesus in the Church in Paris. It was called Society of Jesus (it was an offshoot of neo-Catholicism)[21] wto be called 'Jesuits'.

Table 1.2: Some Jesuit Run Institutions of Mumbai

Institution	*Year*
St. Stanislaus High School (Bandra)	1863
St. Mary's High School (Mazgaon)	1864
St. Xavier's College	1869
St. Xavier's High School (Fort)	1869
Campion School (Colaba)	1943
Holy Family High School (Andheri)	1944
St. Xavier's Institute of Education (Churchgate)	1953
St. Xavier's Boys Academy (Churchgate)	1957
Gyanmata Adivasi Ashram Vidyalaya (Talaserri)	1996
St. Xavier's Institute of Engineering (Mahim)	2005

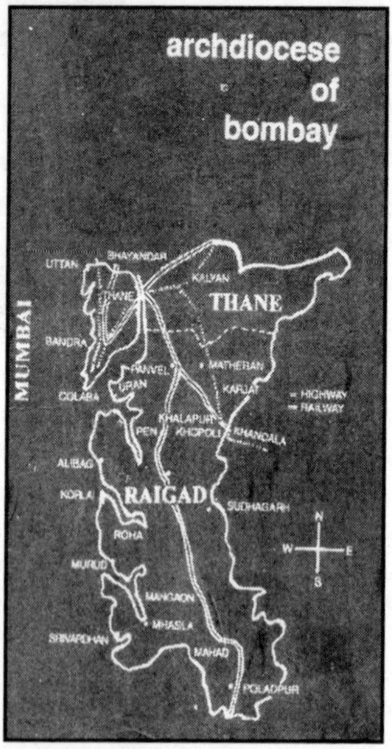

Map 1.3: Map of Archdiocese of Mumbai (Source: *The Directory of Archdiocese of Bombay*, 2004)

21 Rudolph Wittcower, *Art and Architecture in Italy 1600-1750*, Penguin Books, Harmondsworth, 1958, p. 3

The Jesuit Missionaries made the European world acquainted with the astronomy of the Hindus[22].

1.3.2 The Dominican Order

The Dominicans (from the pun 'Domini Canes'., the watch-dogs of the Lord and they are shown as black and white hounds guarding flock an attribute of St. Dominic himself is a black and white dog with a lighted torch in its mouth. Black and white are the colours of the Dominican habit)[23], a religious order known officially as Ordo Praedicalorum (Latin Order of Preachers, Black Friars or Jacobins was founded by a Spanish ecclesiast Dominic de Guzman (1170-1221) in 1216 in Italy to provide defenders of the Roman Catholic faith. It was he who arranged the rosary and instituted it as a religious exercise. St. Dominic almost carries a lily[24] (white as the austerity of his faith)[25]. See picture 1.2, of St. Dominic along with the symbol of Dominican order. This order exercises individual and corporate poverty, but is devoted mainly to preaching and teaching. The Friars of this new order were destined to serve among the people of the crowded cities and towns and not to live in monasteries[26].

This order has a fine record of learning {for example Thomas Aquinas (1225-1275) with his teacher Albertus Magnus} and also a Missionary activity having houses in every part of the Christian world.

---

22 *The Calcutta Review*, Vol. III, January – June 1845, p. 43

23 Peter and Linda Murray, *The Oxford Companion to Christian Art and Architecture*, OUP, New Delhi, 1996, p.138

24 The lily, it may be remarked , is given to those saints in holy orders who were pious from their earliest youth and not to those who had passed a gay time in the world before conversion.(Elizabeth Haig, *Loc.Cit*, p. 234)

25 Elizabeth Haig, *The Floral Symbolism of the Great Masters*, K. Paul, Trench, Trubner & Co. Ltd, London, 1913, pp. 232-33

26 Max Savelle, *A History of World Civilization,* 1960, Holt, Rineheart and Winston Publishers, USA, p. 512

To Praise
To Bless } *TRUTH*
To Preach

Picture 1.2: Statue of St. Dominic and Symbol of Dominican Order (Source: http://en.wikipedia.org/wiki/Saint_Dominic retrieved on 8th February 2009)

The black and white cross and the shield stand for Humility and truth and the dog with the lighted torch in its mouth symbolize "with the help of candle show the light to the world".

1.3.3 The Franciscan Order

Saint Francis of Assisi (1181/1182-1226) founded the Franciscans order. He himself called the members of his order the "little brothers" and this name is perpetuated in the official name which is the Order of Friars-Minor (also called Grey Friars)[27]. But, the official designation has never supplanted the popular name of Franciscans. The real name of Francis was Giovanni Bernardone. His father was a wealthy cloth merchant. As a young man, Francis led a happy and frivolous life and dreamed of heroic exploits. In 1202, he joined the young men of Assisi in a battle against the neighbouring city of

27 R. J. Unstead's *Dictionary of History*, Wardlock Publishers, New York, 1976, p. 92

Perugia. He was captured and endured a year in prison. This process was marked by an encounter with a leper and a call Francis believed he heard from God to repair a ruined Church standing near Assisi.

Picture 1.3: Portrait of St. Francis of Assisi and Stamp issued by India Post (Source:http://blogs.dixcdn.com/erica/wp-content/uploads/2008/09/stfrancis.jpg and http://www.indianpost.com/alpha.php/Alpha/Others retrieved on 8th February 2009)

By 1208, Francis had renounced all his belonging, including the clothes he was wearing and had accepted total poverty in imitation to Jesus Christ. Like the older forms of monastic life, the Franciscan system is founded on chastity, poverty and obedience, with the emphasis on the second.

St. Francis is regarded as patron saint of animals and environment. The Indian government issued a postal stamp on him in April 1983 in light brown colour with environment in background.

Because the Franciscans were not attached to a place or to possessions, they could travel freely as Missionaries. Francis himself travelled throughout Italy and to Spain and Egypt. The early Franciscans devoted themselves to preaching to the caring for the spiritual needs of the people. But the order soon branched out into Education, Missionary and Social work.

The earliest religious order under the Portuguese regime in India was that of the Franciscans of the observance (the two distinct Congregations of the Franciscans include the Conventual's and the Observantie's). In 1517 they were regarded as the first spiritual pastors of the Portuguese in Goa. The Dominicans came to Goa shortly after its conquest, but they did not form themselves into a community till near half a century after[28].

As early as 1319, a party of Dominicans and Franciscans set out for a Universal Mission of Christ's Church. A party of Missionaries who managed to land at the city of Thana, consisted of the Dominican Jordanus and four Franciscans (as mentioned earlier). Jordanus saw that the Christians had gone into hiding, frightened by what had befallen the friars in Thana. Later he went to Sopara and Broach[29] to get in touch with the Christians of whom he had been told at Thana. At Sopara, he instructed Christians in religious doctrine, baptized about ninety persons and administered to them the sacrament of the Holy Eucarist during the fifteen days he stayed with them. During his absence the four Franciscans left behind in Thana were put to death. Fr. Jordanus returned, buried their mangled bodies and carried on their work, suffering some petty persecution. Friar Odoricus, who visited Thana a little later, collected details of the pitiful story of these Franciscans.

The Franciscans were the first and for many years the only Missionaries in Bombay. About the year 1565, they established their first residence and Church 'Our Lady of Expectation (Esperanca)'. Mostly the people of Koli caste were baptized by them. The 1626 attack on Bombay by a fleet of British and Dutch vessels led to a set back for Franciscans.

---

28 Rev. Denis L. Cottineau de Loguen "*A Historical Sketch of Goa: The Metropolis of the Portuguese Settlements in India*" (Madras, 1831), reprint, B. R. Publishing Co, New Delhi, 2006, pp. 52-53

29 Present Bharuch in Gujarat.

St Augustine (354-430)

Picture 1.4: St. Augustine of Augustinian Order
(Source: http://www.suttonlea.org/site/stceciliasprimary/images/staugustine.gif retrieved on 15th February 2009)

1.3.4 The Augustinian Order

The Augustinians were the fourth religious order established in Goa. They owe their origin to St. Augustine himself. It is well known that Martin Luther was a member of this order, and as his defection rendered the Augustinians odious in several catholic countries, they obtained from the Pope leave of changing the colour of their usual habit from black to white.

1.3.5 Establishment of Churches

The existence of Catholic Churches in Mumbai till 1850[30] is evident from the tables below. Table 1.3 shows the churches in Bassein[31] region and Table 1.4 depicting Churches in Salsette region[32].

30 Jenifer Rodrigues, *A History of the Catholic Christian Community in Maharashtra: 1850-1950*, Ph.D Thesis, Mumbai, July 2007, pp.19-20

31 It refers to present Vasai near Mumbai.

32 Mixed region including parts of Bombay and Thane

Table 1.3: Churches in Bassein

Church	*Place and Year*
Order : Franciscan	
Holy Cross	Nirmal, 1577-78
Holy Spirit	Nandakhal, 1573
Our Lady of the Light	Agashi, 1568
Mother of God	Pale (before 1595)
Order : Jesuit	
St. Thomas	Sandor, 1556
Our Lady of Grace	Papady, 1574
St. Michael	Manickpur, 1606

When the revolt against Rome started under Luther, several newly risen powers rejected the authority of the Pope, and of these the Dutch and the English were the most important. These Protestant nations had a double incentive in overthrowing Iberians. They wanted to show their contempt for the Pope and at the same time wrest naval supremacy from the Iberians.

While the early Catholic Missions gave greater importance to formal conversion, the new Protestant Missions were more concerned with the dissemination of the Christian knowledge. Street preaching's, circulation of Bible and Pamphlets and active humanitarian work among the needy were given greater importance in their program than formal Baptism[33].

A paper entitled 'The strength and weakness of the Indian Christian Community' read by Rev. D. L. Joshi before the Indian Christian Association talks of Christianity in India into three stages- the Syrian, the Roman and the Protestant[34].

33 P. Thomas, Christians, *Christianity in India and Pakistan*, Allen & Unwin Publishers, London, 1954, p.150

34 *BG*, September 20, 1902, p. 9

Table 1.4: Churches in Salsette

Church	*Place and Year*
Our Lady of the Emmaculate Conception	Mt. Poinsur, 1544
Most Holy Trinity	Powai, 1557- 1739
St. Thomas	Goregaon, 1560
Our Lady of Nazereth	Bhayander, 1575-78
St. John the Evangelist	Marol, 1579
Holy Cross	Kurla, 1588
St. John the Baptist (Originally St Anthony)	Thane, 1582
St. Blasé	Amboli, 1585-89
Our Lady of Remedy	Poinsur (before 1591)
Holy Magar	Gorai (between 1595-1602)
St. Jerome	Kashmiri, 1595-1602
Our Lady of Egypt	Kalina, 1606-1609
Our Lady of Bethlehem	Dongri, 1613
St. Andrew	Bandra, 1616
St. Sebastian	Marouli (before 1630)
St. Anthony	Malvani,1630-1642..1739
Our Lady of Health	Versova, 1634-42
Our Lady of Perpetual Succor	Manori, 1634-42
Our Lady of the Sea	Utan, 1632-42

1.4 Mission through Church Histories

Closely related to any Mission are the Church histories. They are official Mission histories, which give details of achievements of various Missionaries, names of Mission stations, the number of persons converted and the problems faced by the Missionaries in the Mission fields. They belong to the class of already published Mission histories for example. *The Problems of Success-A History of CMS*

(2 Vols) 1977 by Gordon Hewitt., *Centennial Report of American Marathi Mission* (1913) ed. By A. Clark, W. Hazen and C. Bruce and *The History of London Missionary Society* by R. Lowett (1899). Some of the Magazines and Journals started by the Missionaries in India like *The Examiner* (a catholic journal), The *OCS, Dnyanodaya and Bombay Guardian* serve as sources even for the study of Indian history. The *OCS* news paper has reproduced a number of letters from the other native newspapers as well. Though the contents of the paper represented Missionary side, the facts mentioned therein are important. *Dnyanodaya* (Marathi) has been a major source of the Missionary activities. It started in 1842, regularly appeared before the readers first as fortnightly and then as weekly. *Dnyanodaya* not only pleaded the Missionary cause but also the cause of reform in India. It criticized evil practices and gave wide publicity to various views by reformers.

Now, an ecumenical effort is being made by Church History Association of India (CHAI) to write the Indian Church History with a new perspective. After independence the administrative power in Catholic and Protestant Churches had been transferred to Indian clergy. Indian Church historians had begun the efforts to write Church history. Dr. G. Moraes (President IHC, 1969) and P. J. Thomas have tried to get Church histories into the mainstream of historical writings in India.

It is interesting to note that today even non-Christian secular historians have begun to take interest in Indian Church history in view of the revolutionary effect the Church has produced on the modern Indian Society[35].

After getting a broad outline of Mission and its meaning with focus on some of the Christian Missionary orders, one can safely pass to the distinct contribution rendered by the Missionaries in the field of education, which is presented in the following chapter.

---

35 M. D. David (ed), *Asia and Christianity*, Himalaya Publications, Mumbai, 1985, p. 163

Chapter 2

Social Activities of Missionaries-I
(Educational Mission)

Chapter 2

Social Activities of Missionaries-I (Educational Mission)

2.1 Necessity of Schools

In September 1866, philanthropic traveller Mary Carpenter[36] came to Bombay to look in to the issue of female education. She felt the grand obstacle in the progress of female education was the lack of female teachers. She made suggestion for the establishment of a Female Normal Training School. Her idea was appreciated by Alexander Grant (Director of Public Instruction). Although the Missionaries were interested in educating girls as well as boys, female instruction was largely religious and oriented towards helping the girls become better mothers and housewives. This is visible from Mrs. F. P. Horne's essay entitled 'How to fit girls in Mission Schools to be Good Wives'[37]. It focuses in teaching girls house keeping (How to Cook, How to Buy, How to wash clothing etc). In Mary F. Billington's Book 'Women in India' opposite page 36, a big table entitled 'Vernacular Standards of Examination for Girl Schools and Zenanas' shows needle works and sewing.

---

36 The *Nav Bidhan* (Keshaub Sen break away group) had welcomed Ms. Mary Carpenter to Calcutta. Her Mission was to encourage female education and she was quick to notice the shortage of suitable teachers.

37 *BG*, September 13, 1878, p.10

The *Bombay Guardian* (*BG*) front page[38] mentions about Frere – Fletcher Girls School[39] (earlier the Fort Christian School). The characteristics of the School were that Christians and non – Christian children have been received indiscriminately. The former receiving religious instruction, the latter not, except the parents should wish it. The building of the school had cost about Rs. 75,000 of which Rs. 50,000 was given by Premchand Roychand[40] in the days of the share mania.

Sharda Dwivedi in her book *Premchand Roychand : 1831-1906* Bombay (2006) mentions of Premchand who gave a private donation of Rs. 60,000 to Mary Prescott an Englishwomen with a Proviso that Indian girls would be admitted without any restrictions regarding their numbers or the fees they paid. In the same issue of *BG* the Vernacular Press Bill passed hurriedly through Supreme Court has been mentioned. Rev. James Long[41] (an Irish born Anglican who came in India in 1840 and belonged to CMS) has been described as an ideal Missionary. In this connection in June 1860 as also a year later (before the indigo comMission), Long emphasized the great importance of the Indian Vernacular Press as "A Genuine Exponent of Native Opinion" and "The Barometer of the Native Mind"[42]. He also had interests in Bengali folklore and proverbs[43]. Jame Long's genuine love for the Indians has been displayed by vigorous denunciation of the drawbacks of the British administration in India.

Front page of *BG* of March 6, 1880 mentions …in the palmy days of 1864 Mr. Premchand Roychand, then a person of prodigious influence at whose door the carriages of many might be seen standing

---

38 *BG*, March 23, 1878, front page

39 It was earlier called Miss Prescott's Fort Christian School

40 Premchand Roychand was the first Indian Stock broker who was fluent in the English language (He registered himself as a stock broker in 1849). Roychand promoted J. V. Petit high school, Bombay Scottish and Alexandria Girls School (*Mumbai Mirror*, January 4, 2007, p. 14)

41 He was called Padre Long in Bengal

42 S. R. Mehrotra, *The Emergence of the Indian National Congress*, Rupa & Co., New Delhi, 2004, p. 403

43 G. D. Oddie, *Social Protest in India* 1850-1900, Manohar Publishers, New Delhi, 1979, p. 153

daily, gave four lacks for the erection of the University library and tower.

A long letter by Geo K. Gilder[44] mentioned about Thakoors, Kunbi, Koli, Warli villages around Igatpuri, Mokhara and Jowhar areas. It says… "We believe in the Missionary residing in the very midst of the people among whom he labours and not in civil stations".

Ranu Janoji Salvi wrote a Marathi tract "*Instructive chapters for the Kunbis*" which was a conversation between a Christian schoolmaster and a Kunbi (cultivator who is simple-minded man of an enquiring turn of mind) whose son was learning under the former[45].

The focus on Vernacular Education in the Bombay Presidency had already begun by the end of 1850. The Minutes on Education of the Honourable J. P. Willoughby[46] stressed the fact that the greater attention was being paid to the Vernaculars. The History of Post 1857 Indian education told the tale of a long struggle by the authorities to reverse Macaulayan trend and promote mass education, the ideal being a large pool of literate, skilled minor clerks and petty officials. To this end the Hunter Commission of 1882 headed by William Hunter championed the vernaculars over English as a medium, downgraded literary study, and promoted technical and vocational instructions[47]. Earlier in the "Epitome of News Column-a News from *Poona Observer* of Saturday March 7, 1863 says "There is one direction in which instruction in vernacular languages might be extended with great advantage, with which the educational department has nothing to do; we mean in schools for children of English parents, like the military schools and those of the Education Society of Bombay[48]. To these children a correct knowledge of the Vernacular would be invaluable. Most of them are, in all probability, destined to spend their lives in India. If so, knowledge of the language in some form or other becomes simply necessary; and a correct knowledge of it would

44 *BG*, March 26,1881, pp. 54-55
45 *BG*, September 24, 1881, p. 467
46 *OCS*, December 1850, p. 492
47 Rimi Chatterjee, Empires of the Mind, The History of OUP in India under the Raj, OUP, New Delhi, 2006, p. 7
48 *BG*, March 14, 1863, p. 83

be of immense advantage in many ways. The superiority possessed by a person who knows two languages in common use over a person who knows only one is almost unmeasurable"[49].

In Nineteenth Century, the impossibility of gathering a stated audience by preaching, forced upon the attention of these devoted men the necessity of schools as a means of coming in contact with the people, and gaining their attention to the truth[50]. The Missionaries and government had different ideas about the use of English education in India. Macaulay held the view that western education was to be introduced with the sole objective of training persons for administration. The Missionaries were keen on promoting education as an effective measure to propagate Christianity[51]. Their dedicated efforts filled the educational vacuum created in the aftermath of Peshwa rule.

The first effort of English education in Bombay was made in 1718, with the opening of a school[52] at Fort by Rev. Richard Cobbe, Chaplain to the Hon. East India Company of St. Thomas Church (the oldest English Church in Bombay) to educate poor children in Christian doctrine[53].

The task of promoting the education of Indian people had started well before J. S. Mill entered the India House. The British authorities had taken up the subject as a result of pressure from three groups.

1. The Missionary societies who believed that education would help spread Christianity.
2. Oriental Scholars who wanted the government to patronize art, literature and learning in India for its own sake.

---

49 Toru Dutt (1856-77) who died at 21 years of age could put one foreign language into another foreign language in poetic form. She was well versed in French, German and English and had begun the study of Sanskrit with her father.

50 R. G. Wilder, *Mission Schools in India*, University of Michigan, Boston, 1861, pp. 55-56

51 Mridulla Ramanna, *English Education and Social Change in Bombay City 1815-1858*, Ph.D Thesis, Bombay, 1985, p. 201

52 Called Old Charity School

53 Mridula Ramanna, *Op.Cit*, p. 12

3. Utilitarian like James Mill in 1824 set the tone of the Home government's policy by insisting that the aim of education should be 'useful knowledge'[54].

Nineteenth Century was also marked by the arrival of the first batch of American Missionaries. Gordon Hall did a good deal of street preaching and became a familiar figure in the streets of Bombay but died of cholera in Nasik while doing relief work during the epidemic (1826).

The spirit of 'discoveries' of the sixteenth Century saw Iberian religious zeal which was later followed in the eighteenth Century England by the evangelicals who took their place as the leaders of a 'Missionary movement', one side of which concentrated on the "heathen" at home and the other which concentrated on the "heathen" abroad. This is a phenomenon which is linked up closely with the industrial revolution and modernization of the countries in Europe that began exporting Missionaries. The American Marathi Mission was first to reach the interiors of Maharashtra.

Further, in the later half of the Nineteenth Century it was rightly felt that "Education cannot help being influenced by the social climate in which it was set and one of the aims of education today was vocational"[55].

2.2 Role of Protestant Missionaries

2.2.1 The history of Protestantism in India (1706)

The man who first thought of sending Protestant Missionaries to India was King Frederick of Denmark.[56] The first Protestant Missionaries in India were Lutherians Bartholomaeus Ziegenbalg[57] and Swartz (also

54 George D. Bearce, 'John Stuart Mill and India' *in Journal of the Bombay Branch of the Asiatic Society,* 1954, Vol. 29, part 2, p. 2

55 Srinibas Bhattacharya, *Guidance in Education,* Asia Publishers, New York, 1963, p. 1

56 K. C. Zachariah, *The Syrian Christians of Kerala,* Orient Longman, New Delhi, 2006, p. 82

57 The Department of Posts issued a Postage Stamp on him to commemorate 300th anniversary of his arrival in India in 2006.

spelt Schutze) in South India; Carey, Ward and Marshman in Bengal. Ziegenbalg and Plutsch learnt Tamil without dictionary, grammar or *Munshi* and between 1708-1711 they contrived to translate the New Testament into Tamil. We see pioneer work was done in respect of a critical study of South Indian languages by Missionary enterprise.

Picture 2.1: Stamp released on Bartholomaeus Ziegenbalg by India Post

The mushrooming of Missionary societies and religious congregations in Europe and US particularly from late eighteenth century had its impact in Western India in early 19th century.

In 1772, Charles Grant[58] a founder member of the Clapham sect (important group of evangelicals) advocated Missionary activity in India. Grant supported projects for the spread of Christianity in India[59]. He insisted "Religion is not propagated by force; compulsion is sub service of the rights of private judgment and conscience, and totally contrary to the spirit and genius of Christianity".

William Wilberforce led the parliamentary struggle of Missionaries' legal entry in India. He argued how no other country needed Christianity as much as India did. Charles Marsh, who had been in the Admiralty Court in Madras for many years was an opponent of Wilberforce and regarded the Missionaries as vulgar fanatics' who had succeeded in converting only dregs of the society[60].

58 Grant, though not a Missionary was close to Missionary circles. He emphatically said that English language would acquaint "Hindoos with the literary compositions of the West."

59 G. D. Bearce, *British Attitudes Towards India 1784-1858*, OUP, London, 1961, p. 54

60 Teotonio R. De Souza, "The Christian Missions in the Aftermath of Discoveries" in T. R. De Souza (ed.) *Discoveries Missionary Expansion and Asian*

With the emergence of new state systems the role of Missionaries in social mobility and social change cannot be denied especially in nineteenth century Bombay Presidency. The 1813 charter, which inaugurated a new era in Indian education, also made it possible for Missionaries to work in India on a legal footing. Their basic motive and purpose of providing education was more complex question which might at first appear that they certainly viewed education as a means to an evangelistic end; they were not at this period seriously expecting conversions of the children in their schools, but they did believe that the education that they gave, even if it contained little or no direct Christian teaching, would dispose them to give a favourable hearing to Christian preaching and tracts subsequently[61]. The Peace of 1815 permitted the growing head of educational and scientific zeal and Missionary and humanitarian fervor in Europe to flow more freely. The Government of India too displayed in 1811 and 1815 a ripening consciousness of the ruler's responsibility for the intellectual and moral welfare of the ruled[62].

Two American Missionaries Gordon Hall[63] and Samuel Nott arrived in Bombay on the 11th of February 1813. They had not been allowed to stay in Bombay initially due to the company's objections[64]. Finally, a letter dated 21st December 1813 from the Bombay government gave the desired per Mission for them to engage in Missionary work[65]. Mr. Harriet Newell is said to have joined them on the 7th of March 1814.

The Bombay Mission, the first and oldest Mission of the American Board was the pioneer in the introduction of Protestant Christianity in Western India.

Cultures, Concept, New Delhi 1994, p. 40

61 The contribution of Missionaries to Education in Bengal during the administration of Lord Hastings 1813-23 in *Bengal Past and Present (Journal Since 1907)*, January-June 1967, p. 68

62 *A Short History of the Elphinstone High School 1824-1924*, Bombay, 1925, p. 2

63 He died of Cholera in a village near Nasik in 1826.

64 Preeta Nilesh, 'Law and Social Change'., *Four Judicial Cases in 19th Century Bombay, Ph.D Thesis, Bombay*, December 2000, p. 40

65 *BG*, September 21, 1901, p. 10

Initial years of the Mission

Near the close of 1814 we find on record that they preached in English every Sabbath, in the quarters which had been assigned to them by Government. Also at another place a short distance from the town, they had opened a school, which they hoped would in the end become a boarding school of considerable importance to the Mission.

Of their labors in 1815 we find the following record: "They had acquired such familiarity with the Mahratta (marathi) language that they were able to commence their great work of preaching the Gospel to the heathen. But the reader must not imagine that the heathen came by hundreds on the Sabbath to hear them, instead of this, they had no stated congregation of heathen bearers. They were obliged to go to temples, the markets and other places of public resort and converse with such as would hear them."

2.2.2 The protestant Missionaries in Konkan during British period

The Scottish Missionary society sent its first Missionary Donalt Mitchell[66] in 1822, who was said to have opened his center in Bankot but it got closed by 1831[67]. The locality of his labours was the southern Konkan and he had opened eight simple village schools. On 20th November 1823, he died at Poladpur on the road to Mahabaleshwar. Between 1814-30, Missionaries toured Konkan with the permission of the then British Government. While touring the Missionaries had to face climatic changes, and attack of robbers, snakes etc. In 1829, James Mitchell and Stevenson went on a six weeks tour to Bankot – Poladpur – Mahad- Mahabaleshwar – Wai – Pune. In 1830, John Wilson also went on a six weeks tour to Harnai, Bankot region[68]. Report of the Bombay Mission of the Free Church

66 He was son of a scotch clergyman and brother of Mr. James Mitchell.

67 S. R. Shirgaonkar, *Protestant Christ Missionarianche Maharashtratil Chalwal,* 1813-58, Ph.D Thesis (M), Mumbai, 1972, p. 487

68 *Ibid,* p.119

of Scotland for 1855 was read by Dr. Wilson on 5th January 1856[69] gave details about Rev. Robert Nesbit's[70] life in Poona and Cape of Good Hope. Rev. Nesbit's first sphere of labour was in southern Konkan not far from Mission at Dapoli, following which he was transferred to Bombay to help Dr. Wilson[71].

T. B. Jervis[72] had mentioned in one of his statistical survey that the Missions had by 1824 started their schools in Bombay in both north and south Konkan[73]. He has also mentioned that there were only three Mahar students attending schools at Bankot and Harnai (under the management of Missionaries).

Jervis had also mentioned that in the town of Thana there was a school entirely run at government cost at which all castes were permitted to attend except Manooras ? and Parwaries (Mahars ?). In one of the two charitable schools run by American Missionaries, it was said "the Parwaries sit outside the school room in the Veranda". Even the great Missionaries in those days dare not break the tradition of not allowing these classes to sit inside the school room along with other boys.

The following table highlights the schools connected with the Konkan Missions[74]. The books read in the schools were generally portions of scripture like the Ten Commandments, Catechism and forms of prayer.

---

69 OCS, Vol.VII, January 1856, p.19., Also biographical sketch of Rev. Robert Nesbit of the Free Church of Scotland's Mission in Bombay is given in August 1856's OCS, pp. 306-318

70 One of the free Church Missionaries in India

71 *BG*, November 10, 1888, pp. 714-15

72 He joined his duties in south Konkan (1819) as statistical surveyor. He deserves special mention as the first officer in India who took interest in collecting the educational statistics of indigenous schools.

73 R. V. Parulekar (ed.), *Survey of indigenous education in the province of Bombay*: 1820-1830, reprint, Asia Publishers House, Bombay 1951, p. xix

74 *The Annual Report of the Bombay Auxiliary Scottish Missionary Society* for 1830, p. 19

Table 2.1: List of Schools connected with Konkan Mission

Name of School	*Readers*	*Writers*	*Girls*	*Total*
Hurnee- No.1	36	22	--	58
Ditto – No.2[#]	10	4	--	14
Anjurlem	35	18	--	53
Padlem[#]	12	13	--	25
Paz[#]	3	9	9	21
Moorood No.1	33	10	--	43
Ditto. No.2	38	20	--	58
Boorunwdee	17	18	1	36
Goohagur No.1	42	23	--	65
Ditto No.2	52	39	--	91
Ditto No.3	19	18	--	37
Arem	21	33	--	54
Unjunvel	7	32	--	39
Dabhol No.1	56	25	--	81
Ditto No.2	27	15	2	44
Ditto –3	21	18	3	42
Dhapolee	28	26	3	57
Jalganu	47	34	--	81
Palgud[#]	40	22	--	62
Ditto No.2	26	12	--	48
Shirkul[#]	15	15	--	30
Khed No.1[#]	33	39	2	74
Ditto No.2[#]	27	26	--	53
Moorden[#]	14	13	--	27
Hurnee Girls School[#]	--	--	18	18
Moorood	--	--	14	14

[#] - were discontinued later

2.3 The Scottish Missionaries

The Scottish Missionaries turned towards Bombay in 1822[75]. The first annual examination of the Wilson English School was held on 28th October 1836. The school had seven classes with 209 pupils.

75 They had earlier concentrated on African Continent.

A mention of College division in the second annual examination report of 1837 is seen in which natural history, geometry, astronomy and natural theology were taught by Dr. John Wilson[76].

The below mentioned examples from newspaper sources of nineteenth century especially *The Bombay Guardian* (*BG*) highlights the process of examination in different schools associated with Missionaries.

A public examination of the children of the Bycullah (Byculla) schools was held in the girl's school room on 23rd March 1847. The Honorable Governor presided along with the Chief Justice Sir. D. Pollock. The Rev. Geo Watson, Master of the boy's school was requested to examine some of the upper and one of the lower classes in each school.

The fourth class of boys wrote a piece of English History dictated to them very correctly and answered some questions on English history with great intelligence. The First Class of boys were examined in Euclid, Arithmetic, and a few questions were proposed on the system of the Universe and Etymology and they acquitted themselves very creditably. The V, XXI and XLVII, propositions of the first 'Book of Euclid' were demonstrated; and certain questions in Arithmetic were discussed. They answered the questions proposed to them in Etymology and on the Planetary System and further gave us a reason that the earth was round and planets move in elliptic and not in circular orbits.

The First and Eighth of the Girls Examined

The First Class of Girls answered some questions in History and Geography though the press of time would not allow more than a very few questions to be put. The Prizes were then distributed consisting of a medal, books, flutes and portfolio for the boys and books etc. for the girls[77].

76 Sulochana Krishnamurti, *English Education and its Impact*, Ph.D Thesis, Bombay, 1987, p. 326

77 *The Telegraph and Courier Newspaper*, March 24, 1847, p. 283

2.3.1 Examination of the Free Church Schools

On Saturday 10th April 1847, the Fourth Annual Examination of the General Assembly's Institution in connection with the Free Church of Scotland[78] took place in the Mission House at Ambroli, which was formerly the residence of Rev. Dr. Wilson well adapted for the educational purposes to which it was devoted.

In popularity and usefulness this educational establishment stood second in Bombay next to the Elphinstone Institution. The two page write up[79] on the Honorable Mountstuart Elphinstone begins with news of death of Mt. Elphinstone and how in every respect he was an extraordinary man, possessing great activity of body and mind.

Further a comparison is made between the Free Church Schools and the Elphinstone Institution. In the latter and its local branches, nearly 3000 young people received a liberal and enlightened education and 1067 in Free Church Schools (Table 2.2).

Table 2.2: Classification of Children of Free Church Schools

Young men and boys learning in English	263
Boys learning in Marathi and Gujarati	368
Girls and adult females learning in Marathi	436
Total number under instruction	**1067**

There was remarkable difference in the principles of the above two institutions. Religion was carefully excluded from the plan of the Elphinstone College. In Free Church Schools, it was sought to impart Christian education to the Natives[80] in general and also to train up some of them for preaching and teaching their countrymen. The English Educational Department was ably superintended by the

78 It was called Scottish Missionary Society in 1829, General Assembly of the Church of Scotland in 1835 and finally Bombay Mission of the Free Church of Scotland.

79 *OCS*, February 1860, pp. 66- 68

80 Rev. A Manwaring of the C. M. S. Bombay deprecates the use of the word "Native" but recognises the difficulty of avoiding it especially in writing for home readers whose ideas are so mixed with regard to the "Word Indian"(which would be its best substitute)

Reverends J. M. Mitchell and R. Nesbit. Along with Rev. Wilson[81] they became powerful trio of the Scottish Mission in Maharashtra. Prof. William Henderson[82] was also associated with them.

The Missionaries repeatedly urged the introduction of Christian education and the use of Bible as a class book in government schools. At the Missionary institutions, religious knowledge was imparted in every class. A suggestion was made to introduce Rev. Ganpatrao Navalkar's marathi poem "*The Temptation*" (a Marathi translation from Milton's 'Paradise Regained') in to the Vernacular Mission schools as text book, instead of the poetry usually taught to them mostly comprising of stories of Hindu gods and demons[83].

2.3.2 Examination of the School of the Scottish Orphanage

BG of Friday, 26th December, 1851 speaks of Rev. Dr. Wilson (1804-1875)[84] of reading the report of the Examination of the School of the Scottish Orphanage which took place on Friday i.e. 18th December 1851 on which Dr. Stevenson presided. The number of girls present at the examination was twenty seven. The youngest classes comprising of mostly the orphans, supported by the Scottish Ladies Association and of pure Indian origin were first of all examined. They read an elementary English book and repeated a hymn in that language, after which they were examined in Marathi and in all these exercises, acquitted themselves satisfactorily.

The second class consisting, partly of natives and of children of European parents were next examined. They read the New Testament with much ease and correctness and answered very satisfactorily the questions that were put to them on the meaning of what they read. They were also examined on the map of the world, with the general facts connected with which they showed themselves well acquainted.

---

81 Stevenson, Wilson and Murray Mitchell were the three doctors of the Scottish Church, who with several others were instrumental in establishing the Asiatic Society's Journal, *BG*, January 21, 1905, Front Page.

82 *The Telegraph and Courier*, April 12, 1847, p. 347

83 *BG*, October 1892, front page

84 He founded the oldest Christian Periodical in India i.e. *Oriental Christian Spectator*, the Wilson College Bombay was founded in his memory in 1887.

The highest class, several girls of which defray their own expenses and others were supported by the charitable fund, was examined on scripture History, the History of England and the Geography of Asia and Europe.........

The Annual Examination of the school was conducted by the Rev. W. W. Peyton on Saturday morning, in the presence of a number of ladies and gentlemen, friends of the cause of education. He says "What we witnessed of the examination was exceedingly satisfactory, showing the pupils to be quite at home in the branches of Geography, Astronomy, and Scripture, History etc. Some Essays had been prepared on the Natural History of Girgaum, the part of Bombay where the school is situated, by the elder pupils: while the younger pupils exhibited a great number of specimens which they had collected for the illustration of these lectures". Mr. Peyton seems to desire and successfully endeavor that his pupils should acquire the habit of looking to the world around them for instruction, as well as to books.[85]

2.4 Missionaries-Pioneers in Women's Education

In the beginning of the nineteenth century, educating the girls in the formal educational institutions or the concept of girl's school was totally absent. Most of the women, except a few from the privileged or liberated class, were illiterate and were not regarded as an active section in social activities. Naturally, they were under the heavy influence of all traditions and customs. The process of liberating them from this state of affairs through education has been started by the Missionaries. The girls were perused instructive books at home. In fact there were immense difficulties with which female education has to contend in this country. The Natives themselves did next to nothing. Even the Government did nothing to educate the females. It was said "Unless Missionary efforts reach them they are not reached at all"[86]. Though people were apprehensive about their intentions and did not encourage the girls to attend these schools, the Missionaries had the credit of creating an awareness among educated people of

85 *BG*, May 24,1856, p.163

86 The *Oriental Christian Spectator*, January-February 1849.

the necessity of educating women in the interest of society and of the nation, apart from the interest in women's welfare. An atmosphere in favour of women's education created by the Missionaries helped in providing a ready ground for the future attempts made in this direction by other agencies, including the Government.

Deeply convinced that the Hindus can never be an enlightened and happy people while their wives and mothers are in such a state of degradation, the Missionaries in connection with their other labour, uniformly addressed themselves to this important work of female education. In was felt that "The apathy, incredulity and even active opposition which have been so generally manifested by the natives towards this cause, the success has been as great as could reasonably have been expected"[87].

On evening of 14th April 1882, the annual exhibition and distribution of prizes to the children of all the native female schools in the city connected with the Mission of the Free Church of Scotland in the Bombay Presidency was held at the Ambroli Native Church, in the Girgaum back road. While Rev. R. Stothat occupied the chair, 300 children along with many native Christian converts were examined by Rev. Narayan Sheshadri in respect of the life of Christ. Rev. Sheshadri delivered their answers in a very intelligent manner. Hymns were also sung by some of the Christian convert girls in the Mahratti (marathi) tongue, set to English music on this occasion[88].

First boarding school for girls with the intention of providing shelter to orphan girls, widows and destitute women, were established by the Missions. A report[89] to this effect was given by Mrs. Squires of Church Missionary Society's Girls Boarding School at Girgaum in Bombay.

---

87 Sheela Patwardhan, *"History of Development of Women Education in the Central Division of the Bombay Presidency 1818-1905"*, Ph.D. Thesis, November 1990, Pune, p. 157

88 *BG*, April 15, 1882, p. 231

89 *BG*, June 2,1883, p. 339

Table 2.3: Candidates at first boarding school for girls (1883)

Candidates	*Number*
Christian boarding girls	23
Hindu Girls	93
Boys day scholars (4 Christians)	22
Brahman Widow	01

The school had 23 Christian girl's boarders, besides 93 Hindu girl's day scholars and 22 boy's day scholars, 4 of whom are Christians. Special mention of one of the pupil a Brahman's widow aged about 20 years can be seen.

Meeting of United Free Church girl's boarding school and Sunday school (Composing of Non-Christian children) was held on Saturday (September 6 1902)[90]. Apart from many activities one interesting item was a Marathi dialogue by two Hindu lads on the advantages gained from the railway time table and the blessings obtained from studying the Christian time table (the Bible).

A big write up on Mrs. Sagunabai Mazda[91] originally of Mahar Caste was published[92]. At Ambroli Mission she taught religious lessons to girls. She had a refinement of look and manner unknown to illiterate women and had such a dignity about her that every one who came into contact with her felt that he was in presence of a person whom he must respect. She was proficient equally in English and Marathi, while she was distinguished for her knowledge of singing and the use of the needle. The Missionaries and Converts, who lived in close proximity, formed one large family and the relation between them was really of a tender nature. As if the Missionary was

90 *BG*, September 13,1902, p. ii

91 Perhaps she was related to a converted Hindu Bapu Mazda whose name appears frequently in Vernacular Girls Schools run by Scottish Missionaries. The annual report of the Bombay Auxiliary Missionary Society of the Free Church of Scotland (1857, p.17) mentions the wife of Bapu Mazda, educated in the boarding school was the second pupil of the female schools at the Mission House Ambrolie. She assisted later in the tuition of these schools (from this we may assume that Sagunabai was wife of Bapu Mazda)

92 *BG,* October 22,1887, p. 680

the father and the converts were his children. Niri Yami[93], Dhondi[94] and Umabai[95] were four young women baptized by Dr. Wilson on 2nd December 1855.

Mrs. Narayan Sheshadri was a school companion of Mrs. Mazda, and they both commanded respect for their culture and energy. Mazda ran her meeting of school in her house. She was Head mistress of the high school at Ambroli. She was trained by Mrs. Murry Mitchell and was given a position and employment in the Mission by Dr. Wilson. The policy of the Free Church Mission from the first had been to give the highest education both to male and female and the fruits of that policy were seen all over the country.

After 1882, the secondary schools were fashioned after the image of the English Public Schools. Many of them were boarding schools. Frequently the head master was a 'Clergy Men' and every effort was made to ensure that the teachers were Christians. The curriculum was typically English; classical languages, mathematics, sciences, geography, history and English literature[96].

The work done by the American Mission School for the Blind, at Byculla under the care of Miss Millard has been reported[97]. Miss. Millard's care had brought light and happiness to the darkened lives of many little ones[98]. There were about 50 boys and girls, who were cared for in separate houses, but educated together. The children learnt to read in English from the Braille type, and were well trained in arithmetic. The usual items of industrial work suitable for Blind Institutions were taught by capable instructors; and the school received an excellent report from the Government Educational Inspector. This school was not be confounded with the then opened non-Christian 'Victoria Memorial School for the Blind', which was largely assisted by the Bombay Municipality, who had declined to

---

93 Yami was brought from Ajanta in 1851 by Mr. and Mrs. Wilson.

94 She was originally a pupil in the Ambrolie School (see *OCS*, January 1856, p. 22)

95 She was the young wife of the convert Rewa.

96 Aruna Narayanan, *History of Bombay 1885-1905*, Ph.D. Thesis, Bombay, 1993, p. 182

97 *BG*, June 24, 1905, front page

98 *BG*, July 8, 1905, p. 9

help Miss Millard's work, which was therefore entirely dependent on the private generosity of the Christian public, except for a one third grant from Government towards the cost of education.

2.5 Printing of Text Books

The first printed textbooks, story books were prepared by the Missionaries. Printing the textbook was a real challenge to the Missionaries in the beginning till a few local people could be entrusted with the work. The Church Vernacular Education Society had done a great deal for the vernacular literature of India by supplying excellent reading Books in various languages. Text books for all grades of scholars were provided[99].

Work of the Missionaries in all its different forms include,

- Education
- Evangelistic work
- Church Development
- Training of Christians
- Literature
- Others

Schools constituted one of the most important departments of Missionary labour. Education for many years had taken a prominent place in the work of all Missionaries. The Mission schools were supported by the respective Mission association's funds plus the generous willing donations received from various quarters. Many Europeans were also major donors.[100]

The existence of the Mission's schools relieved government from a considerable annual expenditure. A big report from Rev. J G Deimler on the Church Missionary Society's Western India report[101] says "as long as there are no more government schools then there are at present and the system of education is so antagonistic to Christianity, Missionary Schools are necessary and a great blessing to the people and at the same time they prepare the way for more direct

99 *BG*, February 11, 1882, p. 84

100 Sheela Patwardhan *Op.Cit*, p. 93

101 *BG*, June 6,1863, p. 182

Missionary labour. Without a reading population there remains the difficulty for the Missionary of having no material to work on and these can only be created in schools".

A front page report in *BG*, May 9th 1863 talks of examination of teachers of vernacular schools in Bombay Presidency. Rewards were offered by Christian Vernacular Education Society. Out of 53 Candidates (26 Hindus + 27 Christians) there were 30 (20 were Christians and 10 Hindus) successful candidates, who received gratuities ranging from Rs. 10 to Rs. 30

Table 2.4: Mission's successful candidates (1863)

Number of Successful Candidates	*Name of Mission*
1	Connected with the established work of Scotland Mission
2	Kolhapoor Mission
3	C M S Malligaum Mission
4	Guzerat Mission of the Irish Presbyterian Church
5	Free Church of Scotland's Poona Mission
15	American Board (Ahmednagar)*

All the teachers connected with the American Board were Christian. Sudamji Raghoba of the last mentioned Mission received the highest award of Rs. 30.

The principal subjects of examinations were:

- Evidences of Christianity
- Astronomy
- Genesis and Arithmetic

2.6 Education in Western India

2.6.1 The American Marathi Mission, Church Mission Society and Scottish Mission Society

The Protestant Missionaries of 19th Century Bombay Presidency includes American Marathi Mission, Church Mission Society and Scottish Mission Society.

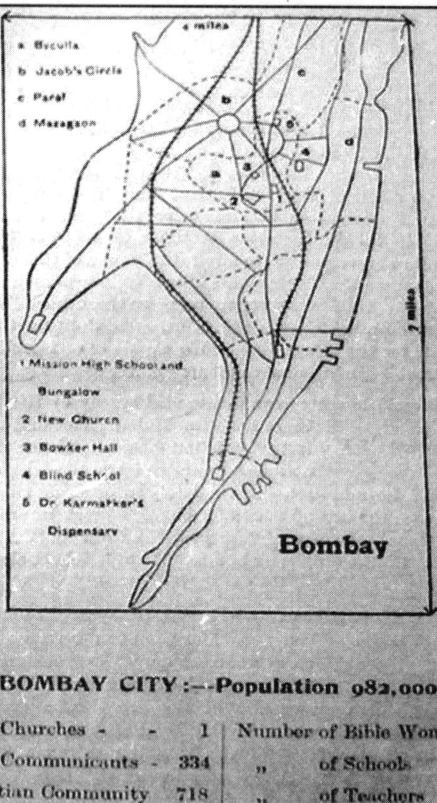

BOMBAY CITY :—Population 982,000.

Number of Churches - -	1	Number of Bible Women -	11
„ of Communicants -	334	„ of Schools - -	14
Total Christian Community	718	„ of Teachers - -	39
Contributions for 1905 Rs. 1303 equal $ 434·33		„ of Christian Pupils	426
		„ Non-Christian „	380
Number of Pastors - - -	1	„ of Sunday Schools	13
„ of Preachers - -	4	„ of S. S. Scholars	786

Map 2.1: Map of Bombay
(Source: American Mission Report of 1903, p. 7)

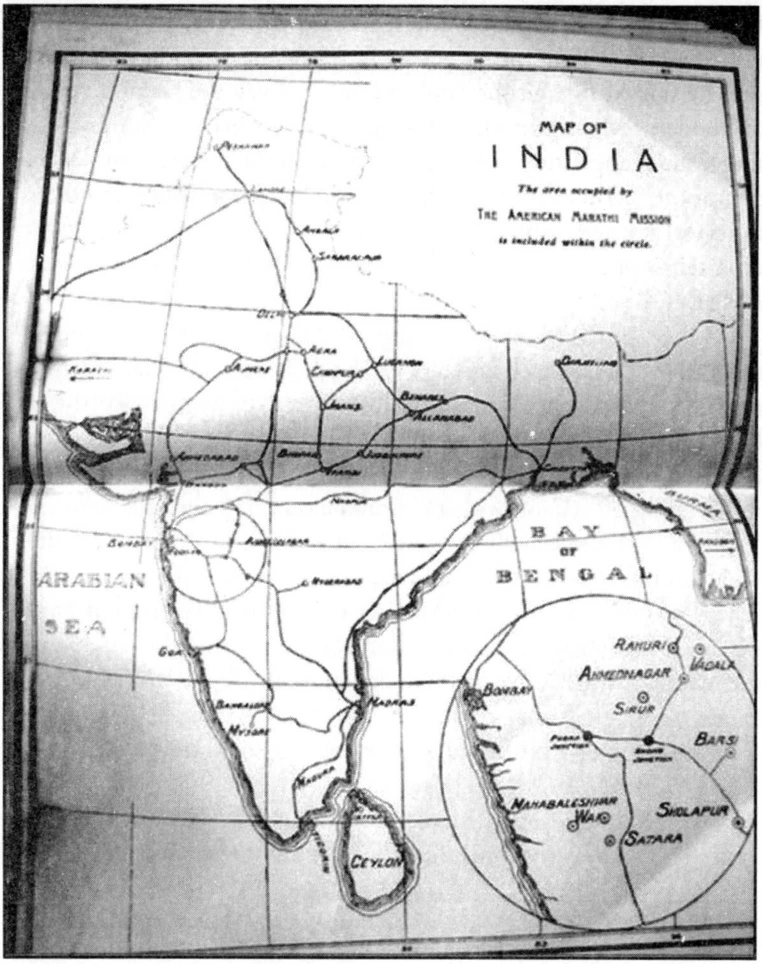

Map 2.2: Map showing area covered by AMM
(Source: R A Hume edited, *Report of AMM,* 1920)

The American Marathi Mission[102](AMM), made a significant breakthrough by opening its first Marathi school for girls in 1824. It was the first of its kind in Western India. By 1831, the AMM diverted its attention in Ahmednagar and made it the Jerusalem of

102 Called Bombay Mission till 1834

Protestant Christianity in Western India[103]. In 1848, Jyotiba Phule visited a girls' school run by AMM in Ahmednagar and in the same year he started first girls' school in Pune[104]. Even the sternest critics of modern Missionary methods were compelled to admit how much the evangelizing agencies have done in the direction of female education[105]. The example of this Mission had been helpful to others in several respects, especially in the matter of placing native churches on a self supporting basis[106]. Rev. Tukaram Nathuji was a pastor at AMM, in Bombay Church, in 1899.

The Church Missionary Society (CMS) was formed in London in 1799 patronised by Church of England. The educational activities of Church Missionary Society (CMS), was also quite praiseworthy. It began its work in Bombay in 1818 and in 1826 started a girl's school. Rev. R. Kenney the first representative of the society was instrumental in founding 10 schools with an enrollment of 310 students between 1820-1826. Later schools were established in Bassein, Thana, Bandra and Nashik. It also founded Robert Money[107] School in 1835. Money school was the host place for Missionary meetings. Translation work occupied the greater part of Mr. Kenny's time during the latter year. He wrote a small tract in Marathi entitled *"Moral and Religious Instruction for Children."* He was also instrumental in translating for the Christian Knowledge Society another small tract called "*The Chief Truths of the Christian Religion*".[108]

In 1880 the Robert Money institution received a government grant of Rs.1810 showing the efficiency of the school. Bible was

---

103 M. D. David, *Missions Cross-Cultural Encounter and Change in Western India*, Manohar, New Delhi, 2001, p. 48

104 Vidyut Bhagwat, *Stree Prashnanchi Vatchaal (M)*, Pratima Prakashan, Pune, 2004, p. 64

105 Mary Frances Billington, *Woman in India*, Chapman & Hall, London,1895, p. 36

106 *BG*, October 6, 1883, p. 627

107 Robert Cotton Money was born in India and for a short time he was serving in the Revenue Department in Southern Konkan. Later he served as an assistant in the Revenue Dept in Southern Konkan and finally as an assistant resident at Bhooj. He died at Solapur on 21st January 1835) from OCS May 1858, Vol 9, No. 5

108 *OCS*, November, 1843, p. 397

taught daily in the school by the Principal Rev. Mr. Carss and Vice Principal Mr. Jackson and Rev. Jani.[109]

The first girls' school of the Scottish Mission was founded by Mrs. Margaret Wilson[110] in Bombay.[111] However the progress of pupils was far from being encouraging between 1830 to 1835. In all she established six girls schools and one of the school is today known as St. Columba High School for Girls. On 24th September 1920, Chattrapati Shahu gave cheque towards donation to the Principal of St. Columba Girls High School, Bombay.[112]

Picture 2.2: American Mission School, Bombay
(**Source** : American Mission Report of 1903, p.6)

Picture 2.3: Margret Wilson (L) and Bombay Church (Former American Board Printing House on right) (Source: American Mission Report of 1900, May 1903, p.192)

109 *BG*, April 24, 1880, p. 89

110 She was the first wife of John Wilson who died on April 19, 1835.

111 George Smith, *The Life of John Wilson*, J. Murray, London, 1879, p. 44

112 In Rumal No. 44, Pudka No. 3, Document No. 12445 of Rajarshi Shahu Chhtrapati of Kolhapur, 1884-1922, Vol. 2, p. 84

Picture 2.4: American Mission Blind School, Bombay
(Source : American Mission Report, December 5th 1901, p.30)

Picture 2.5: Rev. Gordon Hall was the founder of first American Mission outside US [Photograph – A Memorial in his name in Massachusetts (June 1939)]

2.6.2 Alfred Godney High School, Dapoli

In 1889, Society for the Propagation of the Gospel (SPG) Mission started this school as an English Medium School. In 1928, Advocate C. V. Karandikar took lead in saving it by establishing "*Dapoli Shikshan Sanstha*". With co-operation of many the Missions land, building and other infrastructure was purchased. Wrangler Paranjpe, Shri P. V. Kane and Sane Guruji were Alumni of this School.

2.6.3 Literary path for the spread of Christianity among the masses

From the beginning the Missionaries used print as an influential source to spread their message[113]. Missionaries gave impetus to the creation of literary prose. Through small stories, catechisms essays and prayers in marathi, they tried to inculcate spirit of spiritualism and ethical values among the people. They firmly believed that small books written in simple prose would convince more and more people to understand their objectives. The opening of schools by the Missionaries had a desired effect to a certain extent. These schools not only formed a nexus of literacy but also provided opportunities especially to the children of the down-trodden to educate themselves.

In Bombay the Missions along with translations started to write booklets differentiating various aspects of Christianity and Hinduism. The Missionaries resorted to write small didactic essays. Any subject matter could be effectively projected through the essay with brief and lucid introduction, unfurling of central theme and arrived at suitable conclusions. The booklets in the form of didactic essays had been most resourceful weapon in the hands of Missionaries in early stages of propagation of Christianity. However, there had been certain Missionary booklets, which may be considered for their reasonable approach towards family relations, ethical life and other socio-religious problems that required immediate attention. Mrs. Farar, wife of a Christian Missionary from Nasik published in 1835 an essay on better family life entitled 'Hints for the improvement of early education' and 'Discipline' or '*Kutumba Parivartana-niti*'. She had been frank enough to mention in it that she published

113 S. R. Shirgaonkar, *Op.Cit*, p. 30

the book not for personal reputation or money, but that it should be useful as a guide to young children. The other booklets of Mrs. Farar were '*Henry ani Tyacha Sambhalnara Gadi' (Henry and his Bearer), 'Sambhuyachi Gostha'* (1835), '*Chamatkarik Gosthi'* 1835, '*Balbodh Gosthi' (*1836) and '*Yatrekaryacha Vrittanta'* were didactic stories aimed at inculcating virtuous habits among young children's. Scottish Missionary Societies[114], John Wilson[115], Nesbit and Murry Mitchel were engaged in the Missionary work over the Presidency.

Dr. Wilson[116] D D stressed the importance of Indian languages (he was an Orientalist). In 1853, Mr. J. P. Willoughby gave a Bungalow at Mahableshwar for the use of Missionaries to Dr. Wilson[117]. Robert Nesbit (arrived in India in 1827) at Harnai, in Southern Konkan, engaged in the acquisition of the Marathi language; in which he obtained proficiency early. He prepared, revised and lithographed the tracts and schoolbooks[118]. He wrote about 4 small books. Robert presented arguments in favour of Christianity at the cost of Hindu conservatism and traditions. While in Scotland in 1850-51, Rev. Robert Nesbit raised fund for the Buildings (in Bombay) especially for Bombay Mission of the Free Church of Scotland.

Rev. Murry Mitchell (came to India in 1838) contributed about 12 small books in Marathi. Among his collections were such useful titles such as Sanskrit '*Subodh Shlok'* and '*Subodh Abhanga'*. The former contained original Sanskrit *Shlokas* along with Marathi and English translations, while the later was the collection of Tukaram's *Abhangas*

114 Its name changed to General Assembly of the Church of Scotland in 1835 and later Bombay Mission of the Free Church of Scotland.

115 He founded the oldest Christian Periodical in India i.e. *Oriental Christian Spectator* (OCS). Mrs. Wilson explained its necessity in a letter to her sisters dated 20th February1830, in the following words: "Such publication was particularly required in the Presidency, owing to the dearth of information which prevails on religious and Missionary subjects."

116 A special 26 page lecture by John Wilson "The Indian Military Revolt viewed in its Religious Aspect" published in the Report of the Annual Report of the Bombay Auxiliary Missionary Society of the Free Church of Scotland ,1857

117 *BG*, October 17,1903

118 Report of the Annual Report of the Bombay Auxiliary Missionary Society of the Free Church of Scotland 1855, Bombay, p. 9

with their meaning[119]. His work in Marathi "Native Superstitions" (publication of Bombay Tract and Book Society), treats especially of Omens, Portents, Unlucky Days, Incidents, and Phenomenon, etc. showing, Hindus were influenced to a great degree by their belief on superstitions[120]. '*Bala Sondree Tagore*' drawn up by Mrs. Murray Mitchell[121], from a little work published in Bengal.

Table 2.5: Daily Routine at Ambroli House which was Scottish Mission's (Girgaum Church)[122]

Day	*Time*	*Place*	*Language*	*Audience*
Sabbath (Sunday)	Morning 7' O'Clock	Mission House	English	Indo- British Portuguese
Sunday	9' O'Clock	-"-	Marathi	Secondary School Students of Marathi Schools famous (*antedeshiya*) those who desired to get converted to Christianity
-"-	2' O'Clock	-"-	-"-	-"-
-"-	3' O'Clock	-"-	-"-	-"-
-"-	5' O'Clock	Orphanage of Mission	Marathi and Hindustani	Unsheltered or Orphans
Wednesday	7' O'Clock	Mission House	English	Educated People
Thursday	7' O'Clock	-"-	Marathi	Converted
Saturday	5' O'Clock	-"-	-"-	Bible Class for School Teachers
Other days	5' O'Clock	School Rooms	Marathi	Exams for Children on religious education

119 D. A. Dalvi, *Renaissance in the 19th century Maharashtra (1832-1874)*, Ph.D Thesis, Bombay, 1990, p. 452

120 *OCS*, January 1863, Vol. 4, p. 73

121 Rev. Dr. Murry Mitchell with Mrs. Mitchell expects to be present at the Philadelphia Council (PC) in September 1880. The presented report on foreign Missions at PC (Front Page of *BG*, August 21, 1880)

122 S. R. Shirgaonkar, *Op.Cit*, pp. 107-108

2.7 Premier Christian Educational Institutions

The Catholic Mission

The early history of education in Bombay is chiefly a record of Christian Missionary enterprise. The Portuguese, Franciscans were not only the first Missionaries but also the first school masters. But, by 1720 they were replaced by Italian Carmelites. Till 1850, the condition of catholic education was miserable. Catholic Missions did not do effective work during the period from 1720 to 1850. The separation of Society of Jesus (Jesuits) in the Portuguese colonies had a disastrous effect on the Missions the World over and in India quite definitely. However, with the restoration of the society in 1814, and the return of the Jesuits to India a revival in Catholic education began especially with regard to higher education.

Picture 2.6: The symbol of Jesuits

When Bishop Hartmann arrived in Bombay, the catholic education was disorganized while protestant Hindu, Muslim and Parsi educational institutions were forging ahead at a quick pace. There were two primary schools, one the Baretto Foundation at Kavel and the D'Souza School at Mazgaon[123]. Bishop Hartmann

123 Daniel D'Souza, *Capuchin Missions in India,* Sage Publishers, Mangalore, 2000, p. 243

after putting Mazgaon School under the charge of the Jesuits, went on a pastoral tour to Poona, Belgaum, Vengurla and Solapur. He wanted to reorganize the seminary in Bombay which was formed in 1770. It was more dead than alive. The seminarians did not join as a vocation but wanted to make living out of Priesthood. They did not contribute any thing for their support, and when they did they had every thing to their relatives. When Bishop Hartmann took charge there were about a dozen in mates but without a Rector, Professor. This Seminary for a short while was shifted from Bombay to Surat (between 1852- 1855). It was also during Bishop Hartmann's time the vast Bombay Vicariate was divided in to two separate unit - Bombay and Poona. Bombay was to go to Capuchins and Poona to Jesuits. But, the Jesuits wanted their College only in Bombay. And on 13th August 1857, the Capuchins took over Poona and the Jesuits over Bombay. To keep the faithful and the Missionaries informed about the evangelizing activities and other items of concern, the capuchins had started some periodicals. Among them, *"The Examiner"* of Bombay ranks first. It was started by Bishop Hartmann in 1850. Its original name was *Bombay Catholic Examiner*.

Bishop Hartmann was great writer. We have his translation of the new testament in Hindustani and in Urdu made in 1863. All his writings were collected and edited by Fr. Adel Helmus J. under the title *Monumenta Anstasiana* in five volumes[124].

The Jesuit contribution to the study of "Mission lands" has been significant and multifaceted. India was one of their earliest adventures. They introduced the first movable type printing press in Goa in the sixteenth century. They also published "a variety of grammars and guides to vernacular languages."

The efforts of the Catholic Church also deserve a mention here. St. Teresa's High School at Girgaum and European female orphanage at Byculla was opened in 1850. Portuguese school at Dadar Antonio da Silva opened in 1851.[125]

---

124 Daniel D'Souza, "Tibet-Hindustan Mission as the nucleus of North India Mission" in *Indian Missiological Review*, Vol. 12, No. 2, July 1990, p. 124

125 K. S. Cheema, *British policy in Western India with special reference to Bombay City and the Deccan (1830-1875)*, Ph.D. Thesis, 2001, p. 289

2.7.1 St. Xavier's College

St Xaviers College, Mumbai founded in 1869 introduced studies in Science in 1884. The pioneering contribution of three Jesuit Scientists namely Rev. Ethelbert Blatter (1877-1934), Rev. Jean Ferdinand Caius (1877-1944) and Rev. Hermenegild Santapau (1903-1970) needs to be highlighted.

Picture 2.7: St. Xavier's College, Mumbai

Father Blatter was born in Switzerland and came to India in 1903 to be professor of Biology. He began his extensive collection of botanical material, including some interesting and rare specimens, which is still preserved in the Blatter Herbarium. He studied and wrote on the Mangroves, the Ferns, the Mosses, the Grasses and the many varieties of flora in the Bombay Presidency. With over 300 publications to his credit Blatter ranks among pioneers who developed scientific floras of India. In recognition of his contributions to Asiatic Botany he was awarded the Johannes Bruehl Memorial Medal in 1931.

Picture 2.8: Blatter Herbarium Library and Specimens
(Source: DNA, October 30, 2007, Front Page)

Father Caius was also with St. Xaviers College in 1922 but was latter appointed at Haffkine Institute. He also became member of the Bombay Natural History Society.

Father Santapau had researched on the "Flora of the Khandala on the Western Ghats" and was awarded doctorate in Botany for his work. After completing his postdoctoral work in Herbarium from England, he joined St. Xaviers College, Mumbai. His pioneering work as Chief Botanist led him to be appointed as the Director of Botanical Survey of India in 1961. In 1968, he returned back to St. Xaviers College and guided Ph.D students. To his credit he had more than 300 research articles including books. He had wide collection of about 100,000 botanical specimens, which can still be seen in herbariums at Bombay, Kew Gardens (England), Harvard (USA) , Missouri (UP, India) and many national and international herbariums. He served on several Universities and Government committee's and comMissions including CSIR, New Delhi even after his retirement. On his death the then, Indian Prime Minister, Mrs. Indira Gandhi commented "... He had great knowledge of and concern for our plant wealth and wrote extensively on it for experts as well as for laymen". He received the Padmashree award from the Government of India. The above three Jesuit scientists harmonized the heights of scientific research to unravel the mysteries of Nature and the Environment.

St. Xaviers College today supports NGO's like *Jan Seva Mandal* in social involvement programmes. Around 50 village teachers were brought to visit the *IMS Vikrant*[126] in order to give them a wider perspective. Most of these teachers were from villages in North Maharashtra who taught children in morning and work as farmers through the rest of the day. These teachers in turn work with the NGO on village locals on issues like organic farming and water management. Godfrey D'Lima the director of the NGO said, "The main objective of bringing the teachers to visit *IMS Vikrant* was to give them a wider perspective of the naval force and warfare equipment so that they could in turn give their students a first person account about the issues."[127] Unique idea of connecting rural crowd to urban programmes.

126 This ship served the Indian Navy for nearly three decades and played an important role in the 1971 Indo-Pak War.

127 Puneet N. Yadav, 'Barefoot Teachers get a taste of history, in *DNA*, 12th April 2007

refoot Teachers get a taste of history

DNA Newspaper 12-4-7

Seva Mandal brings village teacher to to visit the IMS in order give them a erspective

Teachers from Dhule and Nandurbar districts aboard the IMS

Fact police

A delegation of 50-odd teachers from rural Maharashtra visited IMS Vikrant on Wednesday morning.

The Barefoot Teachers, as they are known, teach children in Dhule and Nandurbar districts of Maharashtra in the mornings and work as farmers through the rest of the day.

The trip was organised by NGO Jan Seva Mandal which also works with the locals on organic farming.

IMS Vikrant, which served the Indian Navy for nearly three decades played an important role in the 1971 Indo-Pak War in which it not only blocked all supplies to the Pakistani troops but also cut off the escape route of the Pakistani army though the sea. The ship was subsequently decommissioned in 1997 and is currently stationed at Mumbai's Naval Dockyard. The ship is now a microcosm of the Indian Navy exhibiting specialised naval areas like diving, naval operations, armament, missiles, naval uniforms and seamanship aspects.

Picture 2.9: St. Xavier College's NGO Connection
(Source : DNA, April 12, 2007, Mumbai)

The Indian Historical Research (Heras Institute) founded by Rev. Henry Heras S. J in 1926 is doing pioneering work in the field of History and Culture.

While the Heras Institute is an autonomous Research Institute, it collaborates with St. Xavier's College in the Doctoral programmes in the Faculty of Arts in the University of Mumbai. In response to a request from colleges affiliated to the University of Mumbai and S.N.D.T. University, the Heras Institute offers a regular programme on Research methodology and the reconstruction of History using the ancient artifacts in the Heras Institute Museum and the Primary sources in the Heras Institute Library. Through Heras Research programme students get to examine ancient artifacts like Mohen-jo-daro seals, Buddhist stupas, Gandhara sculptures, Indian Christian paintings, punch-marked coins, Ivory images and so on . Today the Heras Research Programmes are a big hit among under-graduate students especially of History subject.

2.7.2 Wilson College of Anglican influence

Strictly speaking, Wilson college was started in 1836 (lot of Books on its founder John Wilson have been already written), but the present building was functional since 1889. In 1902, Wilson College was only a two-storied building. In 1905 a third storey was added[128]. It has boys as well as Lady's Hostel. The College Motto is "*Fides, Spes, Cartas*"- Faith, Hope and Love. These qualities have served as a guiding force for all those who managed and maintained the institution throughout the years of its existence. College emblem is Burning Bush, it has blue colour and Thistle the National flower of Scotland, yellow pineapples signify bounty of nature and hospitality and cross of St. Andrews, Patron saint of Scotland can be seen. It was based on the strong set of values that Wilson adopted. Though Scottish by birth, Wilson fitted in with the Indian society where he lived and laboured with a deep understanding of the Indian mind. He advocated the use of the mother tongue in education.

Picture 2.10: Rev. John Wilson and Wilson College, Mumbai

128 M. D. David, *John Wilson and His Institution*, Wilson Education Society, Bombay, 1975, p. 91

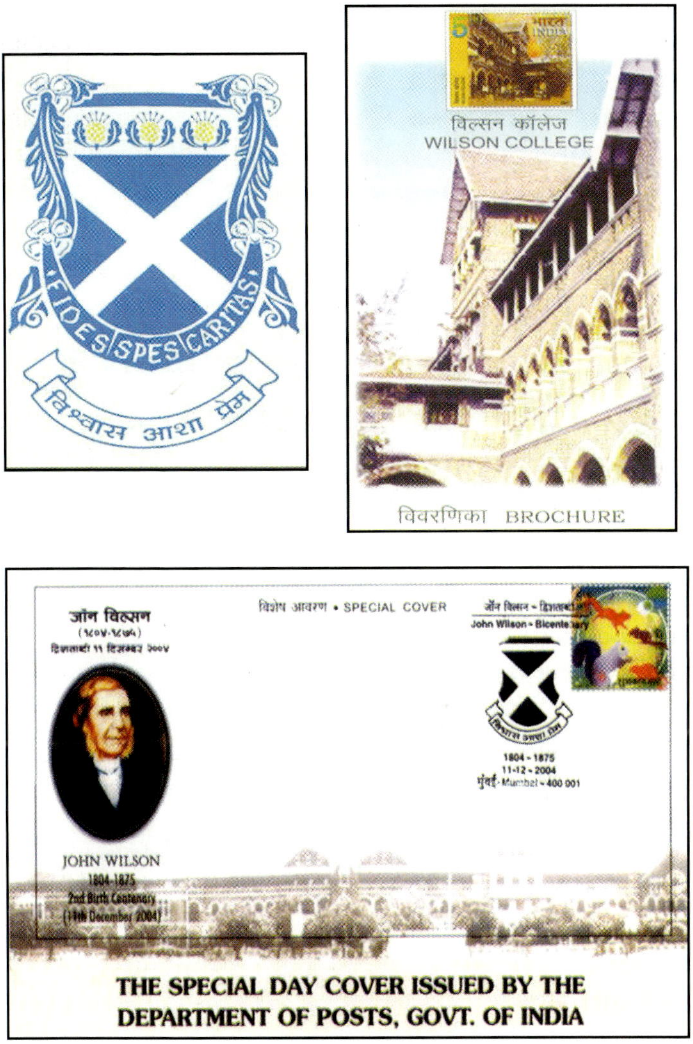

Picture 2.11: Symbol, Brochure and special cover of Wilson College.

2.7.3 Sophia College for Women

Sophia College for Women adopted the motto *Urdhvamula* (roots upwards)-the Sanskrit concept of God being the source of life. Late Fr. Henry Heras inspired its Indian crest.

Mother Anderson believed in a holistic education, with strong emphasis on the formation of values and convictions and a sense of pride in India's culture and heritage. On the first Principals/ College Day, the students wanted to put up a scene from a play of Shakespeare; however, they were gently advised to present one of the plays of Kalidasa instead! During the freedom struggle, Mother Anderson offered to house and look after the children of a freedom fighter couple Alva who were courting imprisonment. The college song and the college Crest and Motto were selected in the early 1940's.

In the Sophia song, the line "Our goal shall be true liberty" is a clear reference to the struggle for national independence. The college motto of *urdhvamula* (roots upwards) is taken from the Bhagavat Gita while the crest is typically Indian in design this is something unique that in pre British time a Britisher chose something from Bhagvat Gita a real effort towards inculturation which late pope John Paul II propagated.

In 2006, Mary Braganza RSCJ, the former principal of Sophia College for Women, 1965-1973 and 1977-1982 was honoured with Padmashri by the Government of India for her contribution in the field of Social Work. The Padmashri is an extremely prestigious national award, presented in recognition of considerable achievement and contribution in various fields. This was the first time that an RSCJ of the Indian Province had received this award. She now prefers to be called Sr. Karuna, she was born on 25th October 1923, the fifth child and first girl among ten brothers and sisters, of whom five became religious. While studying at Xavier's college she was actively involved in the social service and Mission camps to the villages of Talasari and developed a life-long passion to work for rural India and the tribals. She became first Indian Principal of Sophia college in January 1965.

In the mid-1960s, the Kothari Education Commission called for a comprehensive review of the entire educational system, with a focus on issues like science education for all social and national service. Karuna was inspired by this- in fact, her career as principal was to be shaped by these calls. Sophia College and campus saw great expansion and academic innovation during her tenure. She was the moving force behind two academic initiatives on the campus

Picture 2.15: Sr. Mary Braganza

during this period-Sophia Polytechnic, to give education a practical orientation; and Sadhana School for the mentally handicapped to offer quality education even to those rejected by society as being "uneducable".

In 1973, Karuna was able to take a well-deserved sabbatical which was interrupted all too soon by her call to Rome by the then Superior General, Mother Camacho, to serve on her council. After her 3 year stint in Rome, Mary returned to India and to Sophia in June 1977, for a further period of five years as principal. Academic life flourished under her dynamic leadership. After 1980's she was being drawn into involvement at the national level. Her work at St. Joseph's College Torpa, Ranchi District of Jharkhand for more than 12 years saw the birth of a large hostel for the girls of St. Josephs' college, the setting up of a centre for women's development; the establishment of a primary teacher training institute, a *balniketan* and an English medium school, all at Torpa. She can also claim credit for having initiated a unique study that involved mapping indigenous herbs and documenting in a book each and every herb available in the district. Since 2006 she is based in Pune.

Thus, she went into the heart of dacoit territory in Jharkhand and Bihar and in a couple of years; she brought together 10,000 tribal women to take charge of their destinies by participating in the affairs of their villages. Today, the law and order has returned to the otherwise hostile territory that boasts of schools, *balwadis*, playgrounds, medicinal and health farms, village banks and self-help grounds[129]. Detailed work on Mary Braganza's life is carried out by Pearl A Drego[130].

Urdhva Mula, is also the name of a journal of Sophia Centre for Women's Studies and Development with the objective of providing a platform for interdisciplinary dialogue among academicians, students, activists, researchers and policy makers.

Picture 2.16: The Chapel and the staff of library and documentation Unit

2.7.4 Nirmala Niketan College of Social Work

Nirmala Niketan with its motto "the highest law of life is service" was established in 1955 and is run by the parent body, Institute of Social Service, managed by the Daughters of the Heart of Mary. In order to identify themselves with the people the sisters wore a Sari. It is co-educational college providing training at para-professional, Bachelor's and master's level. The academic programmes offered to the students is generic with a developmental slant. It has activities in two directions Social Work and Home Science. It was the first and the only college of the University of Bombay that offered degree in

129 *DNA*, January 26, 2008, p. 7

130 Pearl A. Drego, T*he Charism of Karuna - Life Story of Sister Karuna Mary Braganza,* Alfreruby Publishers, 2011

Home Science[131]. It holds the view that the teaching institutions of social work, specially in under-developed and developing countries have a responsibility towards the social realities of the society. Accordingly, it has evolved its specific commitments with regard to its fieldwork projects. It states that its major emphasis is on urban population- those in urban slums.

Picture 2.17: The logo and symbol of Nirmala Niketan College of Social work, Mumbai

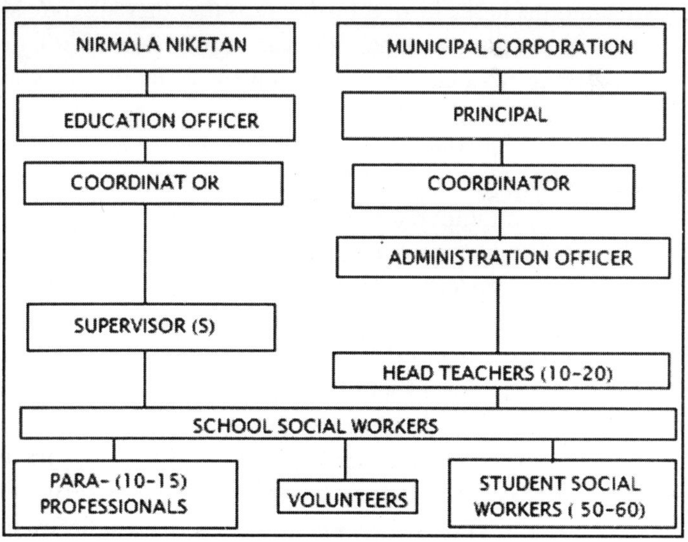

Chart 2.1: School Social Work Program jointly with Municipal corporation of Greater Mumbai

131 *The Examiner*, May 11, 1957, p. 94

The focus is on the systematic and problem aspects of the slum community and possible solutions........ The slums are considered to be the priority areas of work because in spite of the fact that the slum dwellers of Bombay make significant contribution in running the city life, their plight is of untold misery. They lack the basic amenities like water, sanitation, electricity and toilet facilities and live under constant fear of eviction.

In pursuance of its commitments, the college, over the years has evolved and developed numerous field projects like family, service centre, social service syllabus and non-formal education cells etc. in the area of youth health and general welfare. These projects are run on experimental basis and after a certain period of time the effort is made to hand them over to voluntary or governmental organization, as the case may be. The college regards that these field projects besides serving the disadvantaged----- "provide students the opportunity for fieldwork in tune with class room learning and are means for continuous faculty improvement in the field, thus enriching their classroom teaching and giving opportunities to test classroom concepts in the field. It further feels that they also provide opportunity to develop teaching materials suited to social realities and to undertake research which has immediate implications for practice. The social work staff in these projects supervised by the faculty, in turn provide the necessary field based supervision for the students in fieldwork."

One of the most important field projects of Nirmala Niketan in terms of financial and manpower investment is the school social work programme, run in the local municipal schools. The undertaking of this vast financial and technical responsibility by the college should be viewed in terms of its field work priorities as pointed above. Nirmala Niketan which was associated with the initial growth of School Social Work in private schools of Bombay, felt that unlike these schools, the municipal school system was a stable system. Earlier during 1960's some Principals showed receptivity for placement programmes. Fr. Banto who was the Principal of Antonio D"Souza High School, Bombay and also a visiting teacher with the college of social work

Nirmala Niketan and undertook student placement programme in his school.[132]

2.7.5 The Don Bosco Salesians

Picture 2.18: Fr. Maschio and Mother Teresa- marking the 82nd Birthday of the Father with stamp of Mother Teresa and Don Bosco

This Catholic Order founded by St. John Bosco in 1859, in Italy landed in Mumbai in January 1906. Today Matunga in Mumbai is the headquarters of this order. Late Fr. Aurelius Maschio is regarded as a legendry Missionary, preacher and educator. Fr. Maschio was born in Italy in 1909. Shillong was where he started his Missionary

132 Anjali Gandhi, *School Social Work*, Common Wealth Publishers, New Delhi, 1990, p. 65

life. He erected a complex of buildings in the heart of Bombay which cater for the education of thousands of boys. He has literally converted the marshes of Matunga in Mumbai into an academic arena where youths of all religions are trained to be good citizens and men of sound moral character. In the centre of this educational complex, Maschio constructed what he considers the masterpiece of his work, the Shrine of Don Bosco's Madonna, one of the most magnificent shrines in the continent of Asia. Fr. Maschio also published a little magazine "*Don Bosco's Madonna*" through which he spread the message of Christian faith and morals. In his name the award called "Fr. Maschio Platinum Jubilee Award" has been instituted. Among its recipients have been late Mother Teresa, late Vijay Merchant and late Baba Amte.

"Her hands are more used to cleaning the filth from starving near corpses, to coaxing a few to live a little longer to giving to those who cant afford a straw mattress and a blanket…."[133].

The veteran Salesian, Fr. Antonio Alessi, a close friend and collaborator of Fr. Maschio, has described his life-story in a book entitled '*Love without Frontiers*'[134].

The department of Posts, India issued a postage stamp to commemorate hundred years of Don Bosco Salesians in India on 27th February 2006.

2.7.6 St. Teresa Institute of Education

St. Teresa Institute of Education is one of the pioneering Colleges of teacher education in Mumbai. It was established by the sisters of the congregation of Carmellite Religious in 1973. For over four decades now, the College has been rendering yeoman service to the cause of teacher education in and around Mumbai. The College works towards the loafty ideals of creating teachers who are competent and compassionate. The emphasis is on excellence in education and the philosophy of the College is guided by the sublime principles of

133 Benedict Costa, "Much ado about Nuns", in The Illustrated weekly of India, September 20, 1970

134 Louis D'Silva, *The Christian Community and the National Mainstream*, Spicer College Press, Pune, undated, p.162

St. Teresa of Avila, the patron saint of the Carmellites and mother Veronica, the foundress of the CCR congregation.

Picture 2.19: Logo of St. Teresa Institute of Education, Mumbai

2.8 The Vasai Chapter

Vasai a well known suburb of Mumbai situated on the western coastline of India (Konkan). The indigenous name of Bassein was Vasai derived from the Sanskrit verb root *Vas*, 'which means 'to dwell', and therefore Vasai (a dwelling) is a name by which it is still known[135]. During medieval period, the name was changed to *Basai*, which the Portuguese made Baciam and the English, who finally became its masters in 1818, called the port Bassein[136].

For about two hundred and ten years the Portuguese were in possession of Bassein. During this period it gradually rose to a state of 'grandeur and opulence' that obtained for it the noble appellation of ' a Corte do Norte' or ' the Chief city of the North', in relation to the capital of Goa. The Portuguese selected Bassein as their northern capital and port, although Bombay was as much a part of their possessions from the very outset. The choice of Bassein as a port and capital in 1534 was influenced by the sixteenth century navigational needs and favorable geographical factors. India's only male canonized[137] saint Gonsalo Garcia was from Bassein[138] and he

135 R. D' Silva, 'Early Phase of Christianity in Bassein' in the *Proceedings of Indian History Congress*, 33rd session, Muzzafarpur, 1972, p. 342

136 M. D. David, 'Historic Bassein' in *Indica*, Vol. 24, No. 2, September 1987, p. 91

137 Canonised in 1862 for his work carried from India to Japan.

138 Was born inside Bassein Fort

came to the capital of Philippines Manila in 1590 and joined their the Franciscan Missionaries. Since, he knew Japanese well he became an angel for the migrated Christians from Japan.[139] The Christian fisherfolk of Vasai revere the Gonsalo Garcia festival every year in the month of January. The English Physician Dr. John Fryer has written about the property held by religious orders in Bassein in 1674. He further writes that three parts of the city was devoted to their use and that the Jesuit Missionaries had become large property owners and made good money. This money is reported to go to the credit of Missionaries who used to spend it for good works.

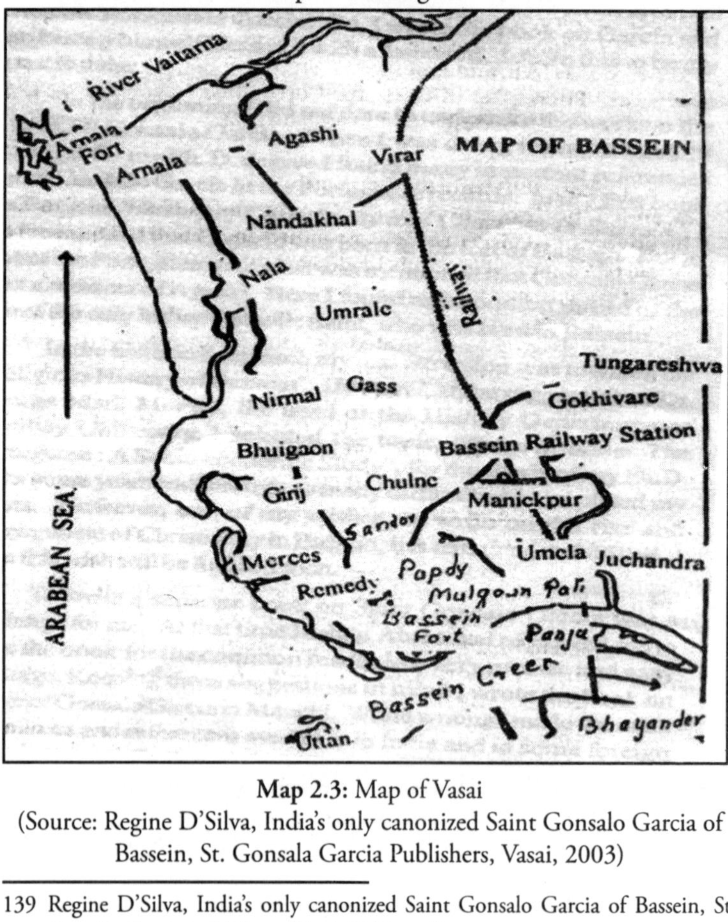

Map 2.3: Map of Vasai
(Source: Regine D'Silva, India's only canonized Saint Gonsalo Garcia of Bassein, St. Gonsala Garcia Publishers, Vasai, 2003)

139 Regine D'Silva, India's only canonized Saint Gonsalo Garcia of Bassein, St. Gonsala Garcia Publishers, Vasai, 2003, p. 40

The converted Christians in and around Vasai came to be known as East Indians, who trace their origins to caste groups like *Agris* (Saltpan workers), *Bhandaris* (Toddy tappers, distillers and musicians), *Kolis* (fishermen), *Kunbis* (Landowners and agriculturists, Kumbhars (Pottery makers)and *Nhavis* (barbers). Since they were converted during Portuguese rule, they were given Portuguese names, but the converts could not correctly pronounce the Portuguese names. The result was that Manuel became Munno, Francis was converted to Fursoo, Gonsalves was known as Gosal. Some of the converts have retained Hindu surnames like Chaudhari, Raut, Mhatre and Karpe[140]. Two type of conversions occurred during the Portuguese rule- Individual and Group conversion and the later was more preferred De Mello, D Castro, D Souza, Soz (Mello Castro, Soz were village names in Portugal). But the *Koli* community even after conversion had traditional surnames as Nago, Tandel, Sonvar, Bombacha etc. Most of the Catholic society in Vasai is from Somvanshi Kshtriya (Panmali) and Samvedi Brahman (North Vasai) Caste. They adopted Portuguese surnames like…

Table 2.6: Typical Christian Surnames in Vasai

Aloj, Alvares, Almeida, Butello, Coelo, Colaso, Carvelo	*Coutinho, Castro, Crasto, DeMello, D'Souza, D'Silva, D'Aubrio, D'Cunha*	*D Cruz, D Costa, De Monto, D'Sa, D'lima, Furtado, Falcav, (Pheraira) Ferera, Frel, Misquita, Machyado, Miranda, Moraes, Murjhelo, Serejo, Silvera, Nunis, Pegad, Sequeira, Lobo, Rego, Rosario.*

Thus in a small community like the Indian Christians, there was a far larger diversity of names than any other. Sometimes the original name need slightly be changed eg. Bheem into Biem, Pawar into Power, Joshi into Jose, Girdher into Gilder etc. In the case of orphans their Christian names were given from the Bible or were named after the European Patrons that supported them hence names

140 These people were probably converted towards the end of Portuguese rule and hence did not change their names.

like Wenright, Dalton, Pemberton, Jones and Price among Indian Christians. Also in Vasai the local folklore had influenced Christian religious hymns especially on Mother Mary. Fr. Francis Correa wrote "*Mauli Nau Mahine Gajbar*" which talks about mother Mary giving birth to Jesus in a cowshed. In 1973, Fr. Hillary Fernandes established the Sanjeevan Kala Kendra to promote indigenisation of the liturgy and music through bhajans, kirtans and traditional Indian dance forms. It used to train young evangelists to enact the Gospel at the time of festivals by moving around the community at Bassein.[141]

St. Xaviers High School (Manikpur) is a marathi medium school for boys which is now more than 50 years old. It is managed by Jesuit Fathers. Attached to the school is the St. Xavier's technical institute. St. John Debritto Adhyapak Vidyala was established 1943 in Manickpur. The School has history of producing many distinguished Father's. St. Anthony's convent (Koliwada) celebrated its golden jubilee in 2007. It is a co-education school managed by sisters of Our Lady of Fatima.

The other prominent schools include, St. Augustine High School, Thomas Baptista Jr. College, Pushpanjali College of Education, St. Antonys Convent School (Koliwada), St. Peter High School (Koliwada), St. Thomas High School (Dev Talav), St. Elizabeth Convent High School and Gonsala Garcia College.

141 Teresa Albuquerque, *To Love is to Serve Catholics of Bombay*,1986, Heras Institute, Bombay, p. 79

Picture 2.20: Education Institutions in Vasai-1

Picture 2.21: Education Institutions in Vasai-2

Picture 2.22: Education Institutions in Vasai-3

2.9 The Kalyan Chapter

The annual report of the Bombay Missionary Society of the Free Church of Scotland, 1855 (pg.21) mentions about an English School opened in the ancient town of Kalyan, having the population of 7000 souls. Dr. George Smyton made liberal contribution for Kalyan. Dr. Wilson had visited Kalyan four times. Mr. Antonius Gabreil comes as teacher at Kalyan[142].

Till the early 1920's the only place of worship for the Catholics (mostly railway workers) of Kalyan was "The Kalyan Church" situated on the east side of the railway lines at Katemanivali. Because of the ever growing population on the west side of the railway lines, the Katemanivali chapel was not only felt to be too small but also very much out of the way and of difficult and dangerous access on account of the many railway tracks that had to be crossed in order to get to the chapel. Already in the 1920's thought was being given to the building of a new Church at a more convenient site on the west side of the railway lines. Near the Kalyan *Mamlatdar's* office, along

142 This report is also covered by *OCS*, January 1856, p. 29

the Kalyan-Murbad road lay a square piece of land on which stood a cross. This plot had been in possession of the catholic community of Kalyan but some how it came to be entered in the city survey records as government land. This the Church authorities learnt in 1922. Appeals from the Bishop of Damaun (Daman) that the land be transferred back to the catholic community of Kalyan began from January 1925 and this was achieved on 5th March 1926 at the time when Fr. Orphino D'Sa was Vicar of St. John the Baptist Church, Thane[143].

The Old Lourdes School

Today the area of Kalyan comes under the Archdiocese of Mumbai. In Kalyan the Lourdes High School was brought to its present status

Picture 2.23: Late Fr. Francis Pereira, Old Lourdes Church, School and foundation stone

143 Leslie J. Ratus and Errol Rozario (ed), Catholic Directory of the Archdiocese of Bombay, 3rd Edition, Ahura Printing Press, Bombay, 1982, p. 84

due to the efforts of late father Francis Pereira who reigned supreme till he retired in April 1983. Fr. Pereira collected funds through fun fairs and premier film shows so that the concrete school building could be constructed. The golden Jubilee volume of the school (1938-1988) speaks about all this. The Old Lourdes Church has been recently renovated.

The Holy Cross School for Girls

The Holy Cross Convent is an English medium girls' school formed in 1974, managed by the Maharashtra Holy Cross Sisters Society. This Society is a member of the Religious congregation namely 'The Sisters of Mercy of the Holy Cross' founded by Fr. Thedosius Florentini and Mother Maria Theresa Scherer in 1856 in Switzerland. The Motto of the school is Truth & Duty.

St. Judes Convent School

One of the prominent Schools of the Kalyan City, it was established on 16th June 1969 on the eastern side of Kalyan. It is run by the 'Church of our Lady of Lourdes' and is dedicated to

Picture 2.24: St. Judes School, the old Chapel and the Parish Priest Fr. Joe Pereira

the idol of its patron. Fr. Joe Pereira was the parish priest of the School. Under his guidance "Life Spring" the Parish bulletin covering various aspects of Parish life is released. Some of the prominent activities of the parish include Sunday Schools, mass for sick and aged, get together for Senior Citizens.

It is noted that the following educational agencies have been employed by the Missionaries in the 19th Century

1. Direct preaching of the Gospel at Central Station
2. Combined Christian and general education, English and Vernacular.*
3. Public lecturing and holding private classes
4. Assisting in translation*
5. Missionary itinerancies[144]*
6. Pastoral care of converts
7. Training converts for the ministry.

Further, it is felt that agencies marked by asterisk proved very effective in bringing social mobility and change in the nineteenth century Indian Society.

The education and medical work of the Missionaries went hand in hand. In fact they represented the two faces of the same coin. The following chapter discusses the medical work of the Missionaries in the greater depth.

144 The Mission according to the ability of its members allotted department of evangelistic Itinerancy. A tour was undertaken by Mr. Narayan Sheshadri to Ratnagiri and other places in the Konkan along with a visit of Hormazdji of Gujarat. The *OCS* of 1845, p.135 highlights the Missionary and ecclesiastical movements like 'Rev. J. Murray Mitchell has returned from Nagpur', 'Rev. Mr. Nesbit returned from a short tour in the Southern Konkan' and 'Rev. Mr. Hume from one in the Northern Konkan'

Chapter 3

Social Activities of Missionaries-II (Medical Mission and Related Works)

Chapter 3

Social Activities of Missionaries-II
(Medical Mission and Related Works)

3.1 Introduction

"The hospital is a powerful educative force, not only in the leveling of the caste barriers but in the spread of common knowledge concerning western medicine and surgery"

...Dr. William Wanless[145]

Like the Christian educational institutions have influenced hundreds of young people every year the work of medical Missions had also touched a large number where in the final motive was welfare of the people.

The First qualified medical Missionary Dr. Clara Swain came to India in November 1869, through the newly formed Women's Foreign Missionary Society at Methodist Episcopal Church from America. She was instrumental in establishing a Women's hospital at Bareilly[146] and after 15 years there, she went to Rajputana, where she worked almost single handedly for next 10 years. Also Ms. Isabela Thoburn started a school with only three girls at Lucknow.

145 Rev. S. N. Suryavanshi, *Physician Extraorinaire- Dr. Sir, Willian James Wanless,* World of Life Publications, Pune, 1991.

146 In 1870, she started a small hospital in equally small room in Bareilly (UP)

Today the Clara Swain hospital at Bareilly and Isabela Girls College at Lucknow tells the story of the work and dedication of the above two ladies. These ladies came to India as the men Missionaries failed to minister to the educational and medical needs of the orthodox Hindu and Muslim families who had Parda System[147].

Miss Funny Butler M. D. was the first qualified medical woman from England to work in India. She came under the auspices of Church of England-Zenana Missionary Society in 1880, and stationed herself at Jabalpur and later in Bhagalpur.[148]

In 1864, a school was started for deaf and mutes by Jesuit Bishop Meurim at his own house in Fort. Later, he was instrumental in establishing a leper asylum and died in the year 1895. This is followed by the work of the Presbyterian Missionaries in Maharashtra. The first issue of *Western India Notes* appeared in January 1893. The Mission hospital of Vengurla (St. Luke's Hospital) with leprosarium and a tuberculosis sanatorium was established. The man behind all this was Dr. Robert H. H. Goheen - the surgical legend attached to Dr. Wanless[149] hospital and research center at Miraj, Kolhapur in Maharashtra. The other pioneering works of Presbyterian Missionaries find there place here. The Presbyterian Missionaries and especially Dr. R. H. H. Goheen's contribution to the AMM school at Vengurla includes the work at Vengurla School' along with the medical Mission work.

The Society of Vincent de Paul looks after Leprosy Home in Trombay and Home for the aged at Kalyan. Father Francis Periera (1902-1985) started the administration of this *Shanti Bhavan* at Kalyan. In 2009, it has 31 male and 5 female inmates.

The All Saints Sisters of the Poor, an Anglican Church Mission founded in 1879, was a pioneer of nursing in Bombay. In 1880, the Bombay government approached them to take up nursing at the J. J.

147 Nalini Keller, *Women under the Cross, Changing Gender roles in Christian Families*, Cosmo, New Delhi, 1997, p. 4

148 Saroj Dhingra, ' Missionary Contribution to the Health Services Development in India' in *St. Francis Xavier His Times and Legacy* ed. Carlo Mata and Kala Acharya, Somaiya Publications, Mumbai, 2007 p. 227

149 Sir William Wanless as a surgeon performed not less those 96,000 operations on all classes of people in India.

and European general hospitals. They were repeatedly commended for their services in the annual reports and a special mention was made of their work during the Hindu-Muslim riots of 1892. They also took up private nursing.[150]

3.2 The American Marathi Mission

This is the oldest Protestant Mission in the Bombay Presidency, Its work having been started in Bombay in 1813, and one happy outcome of these was a large proportion of Missionaries who were the children of those earlier in the field. No other Mission has among its Missionary staff so many who are the sons and daughters of earlier Missionaries. Such a fact speaks volumes for the earlier generation whose Missionary enthusiasm and consecration as witnessed by their children attracting them to similar lines of service and no other Mission working in Marathi language has such a record of past and present Missionaries. There were two leper Asylums at Pui and Poladpur which were supported by the Mission to Lepers in India and the East, but the management was in the hands of AMM. At Pui there were 70 and at Poladpur there were 113 lepers[151].

3.3 Presbyterian Mission of Western India

3.3.1 The Presbyterian Missionaries

The American Presbyterian Mission in Western India was begun by Rev. R. G. Wilder[152] in 1852. Due to certain difficulties arousing between him and Dr. Anderson of the American Board, Wilder carried on the work independently of the Board from 1862 to 1869. Thanks to the friendship between Mr. Wilder and Sir Henry Bartle Frere. The front page *BG* of March 28, 1863 mentions Mr. Wilder's report of his Kolhapur Mission which had five vernacular schools with 250 pupils including 20 girls. It also mentioned about the terrible conflict raging in America (the civil war) doubtlessly

150 Mridualla Ramanna, *Western Medicine and Public Health in Colonial Bombay 1845-1895,* Orient Longman, New Delhi, 2002, p. 58

151 *AMM* report, 1905, p. 14

152 From 1852-1869 he taught classes in English at Kolhapur. Wilder Memorial Church in Kolhapur stands in his name.

diverting attention and funds. It said "only about half the amount subscribed for 1862 has reached us….."

Picture 3.1: Baisinger Memorial Library, Miraj and Dr. Willaim Wanless

Kolhapur Mission was formally taken over by the American Presbyterian Board in 1870 and its work was limited in that state. It covered five stations namely Kolhapur, Ratnagiri, Panhala, Sangali and Miraj and seven outstations – Wadgaon, Herla, Ayatavadi, Kodoli, Borapal, Kuralap and Vengorle. The report of the American Presbyterian Mission in West India mentions the names of various Missionary couples attached to its stations[153].

Table 3.1: Presbyterian Missionary couples attached to the Stations (1886)

Name	*Station*
Mr. & Mrs. Seiler	Kolhapore
Mr. & Mrs. Graham	Sangli
Mr. & Mrs. Goheen	Kolhapur
Mr. & Mrs. Ferris	Panhala
Mr. & Mrs. Tedford	Ratnagiri

153 *BG,* July 3, 1886, p. 420

These Missionaries appear to have been diligently engaged in making known the Gospel in chapels and in the open air and on itinerancies and by means of schools, prisons, hospitals and leper asylums. The schools were mostly vernacular though Mr. Seiler had given a good deal of his time to English Classes[154]. The above report also mentions about Santu, a poor ignorant Mahar, who was now a better teacher than many who have been under Christian instructions from their youth. The Brahman teachers from the Government School at Kodoli used to visit Santu's school twice during a year and expressed surprise at his work. This was considered remarkable as at that time Brahmans did not as a rule take any interest in the education of the lower caste.

Mr. Goheen, perhaps Dr. Goheens father told an interesting incident in connection with the outstation work at Wadgaon. He said "The Mahars who have become Christians at Kini have been subjected to bitter persecutions, especially by the Jain's who are very

Picture 3.2: The Dispensary at Kodoli (Panhala)
(Source: *Bombay Guardian*, 19 January 1895, p.3)

154 *BG,* April 28, 1883, p. 259

numerous in the town. They are nearly all farmers, and when the Christians ask them to give them work as formerly, they heap with an abusive language on them. They say tauntingly go to the *Padri Sahab* who defiled you.

The *BG* of February 1,1896 mentions about Mr. W. H. Hannum securing permission from the collector at Ratnagiri to visit the famous prisoner of the state Theba, the Ex-king of Burma for the express purpose for evangelistic conversations. As the permission was conditional on the wish of the Ex - king two visits were made and the main truths of the Gospel were plainly stated to him. There was a Theodore Carter School managed by Simpson's in Ratnagiri.[155]

Dr. W. J. Wanless of the American Presbyterian Mission, Miraj, Bombay Presidency, proposed[156] with the aid to Dr. A. B. Wilson, to enlarge work which has been carried on for some years with considerable success at the Miraj Hospital namely the training of Indian Christian young men as medical evangelists. Dr. Wanless stated in a circular letter that their curriculum is similar to that of the Government B. J. Medical School in Poona. He further said "In view of the great need in out stations and villages for competent Christian Medical evangelists, and the progress of the present class (four Christian students now in their 3rd and last year) having demonstrated the utility of the Miraj Medical Mission in training men, we desire that the training of Christian Medical Missionary assistants be made a permanent feature of the Miraj Medical Missionary Work. Students in order to be eligible will be required to have passed the middle School Examination or to have studied up to the 7th Anglo-Vernacular Standard. They must be men of good Christian character, and not less then 18 years of age. The Mission also generously proposes to give tuition to students from other Missions provided with scholarships, such students reverting to their own Missions at the close of the course".

Rev. T. B. Tedford, who was transferred from Ratnagiri to Panhala, reported a movement towards Christianity to the Mahar

155 *WIN*, April 1940, Vol. XXI, No. 2, p. 24 (It was a bimonthly bulletin of the Presbyterian Missionaries working in Western India preserved in Baisinger library attached to Wanless Hospital, Miraj, Maharashtra)

156 *BG,* October 7,1899, front page

population. The reports frontispiece carried a fine picture of the young Maharaja of Kolhapur who, was friendly towards the Missionaries. A meeting at Devla of Dr. Babasaheb Ambedkar with the mahars of Dabhola (near Ratnagiri), where Dr. Ambedkar publicly advised the Mahars to send their children's to the Mission schools[157]. The Western India Notes[158] covers Dr. Ambedkar's visit to Nipani and mentions that 'there is no one who speaks to India at present in more challenging and portentous tones as Dr. Ambedkar'.

Vengurla had been a port of the state of Sawantwadi, which was taken over by the British Government in 1812. Since Goa was near, it had influence of the Roman Catholics. The first Protestant Missionary to visit Vengurla was Rev. W. P. Barker, the founder of the Ratnagiri Mission. The others to visit were Rev. W. H. Hannum and Rev. Joseph Milliken Goheen. Rev. Hannum read an instructive paper entitled "A Statistical View of the Presbyterian Church in India at the first General Assembly of the Presbyterian Church of India at Allahabad which is published in *BG* of January 14, 1905 on page 2. Mr. Hannum stressed upon the Missionaries in selecting boys in the vernacular standards, and encouraging and training them in preparation for the sacred office and later be openly enrolled under the care of the Presbyteries, as candidates.

Vengurla became important as it came to have a centre of medical institution from the beginning of the twentieth Century.

3.3.2 Magician of the Surgical Knife

The work of Presbyterian Missionaries in Konkan will be incomplete without the contribution of Dr. Robert H. H. Goheen (1880-1968), a medical doctor by profession who spent most of his life time in Vengurla. Born in Kolhapur in June 11, 1880, he received his M. D. from Rush Medical College of Chicago in 1905 and in the same year he was appointed to the Western India Mission. He was married to Anna. K. Ewing also an Indian born daughter of Presbyterian Missionary parents. At the request of Mr. and Mrs. Hannum, Dr.

157 *WIN*, December 1933, p.18
158 *WIN*, February 1936, p.14

Goheen and his wife were sent to Vengurla since they both had completed their first year of language study and service in Miraj.

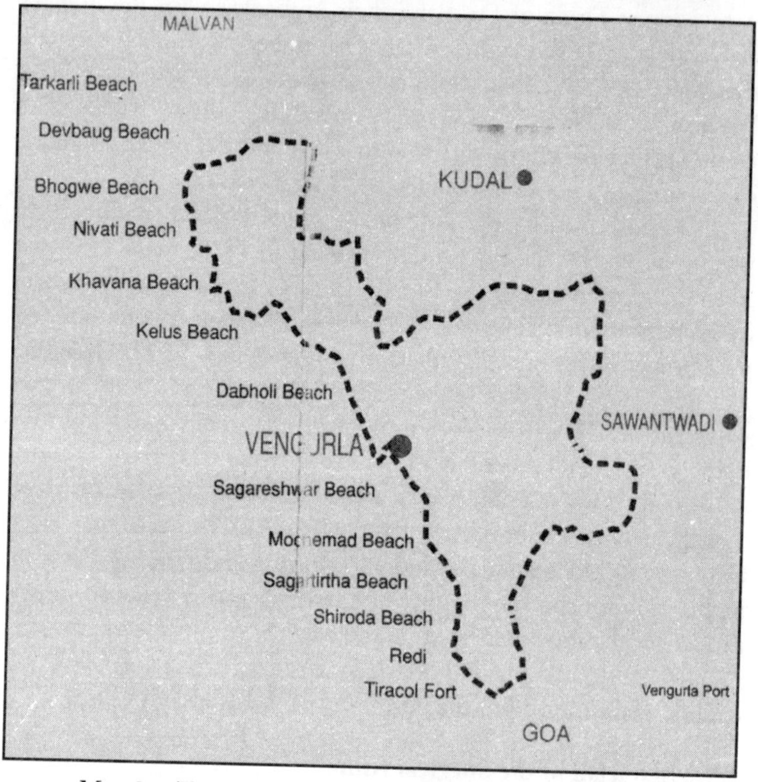

Map 3.1: Tourist Map showing Vengurla Port with beaches (Source : *Paradise on the West Coast- Vengurla*, Coloured Pamphlet issued by the Lions Club of Vengurla, undated)

3.3.3 St. Lukes Hospital, Vengurla

Dr. R. H. H. Goheen started a dispensary in 1907, in a little rented house in Vengurla. There was opposition to Christian influences, which had been very strong, manifested by threatening letters' calling him *Batla*, which meant a converter to Christianity. Later on this opposition slowly and steadily disappeared and the medical

Picture of Joseph M. Goheen and Amanda Goheen (sitting) Robert H. H. Goheen and Anne Ewing Goheen (standing)

(Courtesy: Rober Francis Goheen, Princeton, USA.)

Picture 3.3: The Goheen Family

Young Goheen

1930's

Picture 3.4 : Photograph of Dr. R. H. H. Goheen (Courtesy of Late Dr. Robert F Goheen of USA)

work gathered momentum. Day by day Dr. Goheen's surgical genius grew popular. The treatment he offered to patients who had no hope of survival was so much in advance of his times that it could be described as inspired. There was a uniformly fatal form of malignant malaria which was called cerebral malaria known as black water fever. Fairly early in Dr. Goheen's medical career as he was traveling back on a ship, a British army officer came down with cerebral malaria. Although intravenous quinine had not been used up to that time with nothing to loose, Dr. Goheen compounded some on the spot and several doses later that patient was in reMission. Intravenous quinine is still the treatment of choice, 90 years later according to Dr. Willam E. Lucas.

Dr. Lucas describes another episode that occurred around 1926. During a torrential monsoon downpour, a telegram came from the chief medical officer Dr. De'mello in Goa, "Please come at once my wife is dying..." With his surgical nurse, a trunk full of instruments, saline solution and ether for anesthesia, he went to De'Mello's home. He quickly diagnosed massive intra-abdominal hemorrhage due to a ruptured ectopic pregnancy with a patient in deep shock. Dr. Goheen had no alternative but to operate on the kitchen table. He did all the things a doctor would do and while he operated he collected as much blood as possible in a large basin, filtered it through cheese cloth and infused it back in to the patient. This was done in 1926 while blood transfusion was done only in the late 1930's.

On January 1st 1915, the existing St. Lukes hospital was dedicated by Rev. J. C. R. Ewing[159], father of Mrs. Goheen[160]. While writing about, why the name St. Luke's? (This name was given to the hospital in the year 1927) was chosen for the hospital, Dr. Goheen writes, "In the first place, Luke[161] was a medical doctor and highly

159 In 1887 he was with the Presbyterian Theological Seminary at Saharanpur who attended 23rd North India Conference at Moradabad where twenty four American Missionaries were present.(*BG*, January 22,1887, p. 51)

160 Taken from Dr. Goheen's recollections of the Missionary History of Vengurla written down in 1962 and published on p. 21 of Golden Jubilee souvenir, 1915-65 entitled "*St. Lukes Hospital, Vengurla*"

161 Luke was a physician and may have traveled with St. Paul to Italy. He was the Patron Saint of Painters as well as doctors and Pharmacists [Jack T. (ed), *The complete Dictionary of Symbols*, Chronicle Books LLC, 2005, p. 297]

cultured gentleman. He came to know the apostles of our Lord Jesus Christ and from them obtained the knowledge that enabled him to write the wonderfully beautiful account of our Lords life[162]......"

The dispensary was growing from year to year and in 1912 it had a total of 9,455 patients consisting of 6,307 males and 3,148 females. By 1915, the hospital could accommodate 75 patients. Also a cottage for European patients was added. The children's ward and the nursery near the women's ward were of special interest to visitors. New child welfare centre under the care of Ms. Sunitibai, a trained midwife and welfare worker were in mothers were taught and demonstrated the essentials of proper care, proper bathing and proper feeding[163]. There were also splendid opportunities for the special training of the nurses.

3.3.4 Leprosarium and TB Sanatorium (a great lesson in self sustaining efforts)

The St. Luke's hospital compound had residence for Dr. Goheen's family and for nurses. Later, the hospital work grew in all directions including a Leprosarium in 1918 and T. B. Sanatorium in 1919. Sister Faye arrived in Vengurla to become a Missionary nurse in India. Sr. Faye was energetic vivacious, fun loving and hard working and threw herself for the life of the station. After passing her language examinations, she worked with Dr. R. H. H. Goheen to build up St. Lukes hospital. She organized the school of nursing at Vengurla and while she was incharge, it was considered one of the best in the province. She was active in the organization of the training of Nurses Association of India and took a considerable part in carrying forward this work for many years.

---

162 Probably St. Lukes wrote Acts of the Apostles.

163 *WIN*, January 1939, p. 9

Picture 3.5: Present View of Dr. R. H. H. Goheen's residence at St. Lukes Hospital Compound, facing Balasaheb Khardekar College, Vengurla

Picture 3.6: Present state of Leprosarium and Hill Side Tuberculosis Sanatorium, Vengurla, India

Sister Faye is said to have worked for 19 years in Vengurla Hospital. She was very strict in the sense of maintaining cleanliness and her style of demonstrations for nurses was easily graspable. Her image of dedication, sincerity towards her work and motherly regard for the nurses was clearly visible. Whenever she took the nurses to the sanatorium she would exclaim "well girls this is TB Sanatorium, germs are crawling here, you must keep your sarees up a little and don't allow it to touch the floor". An instance of how careful she was with her nurses… Once she had to send her graduate nurse 'Sarabai' to an outpatient who was suffering from Cholera and needed to be given some intravenous glucose, before the nurse returned, sister Faye got hot water ready for her to take bath. Sister Faye went herself and brought clean clothes for the girl. Even her leather sandals were not spared[164].

164 *WIN*, October 1958, pp. 14-15

At the Leprosarium, the patients were encouraged to work[165] when possible. Some were farmers, who raised peanuts and beans, pumpkins, grains and flowers. Others were interested in poultry culture and so it was being encouraged. Still others were masons, carpenters or labourers and they had been busy on new buildings to improve the living conditions. They had completed a water tank, the building of a latrine with a septic tank, a kitchen and a new men's ward, as well as the beginning of a small carpenter's shop for the men. An article entitled 'Friends Leprosarium'[166], Vengurla by Dr. Daulatrao Satralkar says "This year we have been blessed by the coming as a patient of Mr. Baburao a trained teacher and a zealous Christian man. He has created an altogether Christian and friendly atmosphere in our Leper Home. He conducted literacy classes, taught Indian music, looked after their various social problems and solved them in a true Christian spirit. He also conducted Bible classes and arranged a good *bhajan* band. Due to his efforts there were three adult Baptisms on Easter Sunday. We firmly believe in occupational therapy. This year the patients were kept busy with farming, vegetable growing, weaving rugs, literacy classes, *bhajan* bands, picnics, and celebrations of special days". The Christian festivals and religious services every Sunday were all worthy of mention. The patients managed by themselves a drama depicting the life of Pandita Ramabai. In all these ways the minds and bodies of these sufferers were kept busy most of the time.[167]

In 1958, the leprosarium was closed down and Balniketan Children's home was started in 1973. Earlier in the Report of 1894, of the American Presbyterian Mission in Western India published in *BG* of January 19, 1895 on page3, Rev. Hannum writes of the work of visiting the lepers. He says "At first we were not welcome

165 *WIN*, December 1923, p. 6

166 A very interesting article by Brij Khandelwal entitled Close to Taj, a different monument of Love highlights Japanese- founded Jalma Centre for Leprosy Treatment working for past four decades. Today the total number of leprosy cases in the country has sharply declines. The stigma attached to leprosy has largely gone and the rehabilitation is easier. As a public health programme the success of leprosy eradication is a fulfillment of Mahatma Gandhi's dream" (*Hindustan Times*, February 2, 2008)

167 *WIN*, February 1948, Vol. xxix, No. 1

visitors, and there was no attempt to hide it. Those who were able would go out and draw water, others would say they did not wish to listen to us and go out on the verandah, while only a remnant remained who would pay any heed to the Gospel message. Gradually in answer to prayer they began to remain and listen attentively. Miss. Unsworth[168], in the meantime, learned to play the accordion, and this attracted them very much. For many months past we have been greeted with cordial salaams, and a group of eager longing faces listen to the words of life. Though there is not as yet all the visible fruit that we could desire, the Holy Spirit is truly working in their midst. One little woman quietly and yet confidently acknowledges that Jesus has forgiven her sins and gives her joy. This I believe to be true, so with praises for this we continue on".

Among the diseases most prevalent in this district was tuberculosis. It was becoming more and more prominent as the "Captain of the Men of Death." This was accounted for largely by the vast numbers of men who leaving their homes and free life in the open air, went to Bombay and Karachi to work in mills and offices. As Konkan did not support its population by its agricultural produce, these men had to go elsewhere to a livelihood for themselves and for their families, but many of them paid heavy price indicated above. As late as 1909 majority of Bombay labourers, particularly Konkani Marathas has slowly severed their connections with agriculture, they had not become fully urban, their connection with village remained intact[169].

The TB Sanatorium Building was constructed in 1919, on a Hillside location so that fresh breezes, abundant sunlight etc was available. (In the same year late Robert Francis Goheen was born at Vengurla. There was one ward each for men and for women, and four private cottages, accommodated 22 patients. A winding road up the steep hill provided climbing as one of the routine exercises for those who were able for it.

The town's people were beginning to appreciate the privilege of well-trained girls in their maternity cases. More and more expectant mothers were going to the hospitals early for advice and

168 She ran a Widow's Home in Ratnagiri.

169 Mehdi Mosheni, *Economic History of Bombay in the Nineteenth Century*, Ph.D Thesis, Bombay, 1998, p. 346

treatment. Before this, only midwives had the preference. People were beginning to realize that the service of well-trained individuals was extremely important for their own interest and welfare, as well as for their children. E. H. Evans wrote 'Vengurla through New Eyes-Another Set'[170] wherein he writes about three qualities of the people of Vengurla

1. Friendliness of the people
2. No outstanding glaring evils appear to the casual observer and
3. The efficiency with which the medical work here is being done.

Shriram Mantri in his book in Marathi *Fakan Gajli Vengurleche* published in 2003 from Mumbai covers a chapter on Dr. Goheen entitled 'Surgical magician' (*Shastrakriyecha Jadugar*) and also a separate chapter on Vengurla high school (A. P. Mission high school) discussed below.

Interestingly Mahatma Gandhi and his wife visited Vengurla in 1927. Dr. Goheen mentions him as a great reformer praising his work of *Khadi*[171]. His report mentions about the municipality at Vengurla establishing school for untouchable children in 1927. Gandhiji in his speech gave reasons why Indian cloth-Home spun preferred-Indian rice and other Indian products should be used exclusively. Gandhiji was presented with a silver casket and the flowers but since he needed money and no handsome gifts he sold off the casket for Rs.35 to one Mrs. Roy's. Later Gandhiji said at Civil Disobedience campaign "the future of India will be decided not in her cities but in her villages". Mr. K. T. Paul, one of the great Christian leaders of India has said "India is really there in the villages, the foundations of our body politics and of its problems..." Stephen Neill, a far-visional British Missionary of the younger group, says in his stimulating book on '*Village Problems in India*', "We are dealing here with 1/6th of the human race"[172].

---

170 *WIN*, July 1925, p. 6

171 *WIN*, June 1927, p. 4

172 Kenyon L. Butterfield-*The Christian Mission in rural India*, New York Int, London, 1930 p. 42

The medical and surgical treatment of Dr. Goheen had become legendary in the areas surrounding Vengurla. Most common people in Sawantwadi knew him as Dr. Govind and his former name as 'Bato' was clean forgotten. The treatment he offered to patients who had no hope of survival was so much in advance of his times that it could be described as inspired. In 1936, Dr. R. H. H. Goheen retired as president of Christian Medical Association of India (CMAI). Before the Goheen's left Vengurla in 1939[173], they had also secured funds for the building of the maternity home and the Church (Named Goheen Memorial Church). After them Dr. Daulatrao Satralkar became the first Indian medical superintendent of St. Luke's hospital. Followed by Dr. and Mrs. Marshal, Dr. and Mrs. Evans (1952). This was the first period of early pioneer American Missionaries.

Picture 3.7: Goheen Memorial Church, (Opposite to St. Lukes Hospital) Vengurla

In 1948, Dr. Daulat A. Satralkar was invited with his team of Hospital staff to Kankavli where the Congress leader Appasaheb

173 Austin Fernandes, *History of Sawantwadi From 1800 to 1948*, Ph.D Thesis, Bombay, 2003, p. 285.

Patwardhan[174] in his concluding remarks as Chairman of the meeting paid enthusiastic tribute to the work saying that it was after the teaching of the great Master, Jesus Christ, and that when Indians were seen working according to Jesus teachings, barriers between foreign Missions and the Indian population were broken down and Christianity was seen to belong to India.

The poem reproduced below was written by Dr. R. H. H. Goheen on Vengurla just before he left that place[175].

Vengurla, Where the towny sands
Roll down to bank the sea,-
When on the glistening fronds of palm,
On rugged rocks of gold headlands,
On wrestling waves, lies moonlight calm-
Dreams deep in mystery
But with the singing birds at dawn
Bright colours reappear:
Blue skies, blue seas, green peeple trees
That chattering parrots sit upon,
And rice field cooling every breeze
With spring time twice a year !
The busy market place at noon
Collects a mighty throng:
White flowing roads and brown bear backs
Josle along, but when the moon
Peeps through palm- thatches' little cracks
Old temples flood with song,
And down the winding smooth red road
When stars are in the sky,
A caravan with tinkling bells
On every ox that draws a load,
A sweetly chiming message tells
Of cheerful industry
.... R H H Goheen

174 Detailed paper on 'Appa's work of Social Reconstruction in Konkan (1905-1971) published by Prof. P. B. Kulkarni on p.148 in State level seminar to Explore Historical Wealth of Konkan, February 2003

175 *WIN*, December 1937, Vol. XVIII, front page

3.3.5 The second innings of St. Lukes Hospital

Then from 1953 to 1973, it was the second period of American Doctors like Dr. and Mrs. L. P. Servid, Dr. and Mrs. R. S. Seaton (Ron and Edith), who continued their leadership with able assistance of Indian Doctors namely Dr. R. B. Satwekar, Dr. Eden, Dr. M. K. Dhanawade, Dr. Bhangle and Dr. Sase. In 1956 during the Goa freedom movement, there was bloodshed and many Indian volunteers were seriously injured on the Goa frontier, Dr. Servid then incharge of St. Lukes hospital went in person to treat the wounded.

Dr. & Mrs. L. P. Servid

Picture 3.8: Dr. & Mrs. Lester P. Servid (1952)

Beatrice S. Stevenson's article 'Half a Dozen Hospitals' in WIN, July 1961 talks of Dr. Seaton making repeated trips in the hospital car to check up post operative patients across the town at St. Lukes. It also says the cost of delivering baby and the ten day rest was very cheap (only 3 US $).

St. Luke's Hospital staff at farewell for Dr. and Mrs. Servid who were transferred to Wanless Chest Hospital, Wanlesswadi, in January 1964

Picture 3.9: Farewell to Dr. & Mrs. Servid (1964) before being transferred to Wanless Hospital, Kolhapur (Source: St. Lukes Hospital, Platinum Jubilee Souvenir, 1915-1991, Courtesy: Dr. Ronald and Edith Seaton, USA)

Dr. R. S Seaton & Mrs. Edith Seaton
E. 28, Green Park, New Delhi – 110016

Picture 3.10: Dr. Ronald and Edith Seaton (After 1964, India) and their recent photograph (2008,USA) (Mrs. Edith Seaton speaking on the occasion of distinguished Alumni Award[176])

176 *http://alumni.wooster.edu/daa/seaton.php retrieved on 24.02.09*

An article by Renato De Sa published in *Harpa Goesa* entitled "The Great Surgeon Dr. R. H. H. Goheen and the gratitude of the Goanese family published in 1979 describes Dr. Goheen as the magician of the surgical knife. Dr. Goheen was asked by the governing body of *Santa Casa de Misericordia* of Goa to give one day of his choice for consultations in their hospital at Ribandar to which he readily agreed.

Late Robert F. Goheen wrote about his father as the only western trained physician along the coast south of Bombay... my father drew many patients from Goa, while their ability to pay,

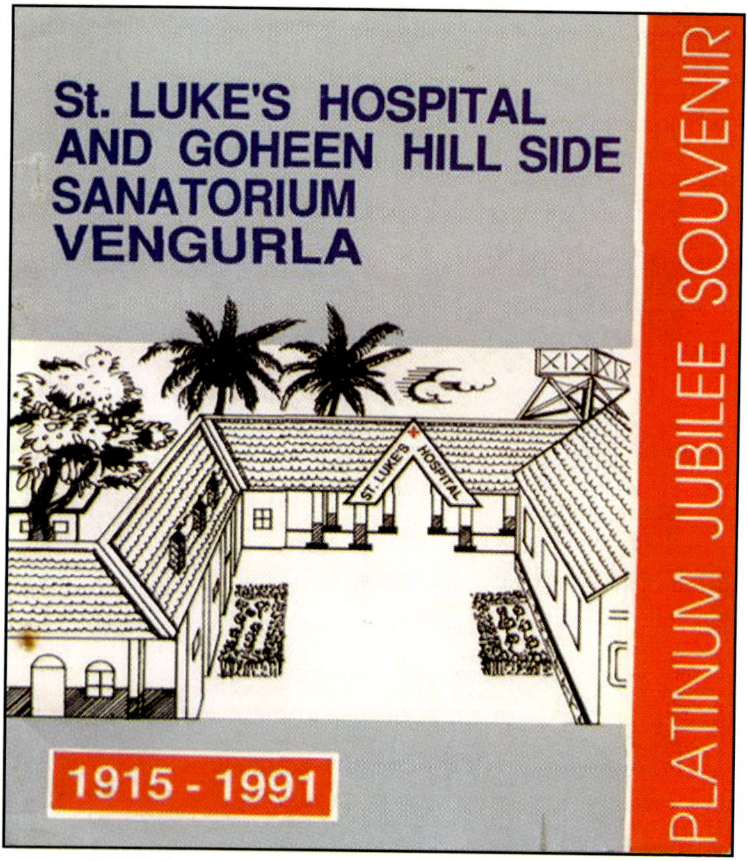

Picture 3.11: Platinum Jubilee Souvenir (1915-1991) showing the St. Luke's Hospital Setup

made possible the treatment of many local farm workers, laborers and fishermen with very limited means. In 1933, Dr. Goheen was awarded the *Kaiser – i– Hind* gold Medal by King George- V for his distinguished medical service to India[177].

3.3.6 Family of Goheen's

Robert F. Goheen son of Dr. R. H. H. Goheen was the joint recipient of the famous Pyne Prize, Princeton University's highest award for scholarship among undergraduates and was truly an honour that only few could reach. Robert Goheen in 1940's is seen to have been congratulated for this splendid work and sterling qualities. It clearly goes against the rumour that Missionary children average up fairly well[178].

Picture 3.12: Young Robert F. Goheen with his recent photograph (2007, Princeton, USA) (Courtesy: Late Robert F. Goheen, USA)

177 *WIN*, December 1933, front page.

178 *WIN*, July 1940, Vol. XXI, No. 3, p. 32

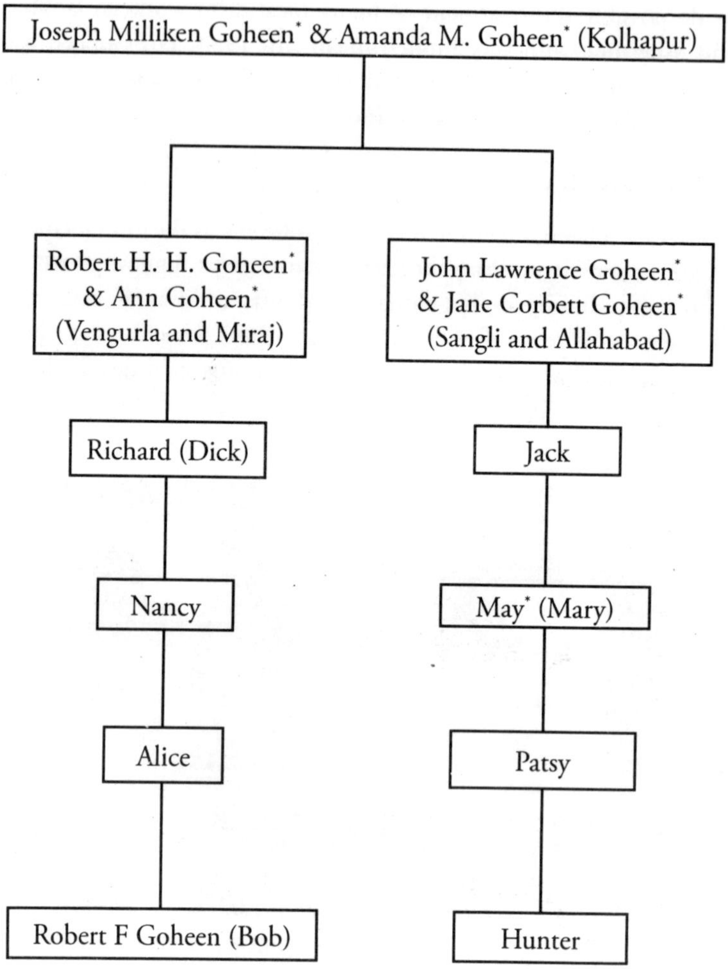

Chart 3.1: Family Tree of Goheens (with the names of major places where they served in India)
(Source: Reconsructed from the information provided by late Prof R. F. Goheen of USA, son of Dr. R. H. H. Goheen who was also ambassador to India in 1970's)
*- Associated with Missionary Work.

3.4 The Vengurla Chapter

3.4.1 Vengurla High School (former APM High School)

The Vengurla Mission High School was established around 1915, Bible was taught in addition to secular subjects. In 1930, friends in Cleveland gave 8000 dollars for the erection of a clinical building of St. Lukes Hospital. Also in the same year the New High School building work started. The building was to be an open air building. Earlier it was only a school for boys. The teachers and students felt a sense of freedom and appreciated the benefit of open air, abundant light , attractive and clean surrounding after occupying the New Vengurla High School building in August 1930. Added advantage of the new building was it was free from close proximity to plague infection[179]. There were 210 boys and 5 girls in the school[180].

Picture 3.13: Vengurla High School

On December 6th 1930, The New High School building was opened. Sardesai Maharaj, the chief of Sawantwadi state was present for this function. G.V. Moses was the principal of the school. Mrs.

179 *WIN*, June 1930, p. 68

180 *WIN*, December 1930, p. 80

Goheen, Mrs. Evans and Mr. Lyon were on the staff of the high school teaching Scripture and English to the boys in matriculation and pre-matriculation classes[181].

Dr. R. H. H. Goheen, who was a strong arm to the school all through the years, spoke on the relation of high school to public health. Rev. H. K. Wright who was principal of the school in the troubling years also gave a steering address.

The school was initially opened by Rev. R. H. Hannum in June 1912 with 24 boys on the roll and 4 teachers on the staff. The school building was made as far as possible open to sunlight and fresh air, to maintain the health of students who spent the best part of their study here. So far the cost of the building was about Rs. 21,000. Most of this money came in form of Christmas Gift from America. The chief of Sawantwadi in his speech said "the progress of school largely depends on the close co-operation of parents and guardians. The absence of this co-operation dampens the enthusiasm of teachers….."

Picture 3.14: Hannum Couple

181 *WIN*, July 1933, p.16

Picture 3.15: Principal Moses of Vengurla High School (1940's)

"Friends, Western Missionaries have done much for the cause of education in India and the people of India have good reason to be grateful to them in this respect. The education institutions run by these Missionaries are often staffed by education experts always keen on trying new scientific methods of education. They have in many instances shown a lead to other private education societies in India".

WIN of October 1940 (page 61) mentions about 25 years of High School. In this school Mrs. Anne Ewing Goheen taught English to generations of young Vengurlekar's. She had also directed a Play "Sacrifice".[182] There is a mention of the Silver Jubilee function of this School. On this occasion Mr. and Mrs. Moses prepared a booklet to celebrate a quarter century of Vengurla Institution. The alumni of Bombay and Vengurla were organized and money was collected to cover the expenses of this occasion. Honorary Mr. Paranjape[183]

182 Shriram Mantri, *Fakan Gajli Vengurleche (M)*, Indraneel Prakashan, Mumbai, 2003.

183 He was Principal of Ferguson College, Pune, Former Minister of the Education of the Bombay Government, Vice Chancellor of Lucknow University and Senior Wrangler of Cambridge University.

an eminent educator was to preside at the above occasion. Since Dr. Paranjape was not of the congress party there was some local opposition for this. Though Mr. Paranjape has received letters that he was betraying his religion by consenting to act as Chairman on the occasion of the silver jubilee of the Mission Institution, he in his lecture made a most unexpected and rigorous defence of Mission work, mentioning especially and medical and educational work. He said "The education contribution of early Missionaries to the progress of India was unique". Dr. Miller of Madras and Dr. Wilson of Bombay were names to be conjured with[184].

During the tenure of Principal Mr. Ramdas, New Novel programme[185] was implemented which received enthusiastic response. The focus was on the want of food and the following schedule was prepared....

Table 3.2: Novel Programme Schedule

Month	*Activity*	*Comment*
June	Vegetable Month	Require hard work
July	Trees	Prize for most trees surviving throughout the year
August	Oratory	Self expression
September	Flowers	----
October	Art	----
November	Music	Prize for student producing best school song
December	Drama	Strengthen Christmas Program
January	Sports	----
February	Animals	----
March	Merit	----
April	*Madhukri Mango*	----

184 Grace Moses "Silver Jubilee of the Vengurla Mission High School" *WIN*, December 1940, p. 1

185 *WIN*, April 1949, p. 24

Apart from these on India's first Independence Day the first of the mango grafts were planted providing the source of income as well as hands on experience in mango grafting. In *WIN* July 1935, an interesting article on mangoes by James E. Napp talks of unique ways to eat mango.

Today also this school celebrates 29th August as its founders day wherein toppers in SSC (Tenth Exams) Exams are given awards after the name of its five founder Principals. Rev. Hannum directed a play on American President from Log House to the White House, Rev. Wright (Rev. Wright was so attached to school that his last wishes were he be cremated in Vengurla Missionary cemetery which was done in 1957). The others included were Rev. G. V. Moses, Rev. Ramdas and Rev. O. Conses.

Table 3.3: List of headmasters from 1939

Headmasters/ Principal	*Year*
Mrs. C. G. Moses (Wife of G.V. Moses)	1939-43
M. S. Ramdas	1944-49
M. C. Gorde	1949-51
G. D. Masoji	1951-55
B. P. Kale	1955-61
E. A. Khabade	1961-67
B. P. Kale	1968-71
G. B. Joshi (He was a Hindu)	1971-74
M. A. Lad	1974-75

Hira D. Bhangle entered as assistant teacher to teach Sanskrit at Vengurla High School in August 1959 when Mr. B. P. Kale was the Headmaster. She writes "I am proud that the school is famous for discipline". She further writes "most of thc Sanskrit scholars are from Konkan". Kalidas Jayanti (Kalidas's birthday) was celebrated with students reciting *shlokas* from Kalidas's world-known poems and staging a piece of drama[186]. Ester Khabade, Head mistress of Vengurla high school writes[187] "The school starts when members of

186 *WIN*, July 1961, p. 12
187 *WIN*, January 1962, p. 20

Picture 3.16: Photograph inside Vengurla High School (List of previous principals at the board on the backside)

the staff and the students get together in the assembly hall. Interesting topics having good morals are chosen for each assembly talk".

"The school has been helping the poor and needy students and without this help they would not be where they are today". In one such incident in the year 1927 one Mr. Thakur failed his matric examination (high school final exam). His interest was in the art of drawing, he wanted to go to Bombay the Sir J. J. School of Art. He needed financial help. He explained his difficulty to principal G. V. Moses., who consulted with Dr. R. H. H. Goheen who was not only willing to help Mr. Thakur financially but also gave him a very good recommendation.

Sister Fay Froese who had served as nursing superintendent in St. Lukes Hospital earlier says about Annual Social Gathering in 1965 at the Vengurla High School "it was interesting to see as many girls as boys among the students and to see many women, probably mothers of the students, attending the function. India has come a long way in the emancipation and education of its women[188].

188 St. Lukes Hospital Vengurla Golden Jubilee 1915-1965, p. 2

3.4.2 Rangnekar English School, Vengurla

Mr. Raghunath Vitthal Rangnekar of Vengurla established this English School for boys in 1939. Mr. Rangnekar was a trained educator anxious to see formal education advanced in Vengurla city and surrounding. The school had earned a good name for success in examinations. By 1944, Mr. Rangnekar due to ill health and being friend of Rev. S. J. Ramdas the new Principal of the Mission high school made plans whereby the Rangnekar English School should come under the management of APM High school. Both parties entered into a formal agreement with mutual goodwill and good faith. With the transfer of management of the school all records, register, books, furniture and other assets were turned over to Mr. Ramdas.

Mr. Ramdas told of this gratitude to god for this happy event. He said "the newly wedded bride of 15 years came to receive her father's blessing" (Vengurla High School). Mr. Ramdas was aware that so many boys of Vengurla had been educated to become clerks; they leave the city to work elsewhere. He wanted to see the kind of schooling that would save the boys and girls of Vengurla. He wanted to see the sons and daughters of land owners complete their education and then return to serve in their own community and upon their own land. There should be schooling with agricultural interests. It need not be an agricultural school as such. Let there be a teacher living in a house with his pupils on an acre of land with gardens and a well, working together to see the land and trees produce fruits to eat and sell.

The study of Bible and teaching of Jesus Christ was to be done with not an effort to proselytize but to spread goodwill love and brotherhood among the children of god[189].

3.4.3 Malgav Camp (Near Vengurla)

Wilbur H. and Mary Lyon in their write-up[190] ' The Rockey Kokan' highlight about a young Vengurla Mahar who was interested in Christianity and was also a trained government teacher.

---

189 Gaylord Knox, "The Rangnekar English School", *WIN*, April 1944, pp. 8-10

190 *WIN*, April 1939, Vol. XX, No. 2

He advised his own people there about cleanliness and model ways of disposing of the carcasses of cattle, urging them not to relent against these imposed duties but to profit by the income there from and to turn a degrading task in to honorable trade. The Missionaries were often amazed, delighted with the friendly response of the *Mahars* of Vengurla.

But the minds that were for centuries denied learning frequently asked or expressed 'How can we learn?'... But after the little self confidence given by Missionaries they showed keenness towards learning.

According to the regulations of the education department the children of the outcastes were supposed to be taught in the same schools as caste children. But when two qualified *Mahars* were made teachers along with half a dozen of other teachers from high castes, the village boycotted the school and reduced the attendance from 250 to 30 in short time[191].

3.5 The Kalyan Chapter

The Holy Cross Hospital

The sisters of Holy Cross School also manage Holy Cross Hospital very close to the School in addition to the home for the Aged "Shanti Bhavan" near by Shantibhavan is run by St.Vincent de Paul Society[192].

Vincent de Paul Society

In Mumbai, the Vincentian organization was born in 1833, when a twenty year old student Frederic Ozanam and his companions set about to help the marginalized, the oppressed and the poor. In Bombay in 1862 Fr. Leo Meurin the Parish Priest of Bhuleshwar Cathedral conducted first conference of St. Vincent de Paul.

One of the most significant activities of the Vincentian's has been the running of the Albless Leprosy Home at Trombay which has completed more than hundred years, sheltering 90 leprosy

191 *WIN*, July 1933, p. 17

192 St. Vincent de Paul (1581-1660) established Daughters of Charity in 1633. They work in hospitals, schools and the homes of the poor (M. V. Woodgate, *St. Vincet de Paul*, Mumbai, 2004, cover page)

Picture 3.17: The Holy Cross Hospital, Kalyan

patients including 9 women. The donors of the Albless bunglow were a parsi merchant family Aduljee Framjee. An AIDS wing has been added on January 28, 1996 with 15 beds. The concept of a institution specifically for shelter and isolation of a special category of sick was a peculiarly European one. Leprosy Asylums and refugees were the most tangible and long lasting symbols of Western India's colonial encounter.

Christian Missionary accounts in the 1830's had hinted at the large number of leprosy sufferers in the coastal districts of Ratnagiri. Socially ostracized and distressed lepers were reported to comprise a substantial number of the inmates of the "asylum for the aged and destitute" set up at the small island fort of Harnai[193]. In fact, Bishop Leo Maurine had put an ambitious proposal to the then government that the premises of one of the old forts–Sion, Matunga, Sewree or Worlee and also Bassein fort be placed at his disposal with a view to

193 Report of the Hurnee Asylum for the Aged and Destitute for 1832-33 in *OCS*, 1833, p. 254

converting them into the head quarters of a leper colony or village but the government refused his idea[194].

Shantibhavan-Home for the aged

Another mile stone in the history of the Vincentian's has been the setting up of a Home for the Aged- Shanti Bhavan at Kalyan where men and women are accommodated and looked after.

Table 3.4: List of Donors of the Society of St. Vincent De Paul, Shanti Bhavan, Home for the Aged, Kalyan.

Donor's	*Amount (Rs)*
National Council of France	65384
National Council of Australia	51963
Council of England and Wales	26546
M. C. C. of Victoria, Australia	8300
St. Mary's (I.S.C. Section)Mazgaon	28000
O. L. of Good Counsel High School, Sion	19503
Holy Cross High School, Kurla	14850
Bombay Scottish Orphanage, Mahim	11650
St. Joseph Convent, SSC Section, Bandra	10,000
Auxilium Convent School Wadala	7380
St. Michael's High School Mahim	7380
St. Stanislaus High School, Bandra	6000
Rosary High School, Dockyard Road, Mazgaon	5785
St. John's High School, Goregaon	5000
St. Aloysius High School, Bandra	3000
St. Mary's High School, Mahim	350
St. Michael's High School, Mahim	6000
Auxiliam Convent Bandra	6000
Don Bosco High School, Matunga	52,000

194 Subadha S. Pandya, *Leprosy in the Bombay Presidency, 1840-1897, Perceptions and Approaches to its Control,* Ph.D Thesis, November 2001, Mumbai, p. 233

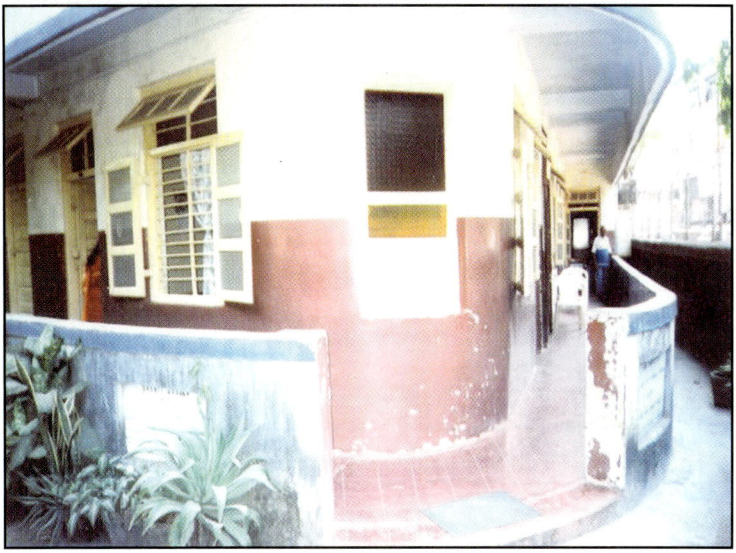

Picture 3.18: Shanti Bhavan (Home for the Aged), Kalyan

The Sanjeevni Foundation

There is a Lourdes Community Centre called "Sanjeevni Foundation". Sister Dhanam has been carrying out active social work for the Prisoner's of Kalyan Jail, Computer Education, Girl Child

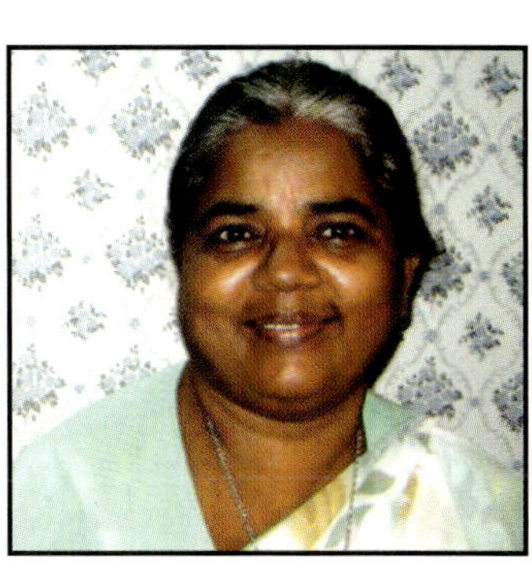

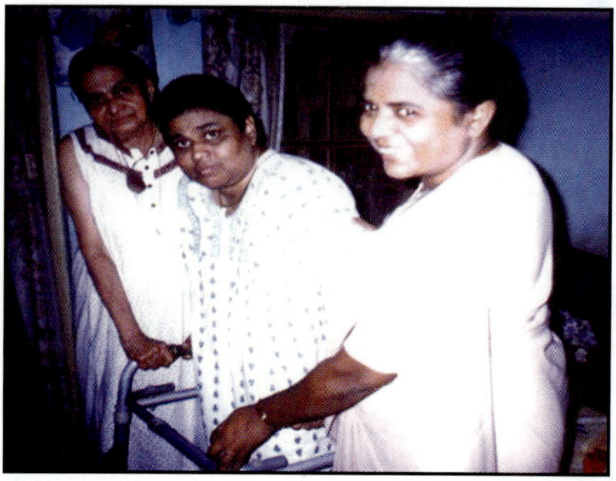

Picture 3.19: Sister Dhanam with her team and Visiting the Sick

Day and other programmes. Sister Dhanam gives family visits for sick patients.

Thus, medical work formed the major part of the Missionary activity after the education work. The other social activities of the Missionary labour namely the industrial training, zenana along with their evangelical counterparts like development of Church and training of Christians are discussed in Chapter four. The relevant issues in connection with women and caste are dealt with.

Chapter 4

Social Activities of Missionaries-III
(Social, Religious and Related Issues)

Chapter 4

Social Activities of Missionaries-III (Social, Religious and Related Issues)

4.1 Introduction

From 1860 onwards English Missionary Women have been playing a pivotal role fostering colonialism and reform because as teachers they gained access to the innermost part of the Indian Home, the Zenana where elite Indian women were kept secluded. This access was totally denied to European men who regarded Indian women as "Pure Heathen", that is women kept secluded in the Zenana. In their role as teachers, women Missionaries not only served as passive agents in that they acted as 'Help Mates' of British imperialism, cultural imperialists providing an education based entirely on English values[195].

The Zenana system preserved important elements of the structure of family life such as the maintenance of separate physical as well as mental domains for men and for women[196].

Indian's were unaccustomed in sending their daughters to schools and hence, Zenana education was started but which was

195 Geraldin H. Forbes, "In Search of the Pure Heathen: Missionary Women in the 19th Century India", EPW, Vol.XXI, No. 17, 1986, pp. 2-8

196 Malavika Karlekar, *Voices from Within: Early Personal Narratives of Bengali Women*, OUP, New Delhi, 1991, p.110

expensive, cumbersome and largely ineffectual. The industrial education came to be regarded at important part of the work of the Mission especially during famines. The evangelical work like preaching of Gospel, establishment of Churches and development of related literature went hand in hand with its other counterparts.

4.2 Industrial Work

In early 1886, the English captured an Arab slave ship and rescued about 25 young slaves. These were brought to Bombay, and had been kept in a hired house until they could be properly provided for. Out of these, 15 of the younger had been given into the charge of Rev. R. Winsor, to be trained in his industrial school at Sirur[197]. This school was called after the name of a generous Parsee donor as Sir D. M. Petit Industrial School. The famine of 1900 brought to the Mission a large number of destitute children, for whom it was necessary to provide industrial training. Boys in connection with the High School at Bombay were taught laundrying, carpentry, fitting etc. Tin-smithing, carpentry, clay modeling, and sewing were taught at Roha.

Rev. G. R. Navalkar had two stations under his charge that is Alibag and Revdanda. An interesting account of the industrial school at Alibag under his direction shows the following statistics. The number of pupils receiving technical instructions was 84 (79?), distributed amongst the caste (Table 4.1).

All these were students of either from the High School or the Vernacular Schools. The interesting part was the willingness of Brahman boys to learn these useful trades, a trend towards occupational mobility can be seen. This willingness is not exceptional, for we can bear witness to the oft-repeated request of the high caste boys in the Mission School at Roha, also in the Konkan, to have a technical class established and only the lack of money has prevented its establishment. Not only had the boys of the school expressed their willingness, but many of the citizens of the place had offered to join such a class[198].

197 *BG*, January 23, 1886, p. 54

198 *BG*, August 28,1886, p. 547

Table 4.1: Industrial School pupil's caste wise

Caste	*Number*
Brahmans	43
Shenvis	1
Prabhus	1
Cultivators	8
Bhandaris	12
Kolis	3
Muslim	1
Beni Israel	9
Christians	1
Total	84 (79?)

4.2.1 The Roha Chapter

While describing the condition of the Church at Roha, situated across the harbour of Bombay, Rev. J. E. Abbot wrote, "The hundred famine children at Roha, 60 boys and 40 girls are bright and active. Aside from the regular book studies, the boys work for 2 hours a day at the carpenter's bench, at the loom, the tin smith's brazier and the sewing machine. The ideal aimed at to teach such industries as will make it possible for the boys to earn their own livelihood in the town and villages of the district where they live so that they may not drift to the cities. All saleable articles made in the workshop are taken by the boys in to the town around and sold. They receive a commission on their sale, thus encouraging them to study the market and lead to the production of things the people want and will buy"[199]. Earlier a long letter of perhaps J. E. Abbot to the Editor of the *Bombay Guardian* dated December 26, 1885 (p. 822), talked of the American Mission Anglo-vernacular School at Roha, but her sister village

199 *BG*, May 03,1902, p. 9

Ashtami has a dark picture of untouchability practiced as to the drinking of water. It also highlights about *Wagris* and *Katkaris* (Indigenous people of the area)

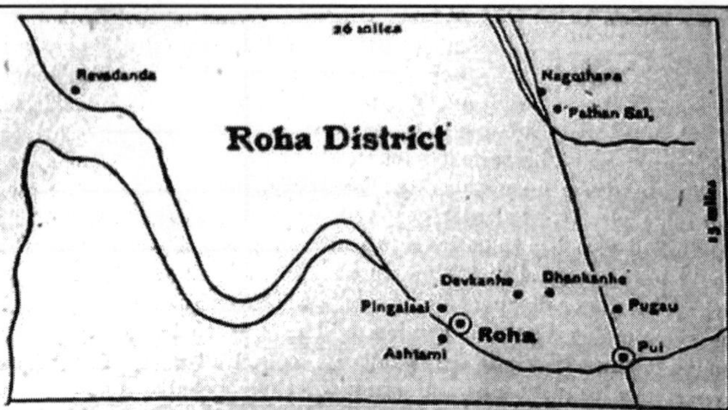

ROHA DISTRICT :—Population 46,000.

Number of Villages	131	Number of Schools	4
" " Churches	3	" " Teachers	9
" " Communicants	221	" " Christian Pupils	90
Total Christian Community	302	" " Non-Christian Pupils	32
Contributions for 1905	Rs. 177 =$39	" " Sunday Schools	4
Number of Preachers	3	" " S. S. Scholars	220
" " Bible-Women	4		
Residing at Ashtami and Poladpur.			

Workers live in Ashtami, Nagothna, Dhankanhe, and Pui. Poladpur, not indicated on the map, is 50 miles to the south.

N.B.—The names Roha and Ashtami on the Map should be transposed, as Roha is south and Ashtami north of the river.

Map 4.1: Map of Roha (Source: American Mission Report of 1905, p.15)

4.2.2 Pandita Ramabai's brain child

Sharada Sadan

On 11th March 1889, Pandita Ramabai started Sharada Sadan, in a house rented on *Chowpatty* behind Wilson College. Vocational Education including other subjects was contained in its curriculum.

Embroidery, knitting, drawing, claymodelling, photography, wood sculpture, ornamental basketry and kindergarten teacher training was taught in the sadan[200]. A report[201] entitled 'News of Ramabai and her Work' talks of her desire to give the Widows of her institution industrial education which would help them to earn a living without leaving their homes. Some of the industries already taught were plain needle work and cutting, making knitted caps and various kinds, embroidery, lace making, knitting, washing and ironing, oil making, gardening and field work, rope making, making brooms, weaving sarees and other cloth, weaving blankets and carpets, spinning wool and thread. To the above was added dairy work, wicker work, grain parching, making bamboo baskets and cane chairs and door mats, *Kalhai* work (Tinning culinary utensil's).

Picture 4.1: Industrial Work, Bombay (American Mission Report of 1900, p. 33)

200 Meera Kosambi (ed) of RCWS Gender Series *"Pandita Ramabai's feminist and Christian Conversion,* Research Centre for Women's Studies, S.N.D.T. Women's University, Bombay, 1995, p. 158

201 *BG*, December 14, 1901, p. 9

Picture 4.2: Christian Women in Bombay Widows Home (American Mission Report of 1900, p. 38)

4.2.3 A Mission–Laundry

In March 9, 1901 (p. 11), BG Fairbank wrote a letter to the editor entitled 'Needed, the Industrial Missions Aid Society'. In the long letter Fairbank wrote "industrial idea is in the air. It has taken hold, and that rightly of most Missions in western India, as well as Missions in other parts of India. The urgent and immediate necessity of industrial training for the thousands of famine children is patent to everyone. Missions on every hand are forced to consider the question of adopting some line of industrial training".

The American Mission school laundry had began in 1903 with one hand machine boilers to heat the water tubs etc. It required four men and six boys regularly. The motive behind establishment of laundry was to provide a new kind of industrial work for the boys of the high school (American Mission Schools, Byculla)[202].

4.3 Zenana Work

Out of the various activities of the Christian Missionaries in India, the Zenana work has made its own mark. Zenana means *Zen* – Woman and *ana*- belonging to. Mission workers in Zenana brought to light special need of the medical health of the women especially those who were shut up in their homes and Zenana's. The below given paragraphs highlight the importance of the Zenana work in general and with special emphasis on the work in coastal belt of Maharashtra. The Zenana work in Madras city is also touched. The spread of Zenana Bible and medical Mission (ZBMM) in to various branches in 1880 is included. The ZBMM work presents the most interesting picture of co-operative Mission work.

The Zenana was the private portion of the home in which women were with more or less stringency in various lands secluded from the outer world. When the term 'Zenana woman' is used it meant one who lived in seclusion.

Out of the various activities of the Christian Missionaries in India, the Zenana work has made its own mark.

Woman after marriage, owing to social restrictions were unable to attend schools, a private teaching facility or private tuition's were arranged by the Missionaries. The agency was known as 'Zenana Mission'. It started Zenana schools which were private houses where English and American ladies connected with Missionary bodies taught girls[203]. The school was staffed by lady teachers to which girls alone were admitted. Miss Carroll gave the origin of the word *Zenana*, which comes from the two words, *Zen*, Woman and *ana* belonging to, at a paper reading session at Bombay District Conference of the

---

202 *BG*, September 10, 1904, p. 11

203 Y. B. Mathur, *Womens Education in India*, 1813-1966, Asia Pub House, Mumbai, 1973, p. 35

M. E. Church[204]. The Report of the Free Church Mission for 1879 mentioned about Miss Paterson, who entered on her Zenana work in Bombay at the beginning of 1879[205].

In December 1885, about 14 Zenana workers were devoted in Bombay. Earlicr in December 1873, Mrs. Crawford a Scots widow[206] had arrived in Bombay to engage in Zenana work. She was sent by the Zenana Bible and Medical Mission but she died in March 1874[207]. She worked for three months with the *Topi*, the Cap unwisely wearing the spine pad, woolen Cholera belts, corsets dictated by convention and the then state of tropical medicine and then dropped dead[208]. The Mission was then left without a medical Missionary.

By 1875, Bombay became one of the biggest Zenana stations. Work was built up not only among the Hindus and Muslims but also among the Bene Israel Jews and Parsis. In 1875, the Bombay Indian female normal school was founded with a school motto 'saved to serve' and Sunderabai Powar[209] was one of its pupils. Founder Maria Butt remarked forty years later that "there were Indian Christain Women of ability and character who were well qualified to inaugurate and carry on important undertakings".

Queen Mary's High school at Girgaum was founded in 1875 by Ms. Harriet Butt under the auspices of the ZBMM to supply the needs of high class Indian girls of the various communities for a liberal education[210]. In 1880, the heroic ladies of the ZBMM began work with the CMS at Nasik[211].

---

204 *BG*, September 1890, p. 3

205 *BG*, July 17, 1880 (front page)

206 She with Lucy Leighton became the first women medical Missionaries. They sailed together for India in November 1873 but Miss Leighton died before reaching India.

207 *BG*, March 28, 1874 , p. 25-26

208 Mridula Ramanna, *Western Medicine and Public Health in Colonial Bombay*, Orient Longman, New Delhi, 2002, p. 196

209 Sunderbai, Manjulabai, Shewantibai, Jaiwantibai are mentioned as quartette sisters in evangelistic efforts. *BG* April 15, 1899, p. 4

210 Ashley Brown, *On The Bombay Coast and Deccan*, Society for promoting Christian Knowledge, London, 1937, p. 238

211 *Ibid*, p. 180

In 1886, a committee of enquiry had made the following suggestions...

1. That in the opinion of this committee, no married woman should be employed as Zenana Mission agent without a written permission from her husband.
2. That no Zenana Mission agent should be employed without the recommendation of the Pastor in charge of the congregation to which she belongs.
3. That in the case of married women, who are Mission agents, husband and wife should live together.
4. That in the case of unmarried women and widows they should live with in the Mission premises under the immediate supervision of lady Superintendent.
5. That young woman may be employed as teachers in schools connected with the Zenana Mission, but that only women of established Christian character and mature age should be employed to visit Zenanas.
6. No Zenana Mission agent should be allowed to ask for presents of clothes or feed in houses she visits.
7. That no Zenana or school teacher and as far as possible, no European Lady Missionary should visit any house or establish a school in any street, without careful inquiry having been previously made regarding the respectability of the house or street.
8. That the special regard should be had to the dress of female agents, and care be taken that it be of such character as not to offend the feelings of the community[212].

Zenana ladies read the Bible for Women eager to learn the Bible and who felt that their spiritual diseases must be healed.[213] In November 1890, out of ten Lady Missionaries of the Zenana Bible and Medical Mission which proceeded to India, Mrs. Trott and Schwartz came to Bombay.

---

212 *BG*, August 28, 1886, p. 553

213 *BG*, December 26, 1885, p. 821

In the 'Book Notices Column', Ms. F. R. Hevergal[214] memorials was published. While writing to a friend who had gone to India to engage in Zenana work she says "I feel how very precious your time will be in acquiring the language and if you spent an hour in writing to me I should feel like David[215] did about the water of the well at Bethlehem"[216].

A front page report in *Bombay Guardian (BG)*, 1881 talks of the Indian Female Normal School and Instruction Society splitting up in to two portions in April 1880, the other portion was called England Zenana Missionary Society in connection with the Church Missionary Society (CMS)[217].

The three Zenana and female education societies (which worked more or less with the CMS)

Table 4.2: Zenana and female education societies (1881)

*** - This branch got split from the Indian female normal school and instruction society in April 1880.**

* The Church of England Zenana Missionary Society. Calcutta, Punjab, Madras, Travancore and Cochin.	Indian female normal school and instruction society (I.F.N.S) North West Province and Bombay Presidency.	The Society for promoting female education in the East (S.P.F.E.E) China.

An amicable division of the field was made, dictated partly by administrative convenience and partly by the wishes of the Missionaries[218]. The *Indian Female Evangelist* of October 1880 says "we have given up Madras and lower Bengal, but we retain the whole of Bombay and upper India except for Amritsar." Though shaken

214 She was attached to Church of Finland.

215 In Old Testament – David a shepherd boy became king at Israel.

216 *BG*, February 12, 1881, p. 667

217 Its centenary celebrations were taken up in London in April 1899.

218 J. C. Pollock, *Shadows fall Apart: The Story of the Zenana Bible and Medical Mission*, Hodder, London, 1958, p. 54

and weakened by the secession, the ZBMM had survived on its original principles.

The ladies connected with the Zenana Mission House in Bombay were going to return to Europe about the first of May due to various reasons especially health reasons. Great regret is expressed by all who were acquainted with the important work done by these ladies. Some 80 or 90 families were regularly visited by these ladies and the number could easily be doubled if they had strength. Some of these ladies were Mrs. Fellon, Ms. Fallen, Ms. Mallock and Ms. Schwarz[219].

Rev. R. A. Squires while speaking at the annual meeting of the Zenana Bible and Medical Mission (ZBMM), pleaded that Western India did not have its full share of attention either from the CMS or the ZBMM. He spoke of the growing willingness of native gentlemen to place Christian ladies at the head of their government institutions for the training of women, and to receive them as nurses in their hospitals. Mr. Squires also spoke of the very admirable work done by the American Missionaries[220]. Earlier in 1892 Ms. Grace, communicated with ZBMM in Europe. She proposed the society to send ZBMM workers to Western India. Ms. Green and Ms. Unsworth were sent to Ratnagiri. The work of the group was purely evangelistic. They visited from Chiplun to Sawantwadi and Goa in the south. They were also associated with Harrison school. Till 1897, they worked under Rev. W. H. Hannum. Later Rev. J. M. Irwin became the honorary secretary of the group. The ZBMM group was associated with Ratnagiri for more than 11years and also for some time in Vengurla[221].

The *Indian Female Evangelist* was the quarterly of the ZBMM which was discontinued in 1893 and was succeeded by the *Zenana or Women's work in India* (a monthly magazine consisting of 16 pages)[222]. In the front page of *BG* of December 9, 1899, information about the sixth annual volume of the *Zenana or Womens Work in India* is mentioned… "It is fully up to its usual standard of interest

219 *BG*, April 30, 1881, p. 130

220 *BG*, June 3, 1893, p. 11

221 Western India Notes (*WIN*), March 1930, p. 21

222 *BG*, August 26, 1893, p. 3

and attractions. Well illustrated with photographs and dainty cuts, with the never failing romance of Missionary life as told by the earnest workers on the field, it would form an excellent Christmas or New year Present for any who are interested in Missionary work. Missionary work among women in India is comparatively little known, and such an intrinsic volume is of incomparably greater interest to the Christian public than the general run of non-illustrated Mission reports".

Miss Evans of the C. E. Zenana Mission said 'If India is to be won for Christ we must get at the hearts of the mothers, as it is only women who can reach the women of India. There is need of lady Missionaries.[223]

4.3.1 Soonderabai Pawar

She was born in a Maratha family in 1856, her father Ramachandra, a student of Wilson College, Mumbai had been baptized. When she was 10 years old her father was transferred from Bombay to Saswad. She and her sisters were educated at home in the absence of a girl school.

At the age of 20 years she was invited to join a training school run by Zenana Bible Mission at Bombay[224]. Later, she became an efficient helper at Pandita Ramabai's Sharada Sadan in Bombay[225].

Miss Fuller of the ZBMM in Bombay wrote about Ramabai "her prayer life was very real, all her activities radiated from that". Ramabai insisted that neither she nor her converts should denationalize themselves. Her example was salutary. There was a tendency among Missionaries, both men and women, to identify Christianity with Western civilization, and though the girls of the other creeds who intended the ZBMM High school at Bombay alongside Europeans and Eurasians were expected to wear their native dress, once converted they were often encouraged to dress as westerners.

---

223 *BG*, November 14, 1903, front page

224 M. D. David, *Missions Cross Cultural Encounter & Change in Western India,* Manohar, New Delhi, 2001, p. 367

225 Jennie Chappell, Pandita Ramabai – *A Great Life in Indian Missions,* Basingstoke: Pickering & Inglis, Great Britain, 1968, p. 40

Later Soonderabai opened the Zenana Training Home at Pune to train Bible women. She revealed her work in the 4th Annual report of the Zenana Training Home[226]. It said "My work is increasing and new girls are coming one by one. Lately I had 120 girls.... One of the girls who had passed the 3 years course in the Bible and was in the highest standard in the school Subhodrabai has gone to assist in the Superintendence of a girl's orphanage at Roha, Konkan district..."

The home was supported by voluntary contributions and had no definite income but the instances of need supplied in answer to prayer, just at the right moment, show that the work was sealed by the Lords blessing. Ms. Pawar had the co-operation and assistance of Ms. Burder whose influence was greatly appreciated. The anti-opium work of Soonderabai Pawar is specially dealt with in chapter eight.

To understand the work of Zenana Mission in better perspective it was advisable to include their activities in city of Madras. The Zenana training home in Poona trained single women as evangelists[227].

4.3.2 Zenana work in Madras City

Ms. Grey Stephens was of Methodist Episcopal Zenana Mission. She said Zenana work is "Womens Work for Women in this large field of India. It is as extensive and as varied as the land itself, for these is no part of India were this work may not be undertaken. The work is the going from house to house among the upper and middle classes of Hindu and Mohammedan women who from custom and caste are obliged to link secluded lives, and have not the privileges of our Christian religion. Zenana work is the means of giving them Bible instructions and if necessary teaching them secular subjects....Only those with the love of Jesus in their hearts, and believing Him to be the true emancipator of women can do this work satisfactorily" [228].

Miss Stephens general work comprised in systematic visiting and teaching of more than five hundred Zenana women

226 *BG*, April 30, 1904, p. 8

227 *Dyanodaya Weekly*, November 13, 1947, p.182 (it was a four page weekly news paper established in 1842 available in Ahmednagar College Library, Maharashtra)

228 *BG*, May 14, 1904, p. 11

1. Nine day schools with nearly 600 pupils
2. Nine Sunday schools, a girls orphanage and the Christian workers
3. Home Editing of the Tamil Women's Friend' "*Mather Mithri*" etc.

Miss Grace published a one page article of a Young Brahmin Convert in *BG* of February 6, 1897 (page 6). It talks of Sooboonagam Ammal daughter of Mr. A. L. Venkataramana Pantulu a sub-judge in the district of Madura whose conversion caused a great stir in Hindu circles. She was married at the age of ten and she came in contact with Zenana when she was between 16 and 17 years of age, and was influenced by ladies of M. E. Zenana Mission (Vepery)[229]. She was always of a very religious turn of mind and for a year and a half she cared for nothing but gradually she became interested in the Bible. By November 1894 she was a changed person. She was baptized in 1896[230], the Hindus performed a mock funeral service of Sooboonagam Ammal within a month after her conversion. Even Krupabai Satthianadhan[231] taught in the Zenanas and also in girl's school. Her desire to initiate a home for Hindu widows could not be realised[232]. The ZBMM was called Bible and Medical Missionary Fellowship (September 1957).[233]

The contributions of sunderabai Powar, Pandita Ramabai and Sooboonagam Ammal towards the Zenana Mission were worth noting. Mission workers in Zenana brought to light the special need of medical health for women, especially those women who were shut up in homes and Zenana's. The stages of growth are subsequently highlighted. Being an inter-denominational society for work among women it was largely an auxiliary force; other Missions were enriched

229 *BG*, February 15, 1896, p. 4

230 Earlier Mr. Raju Naidu was publicly baptized by Dr. Rudisill in 1887 and he was present at Baptism of Sooboo.

231 Krupabai's parents were among the first converts to Christianity in the Bombay presidency.

232 Chandani Lokuge (ed), *Krupabai Satthianadhan - Saguna., The first autobiographical novel in English by an Indian women*, OUP. Delhi, 1998, p. xii

233 Pollock, J. C. *Op Cit*, p. vii

and helped by the work it did[234]. Finally the work of ZBMM presents the most interesting picture of co-operative Mission work.

4.4 Evangelistic Work

The Evangelicals were victorious in securing an Indian Church Establishment, freedom for Missionary work and the appropriation of an annual sum for education. This was the result of repeated petitioning to British parliament for permission to play a role in enlightening Indians. The good offices of Charles Grant[235] and William Wilberforce legalised the entry of Christian Missionaries to India and removed the existing restrictions on their activities. The Missionaries thus supplied British expansionism with ethics of concern[236]. The Protestant Missionaries used evangelization, i.e. mental change through constant use of message from Bible,[237]

Ismail Ibrahim was the first Bohra Muslim in Western India who had embraced Christianity and was baptized by Dr. John Wilson[238]. Mr. Dhanjibhai Nauroji[239] (1820 –1908) converted in 1839 spoke of the narrowness of the way of life to the people of this country when they embraced Christianity. He went on to tell the difficulties which beset him and another Parsi lad (probably Mr. Hormuzdi) when once they had decided to be baptised. He was once shot at but possibly the murderer missed his aim. Another time their butcher was bribed to poison the meat sold to their cook. On the day when Dhanjibhai and his friend had to attend the high court, then called the supreme court of Bombay all Native shops were closed and all the city seemed congregated in and around the court building. A company of English soldiers as well as the police force was there to protect the boys and

234 *BG*, July 18, 1896, p. 3

235 Charles Grant, though not a Missionary circles. He emphatically said the English language would acquaint Hindoos with the literary compositions of the west.

236 Gauri Vishvanathan, *Masks of Conquest, Literary Study and British Rule in India*, Columbia University Press, USA, 1989, p. 36

237 S. R. Shirgaonkar, *Op.Cit*, pp. 37-38

238 *The Annual Report of the Bombay Auxiliary Missionary Society of the Free Church of Scotland*, Bombay, 1855, p. 12

239 Rev. Dhanjibhai Nawroji edited two Anglo Vernacular magazines - *The Gyan Deepika and Bamdad in Gujarati* (*BG*, December 11th 1886, p. 791)

keep order in the crowd. It was exciting to hear Mr. Dhanjibhai how he stood trembling before all the great men of the court with whom on the platform were Sir Jamshedji Jeejebhoy (1783-1853, first Baronate)[240] and other influential Parsis. The boys being of age, it was decided that they could go where they decided – with the Missionaries or their relatives. They went with Dr. Wilson[241]. Rev. S. V. Karmarkar on completion of the Diamond Jubilee of Dhanjibhai's baptism spoke of the bribe of Rs 15,000 which was offered to the brave young converts by the Parsi community if he would return to the religion of his forefathers[242]. Bishop Foster in Bombay spoke about its Parsee population as the proudest native element of India, representing the best business energy and the largest accumulation of wealth, and assuming quite a show of state and elegance[243].

Instance of support for Parsis can be seen when on 29th May 1833., while Col. Van Kennedy was in the chair of the Bombay Branch of the Royal Asiatic Society the name of Manockjee Curstjee was proposed as member by the secretary of the Bombay Native Education society Mr. Robert Money and was seconded by Vans Kennedy himself. But, there was a great opposition to the admission of a native as a member of the society and the proposal was rejected. The editor of the *Oriental Christian Spectator* (OCS), Rev. John Wilson regretted the decision in the following words… "As Manackjee has a respectable knowledge of several of the Asiatic and European languages and is willing and able to advance the interests of the society, we regret the decision which has come to in his case"[244].

240 He helped many news papers and magazines. He was one of the proprietors of the Bombay Courier and also gave financial assistance to the *Bombay Samachar, The Bombay Times and monthly magazine Bidhiasagar.*

241 *BG*, May 6, 1899, p.12

242 *BG*, July 8, 1899, p.11

243 *BG*, April 12, 1884, p. 283

244 as quoted in S. G. Mahajan *History of the Public Library Movement in Western Maharashtra (1805-1921)* Ph.D. Thesis, Pune, 1979, p. 100

4.4.1 Development of the Church

Sir Cowasji Jehangeer[245] (1812-1878) had presented Rs.7000, which was later raised to Rs.13,777 to the trustees of St. Thomas cathedral to erect a fountain opposite the western entrance to the Church. Cowasji Jehangeer writes "all my dearest associations from my school boy days till now are connected with this neighbour hood (the cathedral), and I feel that I shall be wanting in gratitude in heaven which has blessed me here with long life and prosperity, if I did not use every opportunity to do good to my fellow citizen's, by improving that part of my native town which I have always loved as my birth place and as my home" [246]. Commenting upon his catholic charities, the London "Punch" said, "Is Mr. Ready-Money a Parsi? At any rate he is not Parsimonious"[247] . In the front page of *Bombay Guardian*, July 27, 1878, death of Sir Cowasji Jehangeer is covered. He began life as a godown keeper, afterwards became a broker and a singularly successful man of business. He gave donations for building the University Hall, Eye Hospital, Elphinstone College, Surat Hospital, Strangers Home, Street Fountains etc.

J. C. Jehangeer in his book *Life of Sir Cowasji Jehangeer Ready Money* (page 61) says "Sir Cowasji seems to have regarded drinking fountains as supplying one of the chief wants of humanity for he gave 13,540 rupees for the erection of the Regents Park Fountain which bears his name Sir Cowasji Jehangeer Fountain in London in 1869".

Prof. Kellogg of Princeton's spoke of three point to naturalise the Church in Heathen Countries. The standards of doctrine and polity must be adopted as closely as possible to the actual specific conditions of society in each country. All Churches, at one in their fundamental articles of doctrine and polity, waiving minor

---

245 Sir Cowasji Jehangeer had placed a sum of Rs. 5000 or more to the credit of Dr. Birdwood to complete the oriental literature class of the Asiatic Library, so that 'it may be the finest in any library in the world', *BG* February 7, 1863, p. 44

246 *BG*, May 16th 1863, p. 157

247 Rustamji Nasavanji Munshi 'The Life story of the old portuguese Bell' in *The Journal of the Bombay Branch of the Original Royal Asiatic Society*, Vol. XXV (No. 71-73) 1917-21 reprint,1969, p. 146

distinctions, should be organically united. Finally, in due time and order there must be entire ecclesiastical severance from the parent churches in Indians and America[248].

4.4.2 Training of Christians

Rev. C.W. Park's views on self support in Indian Mission speaks about how initially the idea of self help had not dawned and their had been a policy of dispensing benefits dominating for half a century. This led to seeds of dependence planted in the native Christian community. Parents were paid for sending their children to school and chapels. In School- houses built-preachers and teachers were trained and paid at Mission's expense (the Missionaries did pastoral work). In everything they acted as tender parents and the natives were children.

In 1854 a step towards independence was taken in the ordination of two native Pastors over native churches (but here their salaries continued to be paid from Mission funds). It was in 1867 that the Missionaries began to press upon the Christians the obligation to sustain their own pastors. After 15 years of efforts the native Church in connection with the Maratha Mission[249] stood as whole self-sustaining. Further since the beginning of 1882, not a cent of Mission money had been paid to any native pastor. The old policy has been definitely abandoned; the Christians themselves were determined to become independent[250].

4.4.3 Literature

From the beginning the Missionaries used print as an influential source to spread their message[251]. One of the most pressing necessities of India at that moment was a good vernacular literature, which was supplied regularly by the Bombay Tract and Book Society (BTBS). Rev. Narayan Sheshadri, Baba Padmanji, Mr. and Mrs. Murry

---

248 *BG*, January 31st 1880, p. 584

249 The example of the American Marathi Mission has been helpful to others in several respects, especially in the matter of placing native churches on a self-supporting basis.

250 *BG*, March 22, 1884, pp. 179-180

251 S. R. Shirgaonkar, *Op.Cit*, p. 30

Mitchell, Dr. Stevenson, Rev. R. G. Wilder and others regularly contributed their works in this society. Father Hartmann started a diocesan periodical in September 1850 known as *The Bombay Catholic Examiner* [252] or *The Examiner.*

Rev. Kasam Mahomed Dhalwani (called Kassim bhai) translated a Marathi Bible dictionary prepared from its English version. It was edited by Rev. Henry J. Bruce of American Mission, Satara. Most literary works were evangelistic in character. The Centenary of the British and Foreign Bible Society[253] was celebrated in 1904 and brief history of the Bombay Auxiliary to the British and Foreign Bible Society (1813-1904) was published. Dr. Mackinchan gave an account of the work done by the society during the past 90 years of its existence. It was stated that the whole Bible has been translated into 2 principal languages of this Presidency, namely Marathi and Gujarati...[254].

Rev. J. E. Abbott mentioned a strange anomaly in the fact that the Governor of Bombay Sir Edward Nepean, who took the chair at the first meeting of the Bible Society in Bombay, was the very man who refused to allow the first two Missionaries appointed to Western India to settle here. The reason probably was that he himself was personally favourable to the work of Missions, and merely acted in accordance with orders received from higher authority. Knott, Dickinson, Robertson, Wilson, Nesbit, Graves were the honoured names that have been mentioned in connection with Bible translation[255,256].

Evangelism and Work of Mercy are two sides of the same coin. The Christian Missionary activities may be further classified as:

252 In July 1859 *OCS* on p. 273, a word for 'The Bombay Catholic Examiner' can be seen.

253 Its chief aim has been to give the various peoples of the world the divine oracles in their own vernaculars

254 *BG*, June 18,1904, p. 10

255 Graves was the young American who cut the first Marathi type and sent it to America for reproduction

256 *BG*, March 5, 1904, p. 8

Table 4.3: Two chief categories of Missionary activity

Spiritual	*Temporal*
The work of evangelism fell in this category.	In this the material welfare activities in the form of fulfillment of some basic material wants like food, education, health etc were covered. The Christians considered the material gains as the 'Work of Mercy'.

Thus, in Christianity Evangelisation was important, but no less important was the 'Work of Mercy', which follows automatically as an outcome of faith. However, the work could not stand without the faith. The statement implies that evangelisation and works of mercy were complementary to each other. The success of one depends on the well-knit working of the other. Christians maintain that no spiritual or cultural life is possible without the minimum of material comfort and security.[257]

4.5 Prominent Churches in Mumbai

Church is said to be the visible social organization of which Christ remains the head. It governs with legislative, judicial and executive power, the successors of those first appointed to this position, the Apostles were the Bishop of Rome and in them resides the plentitude of powers and jurisdiction as shepherds and rulers of God's people[258].

4.5.1 Methodist Episcopical Church, Grant Road

The Methodist Episcopical Church, Grant Road has a Mission hall where the Gospel was preached in the vernaculars and where native Christians were taught and cared for. Also the zenana workers, temperance advocates, bands of hope, fellowship classes were held there. The Church was the effort of Rev. William Taylor[259], Charles

257 S. K. Bhattacharya, *Christian Missionaries and Indian Societies,* Mohit Publications, New Delhi, 1999, p. 5

258 Nalini Keller, *Women under the Cross, Changing Gender roles in Christian Families*, Cosmo, New Delhi, p. 30

259 He was known as the revivalist feature from California. In 1871 he came by invitation to Bombay.

Harding (AMM of Bombay and Ahmednagar) and Rev. G. O. Bowen[260].

4.5.2 St. Thomas Church, Mumbai[261]

This is the oldest English building and Church in Bombay. Before this Church, there were at least four Portuguese Churches in Bombay and all were Roman Catholic. It was the work of pious and enthusiastic Chaplain Rev. Richard Cobbe. It was opened on the Christmas day of the 1718 to the great joy of the little company of the Christian people. St. Thomas Cathedral is dedicated to St.Thomas who was the first apostle to land on Indian shores. The Cathedral's spire old Porbunder stone, Apse and stained glass windows are awe-inspiring.

A beautiful Gothic style fountain at the entrance designed by Mr. Gilbert Scott was erected at the west entrance at the sole cost of Mr. Cowasji Jehangir Ready Money. He was prompted to do this work by gratitude for the prosperity he had enjoyed in the immediate neighbourhood of which his boyhood and manhood had been spent: the only condition attached to the gift was that it should be a public drinking fountain for the use of the inhabitants of Bombay[262]. It was engraved with the soothing legend "Whosoever drinketh of the water that I shall give him shall never thirst". In 1838 this Church got Cathedral Status and the tower was raised to its present height. The construction of this Church went through lot of ups and downs due to war and trade. Besides being a house of prayer it was also responsible for spreading Anglican education in the city of Bombay. One of the best known schools of India, the Cathedral and the John Cannon School has been always associated with this Church. In 2004, this grade-I heritage structure won a UNESCO Award for heritage conservation

260 *BG*, May 02, 1891, p. 3

261 For details see the article 'St. Thomas the Cathedral Church of Bombay' in the *Calcutta Review*, 1899, p. 215

262 'Renovation of the cathedral Church of Bombay 1864', in *Bombay Pamphlets*, Vol. 6, Education Society's Press, Byculla, 1864, p. 334

Picture 4.3: Fountain Outside St. Thomas Cathedral

4.5.3 Bowen Memorial Church, Colaba

The Bowen Memorial Church[263](named after George Bowen) was opened for public worship in 1890. The Church is on the ground floor with Parsonage above. It is a substantial yet airy and pleasant building excellently situated for Fort and Colaba residents.

The Church was the realization of many years of prayer and toil by its members. It was the first Church organized in Bombay as the result of Bishop Willam Tailor's efforts. The Fort Methodist were able to call this Church their own[264].

263 Bowen Memorial Church is also described in *BG,* June 3, 1893, p. 11

264 *BG,* March 21, 1891, p. 3

Picture 4.4: Bowen Memorial Church

Picture 4.5: Gloria Church, Byculla

4.5.4 Gloria Church, Byculla

This Church is a Gothic structure tower with four commanding turrets which leave the surrounding buildings grappling for attention. Its stained glass windows add to its glory. Earlier it had a giant pipe organ. It is a roman catholic Church.

4.5.5 The Kalina Church, Mumbai

It is more than 400 years old (established in the year 1606) and was serving the villages of Sar (Sahar), Kalyan (Kalina) and Vancolem (Vakola). It is also known as Our lady of Egypt Church.

Picture 4.6: Kalina Church

4.5.6 The Afghan Memorial Church, Colaba

Afghan Church is at the southern end of the Mumbai City. Two years after the conquest of Kabul in 1842, Bishop Carr of Bombay wrote to the English authorities to erect a Church in memory of the martyrs in Afghanistan and that's how the Church got its name. English engineer Henry Cornbeare and architect Willam Butterfield designed the Church in 1847. It was also called St. John the Evangelist and belongs to group of Grade-I heritage site.

4.5.7 The Emmanuel Church, Grant Road

This Church was an effort of CMS in the second half of nineteenth century. By 1874 a Sunday school was established. Music was always an important part of worship. By 1887 the Church had its own pipe organ. This Church was famous for services in English, Marathi and Gujarati languages. It was basically meant for native Christian converts. Recently a book by Raghavendra Kannan entitled *Historic Churches of Bombay* has covered this Church.

Picture 4.7: Afghan Memorial Church **Picture 4.8:** St. Emmanuel Church

4.5.8 St. Peter's Church, Bandra

The foundation stone of St. Peter's Church was laid on April 12, 1852 by Bishop Hartmann who even though troubled by the whole question of double jurisdiction yet produced a volume of constructive work that seems quite incredible[265].

265 Edwina Pio, "Bandra Churches and Shrines", *Heras Institute Seminar on Bandra-* A changing suburb, Bombay, 1986, p. 24

4.6 Women Issues

4.6.1 The First Baniya Remarriage

Karsondas Mulji's friend Seth Madhavdas Raghunath took second wife a widow named Dhankore. Some letters written in 1871 shows the elaborate planning made for this marriage[266]. *The Bombay Guardian*[267] covered information on Late Mr. Madhavdas Raghunathdas as follows – The Valiant Champion of the Hindu Widow. Madhavdas belonged to the *Baniya* Caste and saw that enforced widowhood was a sin or crime and took to himself a young widow for wife. Later his son Bhagwandas Madhavdas became a champion of widow remarriage. He followed the footsteps of his father in encouraging the remarriage of Hindu widows at 'Widow Remarriage Hall' at Girgaum.

The *BG* of November 29, 1890 (page5) says the first widow remarriage among the Pokarna Brahmin caste took place of Kashibai (age 20 years) with Ludha Lakhimdas (30 years). The marriage was performed under the Association for encouraging widow remarriages, the same issue of *BG* mentions about the orphans at poona.

Rakmabai (1860-1950), an educated girl from Sutar[268] community was married to Dadaji at the age of 13. For some time her husband lived as a *Ghar-Jawai*[269]. She refused to live with her husband on grounds that he was illiterate and consumptive. While the lower court upheld that she could not be compelled, her husband Dadaji appealed to the high court and the decision was reverted. She was liable, according to the Anglo-Indian code, and was to be send to prison for six calendar months[270]. She preferred to risk imprisonment than go to her husband. Her decision was no doubt unusual but she was firm about it[271]. The controversy ended in 1887 by mutual agreement[272].

---

266 B. N. Motiwala, *Karsondas Moolji: A Biographical Study* published in 1935

267 *BG*, April 04,1896, front page

268 The Sutars were carpenters who came to play a role in the house construction business in urban areas like Bombay as opportunities opened up.

269 A resident son in law.

270 The Cases of Rakhamabai and Ramabai, *Times of India*, February 8, 1888, p. 6

271 Preeta Nilesh, *Op.Cit*, p. 173

272 Rakmabai brought her independence from Dadaji for a sum of Rs. 2000.

The judgment was both an embarrassment to British Judicial practice and was viewed as an outrage by Behram Malbari who had already begun a campaign both in India and England for an end to 'Infant Marriage'[273].

Rukmabai wrote touching letters by "A Hindu Lady" which won universal Sympathy[274], the case is again reported in a consequent issue of *BG* (April 10, 1886, p. 229). The decision of Mr. Justice Pinhey is highlighted. A long letter by ABC[275] talks of the great stir caused due to Rakhmabai's case. The letter goes against Rakhmabai and says "she is stranger to heroism and she should submit to the yoke laid upon her shoulders by the society of which she is a member.

Arya bhagini was a monthly magazine in Marathi, edited by Mrs. Manakbai Lada, a Hindoo lady of the shenvi community and published under the auspices of Mrs. Radhabai Atmaram Sagoon. This was a new departure in Marathi literature, and congratulated, the daughters of Maharashtra on the fact that one of their number has ventured to sit down in the editorial chair". In this magazine, first number article was on marriage customs, early marriage, the lazy girl and the diligent girl, education of children, cleanliness and true happiness[276].

In the absence of electronic media, the print media especially the press played an important role especially after 1850 in highlighting various changes in the society.

The introductory part deals with Maharaja Libel Case and how the reaction towards Karsondas Mulji was mixed as is highlighted by the press. *Young India*[277] of February 1918 mentions Karsondas Mulji (1832-1871) as a great Bombay reformer. He was a journalist and social reformer and was a leading figure in the social reform movement in the Gujarati Community of Bombay.

He had started his own paper, the *'Satya Prakash'* (printed by Nanabhai Rustamji Ranina) in 1855 for promoting social reform in

273 Uma Chakravarti, *Gendering Caste through a Feminist Lens*, Stree Pub, Calcutta, 2003, p. 133

274 *BG*, March 20,1886, p. 20

275 *BG*, April 17, 1886, pp. 246-47

276 *BG*, March 20, 1886, p. 179

277 It was a weekly newspaper in English edited by Mahatma Gandhi

his own community. He led a crusade against the Maharajas of the Vallabhacharya sect who were worshipped especially by *Kapol Banias* as incarnations of Brahma and Krishna. He began exposing them through the columns of his paper and the *Rast Goftar* and in one of his articles he directly attacked Jadunath Brijaratnaji Maharaj who filed a libel suit in the Supreme Court (Bombay) against Karsondas in 1861.

The BG of March 14, 1863 highlights how Mr. Kursondas Mooljee, on the eve of his departure for England was felicitated for the courage shown by him in exposing the evil practices of the Maharajas (he was honoured as an earnest reformer)[278]. All classes of the community including Europeans, Parsees, Banyas, Bhattias, Marathas etc. honored him. The Meeting was addressed by Rev. Dr. Wilson, Mr. Dadoba Pandurang, Rev. Dr. Murry Mitchell, Hormusjee Dadabhoy etc. The speakers dwelt at length upon the late eventful trial of the Maharaj Libel case, the circumstances which preceded its commencement and those which marked its close, the salutary effects which it was calculated to work upon the debasing religious system of the Vallabhacharyas, the light which it threw upon the hideous practices of their spiritual preceptors and above all, they alluded ineloquent terms to the exertions of Mr. Kursondas in the cause of reform of truth, and morality,....exertions sustained by no hope of gain, but continued to the close of the struggle against a thousand adverse circumstances.

Dr. Wilson stated that a sum of about Rs.5,000 had been subscribed privately, which would be largely increased when the subscription lists will have been circulated more freely. And that it was intended to present Mr. Kursondas with the amount, not as a recompense to him in money for his truly noble efforts in the cause of truth and morality, but merely as a token of the admiration with which his conduct which was looked upon by all the friends of enlightenment in this country. Also Mr. Sorabjee Shapoorjee

278 The case created a great sensation in Bombay and was decided in favour of Karsondas. (B. R. Sunthankar, *Maharashtra* 1858-1920, Manmohan Bhatkal Popular Book Depot, Bombay, 1993, p.107)

Bengalee[279] announced the intention of a Parsee gentleman to found a scholarship in Mr. Kursondas's name in Dr. Bhawoo Dajee's[280] girl's school, and to present him with a piece of plate, for the execution of which an order has been sent to the firm of Messer. Dadabhoy Nowrojee of Liverpool. Karsandas Mulji wrote a Gujarati Work *Ekko Nara* "A Memoir of the Late Philanthropist Sorabji Shapurji Bengalee" of 124 pages.

The Report of the Maharaj Libel Case and of the Bhattia Conspiracy case[281] says "this case is in all respect a most extraordinary one". Also on page 206, it mentions that in 1855 the devout followers of the Maharaj (especially from Bhattia caste) had a caste meeting which fixed hours for females to visit temples.

In the same issue of *BG* a news stating "the followers of the Maharajas in Bombay on hearing Mr. Karsondas's departure to England, taking legal advices as to whether they could not with safety excommunicate him for his intended voyage beyond the limit prescribed in the Shastras" is published.

Again in front page of *BG* of October 10,1863 we see the report about Maharaja Libel case saying "Mr. Kursondass Moolji, the defendant in the libel case is threatened with expulsion from caste, for having visited England..."

BG of October 24, 1863 (page 351) quotes from *Times of India* October 23,1863. " We have been watching with considerable anxiety, the turn matters would take in the case of Mr. Kursondas Mooljee whose visit to Europe was unexpectedly cut short by sickness. Mr. Kursondas is the first man of his caste who has ventured to condemn the traditions which confine the *Banyan* (means *Baniya*

---

279 Sorabji Shapoorji Bengallee who himself was a parsi, neglected the selfish interest of the mill owners of his own community and as a member of the then Bombay Legislative Council, proposed a quite radical factory legislation.

280 He is regarded as first Indian Indologist. Dr. Wilson said "The late Dr. Bhau Daji had indeed proved conspicuous ornaments of the society. The learned doctor had already a European as well as an Indian reputation (G. M. Laud, *Dr. Bhau Daji Lad Parsekar - A Biography 1821-1874*, Dept. of Information and Publicity, Govt. of Goa, Goa, 1974, p. 61)

281 This was published in 1862 Bombay. Dr. Bhawoo's name occurs in this report on p. 149 and p. 183.

caste) to these seas. For absurd as it may appear, it is nevertheless true, that while the *Banyans'* may flock in tribes to the Arabian or African coast, a tradition of the caste forbids their visiting Europe. It required special courage on the part of Mr. Kursondass to break through this bondage for it was inevitable that he should have numerous caste enemies, owing to his having been defendant in the late action for libel in the supreme court. Every friend of the Maharaja was of course the enemy of Mr. Kursondass.

The write-up further says "Mr. Kursondass has taken another step also. He has withdrawn the name from the *Buddhevarduk* society[282], for the indecision which it has evinced as to consorting with Mr. Kursondass Mooljee….."

The Hon'ble Mr. Prema bhaee's family and those of Mr. Candass Narrondass, Mr. Premchund Roychund, and others had all with equal courage and good sense quietly ranged themselves on the side of reason and common sense having either themselves dined with Mr. Kursondass, or knowingly and purposely dined with those who have dined with him.

On his return, he was excommunicated by his community and was subjected to such fierce persecution that he was forced to leave Bombay to serve in one of the Kathiawad States.

4.6.2 The Wrongs of Indian Womanhood

The *BG*, January 14, 1889 (page 4) issue talks about the *Devdasi* system. In Western India there is another class called *Bhavins* who are peculiar to the Konkan and Goa, and the name, says a Hindu writer, is applied to women in the service of the idols in temples in Goa and places round about and in parts of the Konkan. Some of these women are presented to the gods in infancy by their parents as the *Muralis* are. Their business is to attend the temple lamps, and keep them trimmed, to sweep and smear the floor, to turn the *Chauri* over the idol, serve the *Huka* to the congregation, and to serve the visitors of the temple. They always trim a lamp with their fingers and not with small sticks as other Hindus do. The trimming of the lamp

282 He was active in this society with his supporters Narmada Lal Shankar, a renowned Gujarati Poet and Mahipat Ram an eminent educationist.

with the fingers by any other than a Bhavin is supposed to bring poverty, and this is particularly observed in all Hindu houses. They were descendants of pure Marathas.

The *BG*, January 21 issue (page 3) of *BG* talks about the 'Nautch Girl'... "The nautch-girl often begins her career of training under teachers as early as five years of age. She is taught to read, dance and sing, and every seductive art. Her songs were usually amorous. As a large proportion of these women were childless, their ranks were re-enforced by adoption of little girls, who were bought or obtained in other ways. Illegitimate children were often passed on to them, and in the periodical famines that occur in this country large numbers of girls find a home with this class. The write-up also highlights how occasionally young widows are attracted to the above profession. Dr. Bhandarkar's views on Nautch girl (*BG* of September 15, 1894) is quoted in *BG* of February 11, 1899 as "I have always been of the opinion that he who patronises dancing girls does not sufficiently hate the immoral life which they professedly lead, or value as highly as he ought to do female purity which is the soil on which the noble qualities of women grow. The institution of Nautch cannot but have a debasing effect on the morality of men and women. I shall not without strong proof, believe in a man's faithful husband, if he takes a delight in giving Nautch parties and attending them. To have a Nautch at one's own house is to give an object lesson in immorality to the boys and girls in the family and especially to the former. As long as the Nautch is fashionable among us, and is freely indulged in, it is impossible that the morality of our men should greatly improve and our respect for women should increase, and in a country in which women are trampled upon, there can be no great advance in social and moral matters."

The Voice of India a Fortnightly magazine edited by Behramji Malabari of 1884 gives the below list of weeklies in Bombay

Table 4.4: List of weeklies of Bombay (1884)

Anglo-Marathi Weekly	*English Weekly*	*Anglo-Gujarati*
Indu Prakash *Native Opinion*[283] *Deen Bandhu* *Subodh Patrika*	*Indian Spectator* *Native Patriot*	*The Chronicle* *The Samachar* *Gujarati Daily* *Kaiser-i-Hind* *Satya Mitra* *Akhbar –e soudagar*

We see in some of the newspapers periphery analysis of issues related to women, indigo cultivators, and temperance movement emerging in the nineteenth century.

4.7 Others

4.7.1 The Blue Mutiny (1859-62)

Indigo planting in India was a cruel and oppressive system, almost a kind of forced labour. Reverend James Long (1814-1887)[284] was imprisoned in 1861 for translating the *Nil Darpan*[285] (in English). He was very sympathetic to the indigo cultivators and due to his above work he was indicated for libel for it was considered an offence and was fined Rs1,000 and one month imprisonment. Kali Prasanna Sinha a well known Bengali writer and millionaire had stepped forward and paid the fine. He became a martyr in the eyes of Indians[286]. His genuine love for the Indians can be seen in the letter below.

283 V. N. Mandlik (1833-1889) started this news magazine in 1865 with the aim to publish the opinion of Indians without any regard for the reaction from the government.

284 His write-up 'The Portuguese in North India' published in Selection from the *Calcutta Review*, 1846, pp. 64-113

285 'Blue Mutiny' continued to disturb the peace of rural Bengal.

286 S. R. Mehrotra, *The Emergence of the Indian National Congress*, Rupa and Co, New Delhi, 2004, p. 342

A letter dated 15th July 1861[287] by James Long says that *Nil Darpan* is a genuine expression of Native feeling on the subject of Indigo planting. In the concluding part of this long letter, Long writes "my humble labors as a Missionary in this country have taught me to commiserate the sufferings of the masses of the people of this land, and while I have learned to respect the energy and genius of many of my own countrymen, I have at the same time earnestly wished to urge them to show mercy to the poor, and thus to recommend those principles in the Gospel of doing justice, loving mercy and walking humbly with God which Christian Missions have always been designed to promulgate. If I suffer in this cause, it will only be in common with multitudes of far worthier men, who have suffered the loss of all things in the cause of truth, righteousness, and humanity".

4.7.2 The Caste Issue

It is a sad fact that inspite of Christianity being a progressive religion, it succumbed to the caste orthodoxy of the hidebound society of those times. A letter entitled "Should Indian Christians state their original caste at the coming census?" was published[288]. It says "Dear Sir, - I was grieved to notice in the circular issued by the census commissioner the following suggestions… As regards column 8 (caste or tribe), Native Christians should be directed to return the name of the caste to which they belonged before their acceptance of Christianity. Children (i.e. young or adult descendants) of converts should give the original caste of their male parent. Also I was painfully astonished to find that at the advice of the American and S.P.C.K. Missionaries of Ahmednagar this clause was inserted. The desire of the Missionaries to ask the Indian Christians to state their caste is quite unchristian. For caste is founded upon pride and selfishness of the Hindus, and therefore, no Christian Missionary, directly or indirectly ought ever to have anything to do in keeping up this cursed and baneful system. The teaching and spirit of Jesus Christ not only ignores but discards the abominable caste principle. The last command of Jesus, "that ye love one another even as I have

287 Published in *The Times of India* July 31,1861, p. 3

288 *BG*, December 8, 1900, p. 11

loved you", does not harbour for a moment any high or low degree in man....why should then such godly Missionaries advice such an unchristian method of treating Indian Christians who are born in the divine family, through the name spirit who brought them out of bondage of sin and death? Is it necessary for these servants of God to enumerate their converts according to castes? Can we conceive of the Holy spirit making a census of His conversions in the following manners:- 50,000 Mahar souls, 10,000 Mang souls, 5,000 Bhangi souls and 1,000 Brahmin soul brought to the knowledge of Jesus Christ!. I would urge upon every Indian Christian to utterly ignore caste, as it is unchristian and unchristlike. He or she can mention the nationality as Maratha, Bengalee, Tamil, Telugu, Canarese or Gujerathi Christian, if one can possibly do so. For there are instances where the children of the 3rd and 4th generation have no particular nationality like the Americans who are now fast becoming a hybrid race. It is better therefore, to denominate ourselves as Indian Christians". In an yet identical letter published[289] read "I have known of cases where Christian converts and their children were obliged to state their castes by the authoritative order of the Government Officials in the lower courts. Their names are written down in the official documents as so and so Mang Christian; so and so Mahar Christian. This practice is very common in the Deccan, and to it I take a very strong objection. When a Bhangi (sweeper) or Mahar (Pariah) becomes a Muslim, is he ever called a Bhangi Muslim or a Mahar Muslim? Why should then a Christian convert be disgraced by such epithets in the official documents of a Christian Government? Even if it is made optional, it will still be a source of great annoyance to the Indian Christians; and, moreover, it will give its sanction to a thing which is quite unchristian".

The *Bombay Guardian* which was an ardent supporter of the Missionary standpoint alleged that invitations to a meeting at the seminary (for Prabhu boys) included a statement prohibiting Mahar converts from attending. The paper asked why only Mahars were forbidden while converted Brahmins, Muslims, Parsis and Portuguese were admitted[290].

289 *BG*, December 15, 1900, p.12

290 *BG*, September 20, 1856, front page

The literary works formed the integral part to propagate education as well as Christian literature. The Missionaries used the publication tool for teaching and preaching in vernacular languages thereby creating a larger impact on the local populace. It formed a platform for the exchange of ideas not only in India but with other countries as well. It provided the evidence for documentation of Missionary work carried out in this part of the country. The literary work thus formed an important tool for the propagation of knowledge and is discussed in following chapter.

Chapter 5

Literary Works of Christian Missionaries

5.1 Introduction

The decade following the revolt of 1857 witnessed a remarkable growth in the vernacular newspapers and periodicals in Bengal. There were 87 Bengali newspapers and periodicals. The press at registration of books at 1867 was intended to keep a record of the rapidly increasing number of periodicals, journals and various other sought's of publications that were coming in to existence[291].

The Vernacular education was given due importance by the Missionaries. The American Mission Report for 1894 highlighted Mr. Abbott's views on The Vernacular Press- "I have given more time this year to the reading of the vernacular papers in order to note the attitude they assume to the questions of the day. These papers may be divided into 3 classes: those ready to advocate reform; those on the fence, now for, now against, what to us seem reformed ideas, and thirdly those who say the old is better. Politically they are much more of a unit. They may differ in opinion as to individual measures of the Government, but it is essentially an opposition press. Their criticism is very free. It is difficult to exactly gauge its attitude to

291 M. S. Bose, 'The Vernacular Press Act in Indian Nationalism' *in Bengal Past and Present*, July – December 1978

Christianity for the reason that consistency is not their forte. The same paper may one day have an article friendly to Christianity, and the next one, bitter and caustic. One day, we hear of the devoted labours of Missionaries, who have done so much for India, the next we may see Missionaries caricatured and their work ascribed to the lowest motives. On the whole, however a great improvement is to be noticed in the attitude of the press. This improved tone is doubtless, due to a better knowledge of what Christianity is and the greater respect in which the Indian Christians are held".

Table 5.1: Works of Alexander Duff and Mary Carpenter

Name	*Work*
Alexander Duff	India and the India Missions, 1839
Mary Carpenter (1807-1877)	*Our Convicts* (in 2 vols in1864), *Six Months in India*, 1868. She also ed. *Sermons on Practical Subjects by Rev. Lant*[292] Carpenter 1875.

Mary Carpenter embarked for India at the age of fifty-nine and made four trips to India between 1866 and 1876[293]. She dedicated her volumes of *Six Months in India* to Rajah Ram Mohan Roy[294]. On page 102 of her first volume, she mentioned the importance of establishment of a Female Normal Training School for the improvement of female education. In the other volume, she mentioned the pleasure of meeting Student's Society's President Dr. Bhau Daji, and also mentioned about her visit to the Church Mission Schools especially the Robert Money Institution. In the same volume on p. 18, she praised Dr. Wilson's School and College.

---

292 Mary was Dr. Lant's Eldest daughter. Lant was a prominent Utiliitarian minister and school instructor and fervent anti-slavery activist.

293 Indira Ghose, *Women Travellers in Colonial India*, OUP, New Delhi, 1998, p. 115

294 Indian reformer Roy had visited Bristol on the invitation of Dr. Lant

"It does the highest credit to the admirable superintendence it receives from that benevolent and learned man. In this institution there is really no distinction of caste, creed or nationality. She adds the Parsees have left the school, since 2 of their boys embraced Christianity many years ago."

5.2 BTBS and Vernacular Christian Education

The Bombay Tract and Book Society:

The object of the BTBS society formed in 1828 was to provide information to the natives of this country in language that they understand. It was the truths of God's word in forms adapted which would arrest their hearts. Its object was identical with that of the Missionary and that "it must commend itself to all who receive the Bible as a revelation from God and desire to see it so received by all". In 1850, this Society had a record of printing as many as 74,809 books and circulating 67,514 books by sale[295].

The main aim of BTBS was to develop Christian Vernacular literature. It also issued works like *The Life of Mohammed* in English (174pages), *Pandharpur and Vittoba* (in marathi, 69 pages) [296]. The *OCS* of April 1858 (p.132) mentions new publications in 1857 of the BT &BS as follows:

1. The Scripture Manual in Marathi by Rev. R. G. Wilder (his commentary on Mathew's Gospel in Marathi was published in 1858[297])
2. Sin - its nature and results a tract in Marathi by Rev. Narayan Sheshadri
3. Discussions by the Sea Side in English by Bramhachari Bawa, a Brahmin and Christian Missionaries (especially with Mr. George Bowen) in 1857.

It is interesting to look into the three Annual Meeting of the BTBS society which were published in the form of a special

295 *BG*, Friday April 11, 1851
296 *BG*, Saturday, September 06, 1856, p. 283
297 *OCS*, July 1860, p. 276

Supplement to *The Bombay Guardian* of 1857, 1858 and 1859. It highlighted the 31st Anniversary of the Bombay Tract and Book Society and covered information about Marathi translation of an English Tract "*Eric, The Russian Slave*" by Rev. Narayan Sheshadri. The annual meeting of the Bombay Tract and Book Society was held at the Free Church, Esplanade. Major General Lester presided the meeting. Prayer was offered by Rev. Daji Pandurang[298], among others Narayan Sheshadri was also present.

In the report read by the secretary a list of books can be traced.,

1. *A Manual of Christian Duties* by Baba Padmanji in marathi.

   It looked at the native Christian in his various relations, and portrayed the duties connected with these relations. The subject was a very important one, and had been successfully treated. It was a purely original work, as indeed it required to be for no European work on morals treat of relations such as exist in India.

2. *Historical Evidence for the Truth of the Christian Scriptures* by Rev. Narayan Sheshadri also in marathi.

   It was a work of about 82 or 100 pages, sold for one anna and discusses the genuineness, antiquity and authenticity of the Bible. This work was fitted to be useful in familiarizing the people of our country with the nature of reliable evidence, and the principles upon which religious inquiries should be conducted.

   Four tracts on important Hindu festivals had been prepared by Sheshadri and obtained a wide circulation.

3. *What is Truth*? by Dr. J. Craig

   It consisted of passages of scriptures, so arranged as to exhibit in their due order the main doctrines of

298 Rev. Deacon Daji Pandurang was admitted to the order of priesthood at St. Thomas Cathedral on Sunday the 20th March 1859 (Source. *BG*, Saturday March 26, 1859, front page)

Christianity. This book was prepared for the society by Dr. Craig.

4. *Bala Soondaree Tagore*, an English work by Mrs. Murry Mitchell.

   By this time it had been already noticed in Public journals that Mr. Narayan Sheshadri has rendered it into Marathi, and this version has been published.

5. *Hints to Mothers* is a Marathi tract from the English by Rev. Appaji Bapooji.

   This book treated the importance of maternal prayer.

6. *The Elements of Sacred Truth*, in English by Rev. J. Murry Mitchell,

It was designed to exhibit the leading doctrine of Christianity. The same author's book named *Tookaram* was in press by this time[299].

In also depicted how in 1858 the Missionary operations were interrupted due to 1857 rising by Indians.

The BTBS of 26th February 1859 mentioned the death of Rev. Dr. J. Stevenson in Scotland (due to injuries caused due to a fall from a horse) in August 1858. Dr. Stevenson was a friend of the Bombay Tract and Book Society from the very hour of its formation.

It thus read …"Dr. Stevenson arrived in Bombay in February 1824 as a Missionary of the Scottish Missionary Society; labored in the Southern Concan (Konkan) till 1830 and in Poona till 1835, then he accepted one of the Chaplain ships of the Scotch Church in Bombay and finally left India in 1854. Dr. Stevenson prepared a Marathi Grammar and also an English Grammar in Marathi. He edited a portion of the Rig Veda and contributed a great many articles on various oriental topics to the Bombay Branch of the Royal Asiatic Society. He was one of the originators of the *Bombay Guardian* and during the first 3 years of its existence took a constant and prominent part in the editorship"[300].

---

299 Special Supplement to *BG*, March 07, 1857 (Opposite p. 80)

300 *BG*, September 18, 1858 , Front Page

The BTBS Society had no regular sub-agencies of its own for selling books, but the work entirely rested on the co-operation of Missionaries[301]. The main pillars of the native Church namely Rev. Narayan Sheshadri and Baba Padmanji and others like Mr. and Mrs. Murry Mitchell, Dr. Stevenson, Rev. R.G.Wilder regularly contributed their works to this society.

Mention of a Marathi Monthly *Ooday Prabha* (*OP*), *The Dawn* conducted by Mr. Baba Padmanjee[302] (1831-1906) and other native Christians can be seen in front page of *BG*[303]. The August 1856, issue of *OP* carried third chapter of an original work on *Evidences of Christianity*.

Padmanjee was also called father and founder of Christian Marathi Literature, wrote a monthly series for BTBS "A Few Discriminative Thoughts on Caste", wherein in the first part of the little Book caste is shown to be

Opposed to nature,
Opposed to reason,
Opposed to morals,
Opposed to True Religion

In the second part, the evils resulting from caste were considered, and the concluding section relates to Brahminism[304]. He also wrote *Examinations of the Claims of Deism* in Marathi which was an exhaustive work on a subject that is exciting a good deal of attention among the educated young men of this (Bombay) Presidency.

The Oriental Christian Spectator (OCS) (March –April 1963) mentioned about a compendium of Molesworth's Marathi and English dictionary by Baba Padmanji. This work like the authors compendium of Major Candy's English and Marathi dictionary was a great success affording ample proof of the judgement, taste, deiligence, ability and general competency for vernacular literary

301 *BG*, March 4, 1905 p. 3

302 He was baptized in 1854 and became prominent after his Marathi work *Yamuna Paryatan* was published.

303 *BG*, August 16, 1856

304 *BG*, July 16, 1881, p. 307

work of Baba Padmanji. He also translated form English to Marathi, the work of Dr. H. Bonar "*The sins of Our Holy Things borne by Christ*" (this was publication of BTBS)[305]. His write-up in Gujarati on *Help to Marathi Students and Authors* can be seen in 1860 (Vol.1) issue of *Bamdad.*

Rev. T. Davis read the report of the Bombay Auxiliary Bible and Tract Societies[306]. He mentioned the publication of the Marathi Hymn Book by Marathi editor Rev. Baba Padmanji. Mr. Padmanji had also privately prepared an important work consisting of Holiletics on select passages of the proverbs freely translated from the Pulpit commentary[307].

Rev. Haripantanche Charitra a marathi work was published by Bombay Tract and Book Society. It was a memoir of late Hari Ramchandra Khisti[308] prepared by his son in law Rev. Appaji Bapuji. Haripant, his wife and his brother were baptized at Ahmednagar by Rev. Mr. Ballentine in 1839 which created a great sensation. Mrs. Haripant was actively engaged in Zenana work during 1880's[309].

Scottish Missionary Rev. J. Murry Mitchell (MA.,LLD) came to India in 1838 and spent most of his time in Western India and wrote his work *Tookaram* in 1857[310] and also contributed more than 10 books in Marathi. His marathi work *Native Superstitions* (Published by BTBS) treats especially of Omens, Portents, Unlucky Days, Incidents and phenomenon etc showing Hindus were influenced to a great degree by their belief on superstitions[311].

Noteworthy publications of the society include, *A Manual of Christian Duties* (was of about 100 pages and was sold at 2 annas a copy), this Book was chiefly for the benefit of Native Christians. The great principles of Christian obligation are the same in all ages and

---

305 *OCS*, January 1863, Vol. 4, p. 73

306 Advertisement of Bombay Auxiliary Bombay Society can be seen in many issues of *BG* (1896)

307 *BG*, March 21,1896, p.11

308 He was for many year Pastor of the American Mission Church at Ahmednagar.

309 *BG*, September 15, 1883, p. 580

310 *BG*, March 7, 1857, Opposite p. 80

311 *OCS*, Jan 1863, Vol. 4, p. 73

in all lands; but the application of these principles must constitute study in every age and in every nation.

Rev. R. G.Wilder prepared *The Scripture Manual* in Marathi and also translated *Kindness to Animals*[312] written by Charlotte Elizabeth in Marathi.

The Annual Meeting report of BTBS[313] as mentioned above, was published in the form of a special supplement to *The Bombay Guardian* weekly Newspaper[314]. According to 1858, Supplement 30 works[315] averaging 50 pages each with an aggregate of 80,100 copies were printed in 1857 its also mentioned that due to the difficulties that arose out of the disturbed state of the country the copies were less compared to 1856.

Commenting on the Thirtieth Anniversary of the BTBS, Rev. Sheshadri said … "during all this period, the progress of our Society has been upwards and onwards, and, had it not been for circumstances over which we have had no control, its progress during the past year would have been as satisfactory and encouraging as in bygone years…"

Dr. Stevenson was one of the small band that met in the Fort on 10th December 1827, for the purpose of organizing a Religious Tract Society. He also wrote a valuable Tract in Marathi *"Discussions in Poona"* . As mentioned above the monthly publication of the periodical *The Bamdad* finds mention here. Also we find mention of Calcutta Tract Society's work. The report showed an increase in publications (including imported publications) compared to 1857 as follows:

Total 54,283 Tracts and Books issued in 1858
Marathi 36,614
Gujarati 9,446

312 Published by BTBS see *BG,* June 21, 1856, p. 196

313 The first annual meeting of this Society was held in 1833.

314 This weekly was established in March 1851 - the last issue of this weekly available in Maharashtra State Archives Mumbai is of July 22 1905. Initially it was published every Friday and later every Saturday. It had circulation in India, Europe, America, Australia , China etc.

315 In the second page of Supplemnt of 1858 a big list of poetry, scriptures, lives of British reformers like Bradford, Latimer, Knox, Bacon etc is given

English 6,284
Hindustani 1,940
Portuguese 209
Bengali 216
Malayalam 102

The list of works printed in 1858 shows total of 33,800 against a total of 78,600 in 1857. This shows printing has fallen to much less than one-half of what it was in 1857. It said "There are many of the works on our list that need to be reprinted: and we have on hand the manuscripts of new works which we are not able to commit to the press, because we have no means of paying for the printing of them". Dr. Wilson (in the absence of Rev. Broadley) moved a Resolution.

Front Page of *BG*[316] said "We willingly give place to the following circular of the BTBS, and solicit for it the attention of our readers... The operations of the BTBS are increasing in extent and importance. The object of this Society is to present to the Natives of this country in languages that they understand, the truths of God's word in forms adapted to arrest their hearts. BTBS is now engaged in disseminating works in Marathi, Gujarat, Hindustani, English, Portuguese and other languages." The names of Rev. George Bowen from Bombay and Rev. J. Murray Mitchell from Poona were mentioned which shows they were actively associated with BTBS. Thus, the immediate role of BTBS was to develop Christian Vernacular literature in the Bombay Presidency. There was also the Christian Endeavour Society connected with the American Mission School at Bombay[317].

The following Advertisement of BTBS can be seen in many issues of *BG* of 1856.

Books at Reduced Prices

The following works are sold by the BTBS to students and parties requiring them for benevolent distribution at 30% below the English retail prices:-

316 *BG*, September 6, 1856
317 *BG*, November 16, 1895, p. 4

Evidence of Christianity
Alexander's Evidence of Christianity
Bible the Best Teacher
Bogue's Divine Authority of the New Testament
etc.

Biblical Works
Angus's Bible Hand- Book
Barnes's Notes on Gospels
Companion to the Bible
Geography of the Bible, etc.

Practical Religion and Christian Doctrines
Abbot's Young Christian
Bunyan's Pilgrim's Progress
Family Prayers
Wilberforce's Practical view, etc

Natural History
Bird's Botanical Ladder for the young History of insects.
Light:Its properties and effects
Natural History of Birds
Natural History of Reptiles
Shells and their Inmates
The Atmosphere
Young Botanists, etc.

Ancient and Modern History
History of the Church of Christ, 6 Vols
History of Greece
History of Rome, etc.

Sacred Poetry
Christian Lyrics
Christian Harp
Cottage Hymns
The Book of Pslams

Educational Works not mentioned above were to be sold at 30% less. Mention was also made that publications of the London Religious Tract Society and BTBS (Works in English, Marathi, Gujarati, Hindustani, Hindu, Sanskrit, Portuguese).

On 19th January 1878, following small advertisement of BTBS seen

A LARGE AND HANDSOME STOCK OF BOUND BOOKS, suitable for PRESENTATION

School Prizes, etc has been lately received at the Department (Kalbadevi, Bombay) and the Superintendent would invite all to an early inspection. A good supply of the following was also on hand:

Christmas and New Years Cards.
Childrens Story Books
Picture Toy Books on Paper or Linen
Watts Catechisms and Hymns
Bibles and Bible Handbooks
Large Texts and Text Rolls
Theological Works
Histories and Biographies
General Science Series

C.V.E.S.[318] Educational series in English and the Vernacular included the following:

Practical and Devotional Works
Poetry and Hymns
Tracts and Small Books

Also it carried news about the large supply of back numbers of periodicals which may be had at half price. From April 1878 to June 1878 no advertisements of BTBS were seen, only small advertisement of English and Marathi Dictionary of Baba Padmanji is visible.

The July 1878 and October 19, 1878 BTBS advertisement shows a small list of Books related to Christianity

318 Christian Vernacular Education Society

Hints and help for Teachers and Parents (July 1878)
Farrar's Life of Christ 2 vols
History of the reign of Philip II 3 vols
Civil War in America 2 vols
Morning by morning
Evening by evening
Law's serious call
Elements of moral Science
Vaughan's Family Prayers
Faith and Victory
Land and Moab
Ten years on the Euphrates
Sacred Songs and Solos-music

By June 1880, BTBS had commenced the publication of a series of papers for educated natives, entitled "Papers for thoughtful readers"[319]. Again in January 01, 1881 on page 584 full page advertisement showing various books can be seen. On January 7 1888 (p.16, the last Page of *BG*) A full page add of BTBS showed... The Bombay Christian Almanac[320] for 1888. It started with 'The Exterior of the Almanac is more attractive than ever'

The contents included:
Scientific-*A first lesson in Botany*
Biographical-*H. M. Stanley*
Religious-*Christ in the Temple; God's Work-* etc
Descriptive-*Melbourne in 1840 and 1887*
Temperance-*Alcohol and Insanity*
Missionary-*The Moravians*

Miscellaneous- *Finishing touches, Home after work, Four great empires, The usual directory of Missionary, Benevolent and Christian Education Societies* etc.

The Times of India review of 1887 Almanac of BTBS said... "The work contains a great deal of useful and interesting information, with

319 *BG*, June 19,1880, front page.
320 Price was 8 Anna's

reference not only to Missionary and other religious organizations, but to secular affairs, and we have no doubt that it will be highly appreciated by the public. A feature of the work is illustrations of sacred scenes…"

The April, May and June issues of *BG* of 1888 show a big list of books of BTBS. The 1889 issues of *BG* showed half page add of BTBS Books seen like…

Christianity East and West: An Ecclesiastical Pilgrimage by T Grieve Clark

The Nun of Kenmare- an autobiography

Bible Animals and the Lessons taught by them- Richard Newton.

The 1890 issues cover half page advertisement showing books like…

The Trinity of Evil-Infidelity, Impurity, Intemperance by Canon Wilberforce

The Lives of Three Bishops-Fraser, Bickersteth and Hannington (Bullock).

Advertisements of BTBS were missing in 1895 issues but advertisement of Bombay Auxiliary Bible Society (BABS) was seen in small columns. The BABS had earlier published the 8th version of the Gujrathi New Testament[321]. The work of Bombay Auxiliary to the British and Foreign Bible Society for the year 1900 centered around three main divisions i.e. Translating, Printing and Selling.

A big report of the Annual Meeting of the Bombay Bible and Tract Societies covered, Rev. A. B. Wann's abstract of the Report of the Bombay Book and Tract Society, making the preliminary remark that the society did not exist to supply the popular taste but to form it. The total sales has been Rs.34,000, English, Marathi, Gujarati, Christian Almanac have been issued. 35,000 tracts and books had been printed. He expressed sorry state of affair that the subscription list had gone down only Rs. 845, being collected[322]. The advertisements of BTBS could also be seen on the last page of *BG* 1905.

321 *BG*, March 02, 1889, p. 132

322 *BG*, March 23,1889, p. 179

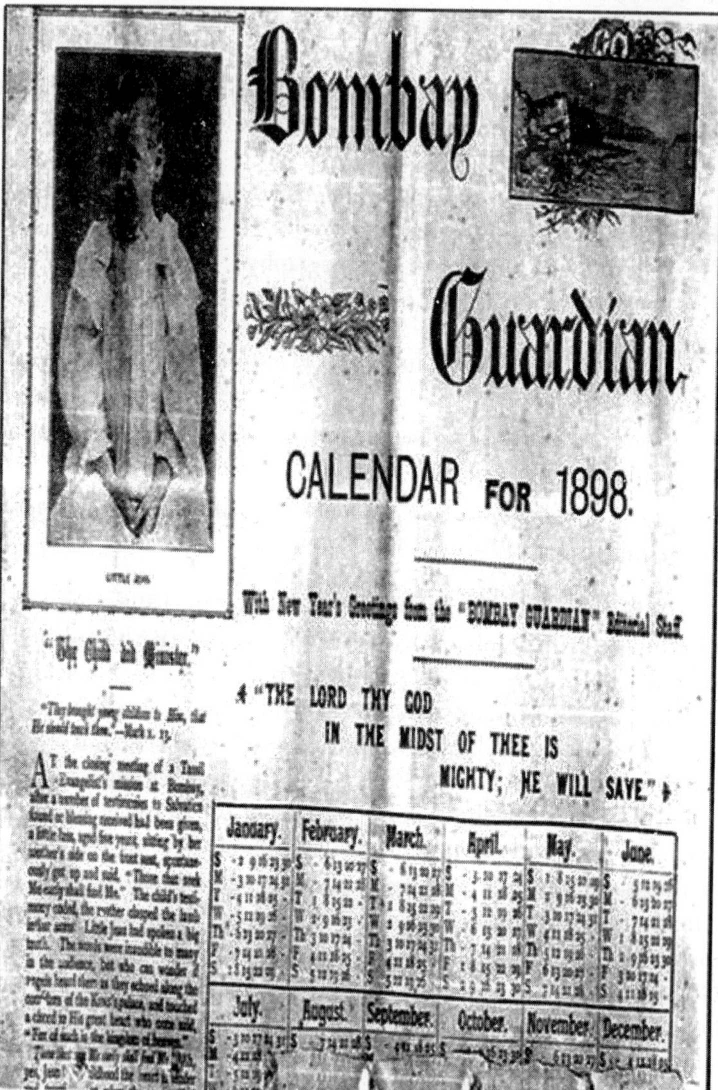

Slide 5.1: The above calendar could be seen in Bombay Guardian, 1898.

480 THE BOMBAY GUARDIAN. July 28.

BOMBAY TRACT AND BOOK SOCIETY.

The attention of the Friends of the Society, and of the Public generally, is invited to this selection from the stock of books now on sale at the depot. (*Address—The Superintendent.*)

Books in Cases.

New Biographical Works.

A Discount of 10 per cent is allowed off the prices of English books (except periodical and those marked nett) when purchases are made within one calendar month to the value of Rs. 10 and upwards. Payment either in cash or on presentation of account at the beginning of the month succeeding the purchases.

Printed and Published for the Proprietor by ... at the ANGLO-VERNACULAR PRINTING PRESS Two Tanks, Bombay.

Slide 5.2: Full page Advertisement in BTBS
Source: *BG*, July 28, 1898

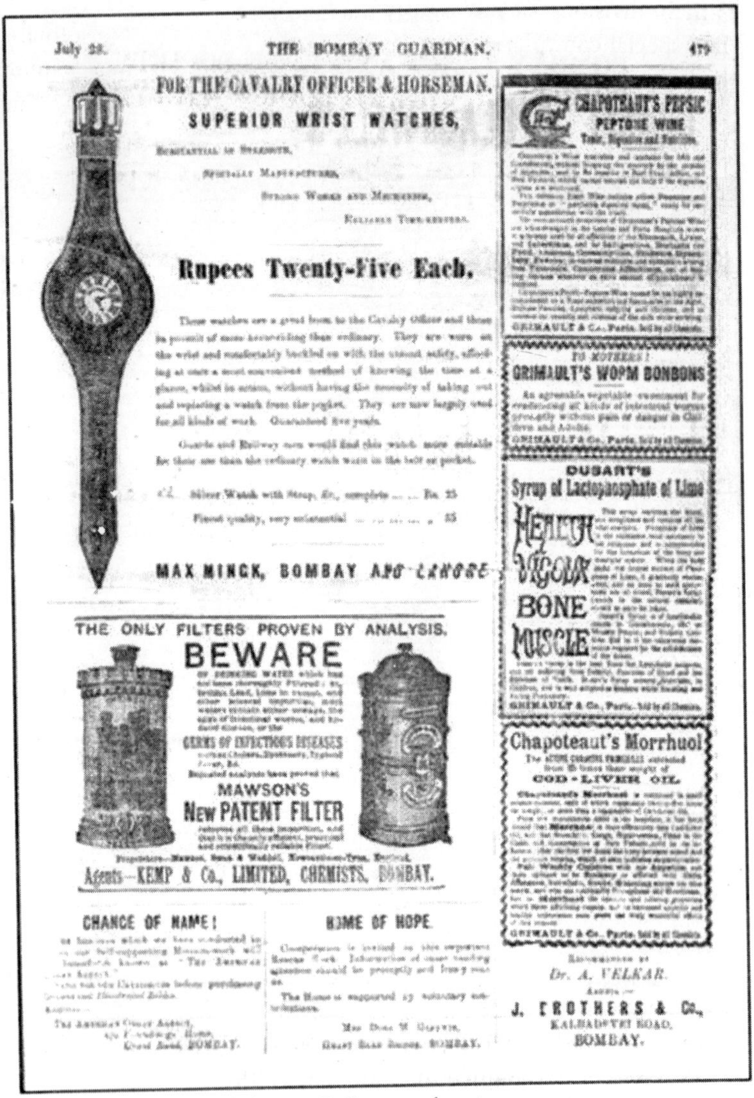

Slide 5.3: Full page advertisement
Source: BG, July 28, 1898

5.3 The Bombay Auxiliary and Foreign Bible Society

The work of the above society for the year 1900 was centered around 3 main divisions, i.e., Translating, Printing and Selling. The Society had special committee which at the suggestion of Pandita Ramabai had sanctioned the printing of certain portions in very large Marathi and Gujrathi type, suitable for old people or those who are beginning to read.

5.3.1 Circulation

A little incident related by lady Missionary showed that the scriptures were not only bought but read intelligently by the people. She wrote "We have spent 26 days in the district lately and sold 327 Gospels. One little thing happened that greatly encouraged me to keep on trying to sell to all I met by the way. In Kudal Bazaar (South Konkan) day a women was in doubt as to which Gospel to take when a young men stepped up and said, 'take Mark, there are some wonderful things in that'. Then to a man he said, 'if you want the whole story, take Luke and John, the one, without the other is only confusing'. I asked him how he knew, and he said that I had sold him some Gospels in the road one day. Last year, at Kankavali Bazaar (South Konkan)we sold 90 Gospels and this year 121"[323].

The unique work[324] prepared primarily for the use of students in the universities and colleges of the United States and Canada who were making a study of foreign Missions had been published. The copious index in the book made the contents easily accessible. The statistical tables in the atlas showed at a glance what has been done or is being done; every known Mission station was placed in alphabetic order with initials of Mission at work.

5.3.2 Missionary Agencies, Methods and Prospects

Questions affecting Missionary problems were discussed, such as the affects of the Boxer rising in China on the Christians and

323 *BG*, March 16, 1901, p. 11

324 Harlan P. Beach, *A Geography and Atlas of Protestant Missions*: 2 Volumes published from New York. The following review is published in *BG*, July 04, 1903, p. 10

general population. Sir Charles Elliott urged the appointment of native bishops, based his argument on the experience of the civil administration in India. It contains a note of Dr. Sherwood and Dr. Pierson's work 'Missionary Review of the World' of January 1888 (New York and London)[325]. There is a mention of "*The Missionary Review* which was ably and successfully edited by the late Rev. R.S. Wilder for 10 years and which had merged into the publication. A memorial notice of Mr. Wilder and his portrait had been presented. This was with an editorial on the Literature of Missions, one, on Missionary problems in India by Rev. E. A. Lawrence it said "It is difficult and painful to express my disappointment with most features of Mission operations in the Presidency Cities of India. The educational work indeed is excellent, in some cases, unequalled. The Christian college in Madras, at the head of which is Dr. Miller of the Scotch Presbyterian Church, may well rank as the best institution of learning in India. But, other forms of work languish. Not only that in many cases the fat school-kine have swallowed up the lean evangelistic kine, and there is an actual famine of God's preached word for the heathen".

After 1835, Minute of Lord Macaulay, Mission's institutions established themselves as separate and independent institutions, preparing students not only for the new government entrance examinations, but also to offer to eager minds the new outlook upon life which came to them from the assimilation of ideas which were at that time fresh and thrilling. To the Missionaries themselves came all the inspiration of being engaged upon a task, every part of which seemed to them the process of opening closed minds to liberating influences. There were some valued Missionary men in the 19th century having access to the government officials namely Dr. Duff (Calcutta), Dr. Miller (Madras), Dr. Wilson (Bombay), Dr. Ewing (Lahore) etc. All these Missionaries were able to exert a profound influence upon university and government policy. The policy of 1854, not only gave freedom to the Missionary institutions but to all private institutions which should fulfill the not very onerous conditions which qualified for grant in aid. The period between 1859-1904 was regarded as the great period of the Christian Colleges. The victory of Japan over

325 *BG*, January 21, 1888, p. 35

Russia in 1905 had very important consequences in India. It gave emotional direction to the nationalist movement, and the political demands based there on. Of far, the greater consequence was the revelation that the success of Japan had depended on her economic power and highly scientific technical ability. Thus, the events of the year 1905 gave birth in India to an economic nationalism, the results of which have been very remarkable. First, the effects on University Curricula were marked. Better provision was made for the teachings of the basic natural sciences and economics[326].

National Missionary society founded in 1905, was an indigenous Missionary movement working in various parts of India. It supported 112 Missionaries and helpers working in about 47 centers in eight different provinces and in nine different languages. Its policy was not to establish independent churches but to work along side of the older Missions and Churches, contributing to the up building of these[327].

Table 5.2: List of active Missionaries (1835)

Stations[328]	*Names of Missionaries*	*Societies*
Bombay	Rev. A Graves, Rev. C. Stone, Rev. D O Allen, Rev. W. Ramsey, Rev. W Hervey, Rev. H. Read	American
Hurnee and Bankote	Rev. J. Cooper, Rev. J. Mitchell	Scottish
Poona	Rev. J. Stevenson, Rev. R. Nesbit	Scottish

Wilson's English school in Bombay opened in 1832, in Military Square in the Fort jointly with Rev. Robert Nesbit became the pioneering institution in many respects and it became the nucleus of the varied academic, intellectual and religious activities which he conducted[329]. The Wilson College owes its origin to this school. The

326 Report of the *Commission on Christian Higher Education in India*, 1931, *OUP*, London, p. 35

327 *Ibid*, p. 61

328 *OCS*, December 1831, p. 475

329 Sulochana Krishnamoorthy, *Op.Cit*, p. 49

following paragraphs contains the substance of a report entitled 'The Opening of the Wilson Memorial College' which appeared in *BG*. The report runs as follows

"Sixty years ago Dr. J. Wilson landed in Bombay, where he lived and worked, with two interruptions of one and four years respectively for forty six years. In the early days of his career, he appears to have preached the Gospel with much faithfulness and clearness. He then seems to have become disheartened at the tremendous powers of evil against him in India, and to have somewhat lost faith in the declaration of God's word...The outcome of this departure from Christ's simple commands was the great secular education work which has dominated, to so large an extent, the Missionary work of the city of Bombay for the past fifty years ....It is to perpetuate the fruitless imitation of Mission work inaugurated by Dr. Wilson in the later part of his life that the Memorial College has been erected. The Wilson Memorial College is a splendid erection on the Chowpatty sea-face, Bombay, the cost of which has been Rs.1,78,000 of which the Government has contributed Rs. 87,000 in addition to giving the land, and the remaining amount Rs. 70,000 have been contributed by (to quote Lord Reay) 'Shepherds and widows, gillies and crofters' in Scotland under the impression that they were giving to Missionary work; and Six Native Chiefs have given large sums. It was opened on the 14th...Many speakers spoke, Prof. Lindsay of the Free Church College, Glasgow insisted upon the fact that this was a Christian College, whilst the Government Schools were strictly neutral. Rev. Dhanjibhai Nauroji followed with some remarks on his old Principal Dr.Wilson whom he knew some fifty years ago".

The paragraph show there was no reference to Jesus Christ (and God) in students address[330].

5.3.3 Related Work

The Jesuit Missions work in Bombay from 1854 under the leadership of Bishop Anastasius Hartmann[331] (Order of Friars Minor) has been

330 *BG*, March 16, 1889, p. 171

331 Earlier named Joseph Louis. Today there is Hartman Ashram and Hartman School in Bareilly.

equally important and Father Joseph Velinkar has already covered about it in his latest book *German Jesuits on the West Coast of India 1854-2004*. Hartmann was best known for his statesmanship and dedication to the cause of education. His efforts contributed to the establishment of St. Xaviers College and seven other schools styled on Modern educational Western lines.

In front page of *BG* March 9, 1878 - The Bombay Catholic Examiner is quoted as saying the last words of Pope Pius the Ninth were *Col Vostro Santo aiuoto*, which is translated 'by thy holy grace'. *BG* sites the proper translation as "with your holy aid".

Also in front page a big write-up on Bombay Catholic Examiner's account of the secession of a large body of Native Christians in the Ahmednagar Collectorate[332], from the S.P.G. Mission to the R.C. Church has been highlighted (possibly due to the inclination of Bishop Douglas towards Rome).

Thus we see direct and indirect changes being brought in Bombay by the efforts of various Missionary works. The *Bombay Guardian* covered experiences which the Missionaries faced, the October 9, 1897 issue highlights Bishop J. M. Thoburn's writeup 'The most Hopeful Missionary Period of the World'. He said "I came to India 38 years ago. In those far-off days the tokens of success which the Missionaries were able to point out were few indeed. The Indian Mutiny had just been quelled, and a spirit of fear and suspicion was still widely prevalent among the people. The Missionary was looked upon with a measure of distrust such as is seldom manifested at the present day".

The Bombay Guardian also covered information on Mahars in its 1885, 1892, 1896, and 1905 issues. It focused on how the advent of the British led to an effort towards their social regeneration. The Missionaries found the Mahars to be co-operative listeners when they preached to them, whereas the Brahmin audience tended to be wrangling and argumentative[333].

A small report in February 18, 1882 (p. 105) reads... "The school for Mohammedan children in Bombay established by the

332 American Mission's work there was already 40 years old.

333 M. D. David, Missions: Cross-Cultural Encounter and change in Western India, Manohar, Delhi, 2001, p. 303

Anjuman-I-Islam with Government aid, contains 429 pupils. Prizes were distributed in the Town Hall on Wednesday 15th February. The Bombay Corporation have voted Rs. 5,000 a year towards the maintenance of the school. If we ask why these Mohammedan children may not avail themselves of the education furnished in the Government schools, we are told that they cannot in the latter acquire an English education through the medium of Hindustani". This shows that perhaps there were more Hindi/Vernacular Medium Government Schools at that time.

An anonymous Letter focused on a staunch believer in Judaism. He had attended services and lectures in the Prarthana Samaj and the Arya Samaj, but he found out that the Samajist's have preached, talked and prayed vehemently for social and religious reforms for years together. And in fact they have done nothing practical. Later, he read the Bible and books on Christian literature. Finally, on 25th December, 1881 he, his wife and three children received the rite of Baptism in the Grant Road Church[334].

The *Bombay Guardian* of June 21, 1856 (p.196) published a reaction of an article denouncing the Missionaries and Philanthropists of this (Bombay) city, for allowing the horses of the buggywallas to be so cruelly treated as they are. The article begins thus…"It is a most singular thing that, overstocked as Bombay is with Philanthropists and Missionaries, no one has yet thought of instituting a society for the protection of cruelty to animals. Any resident in Bombay who has the least feeling in his soul, must have observed that the institution of such a society is now absolutely requisite…. Why are not our tender hearted philanthropists and Missionaries standing forward in defence of the dumb creation. Surely the African Savages, the Hindoo idolaters, or the apostate Christians cannot take up all their time! Surely they see this horrible cruelty practiced on animals every day…Why do they not put in practice a little active Philanthropy, and save the poor animals from such hellish tortures. Horses cannot be converted to Christianity, we are aware, but, although they might not repay the pains of a Missionary, surely, virtue being its own reward, Missionaries might found a society for

334 *BG*, January 21, 1882, p. 38

the prevention of cruelty to animals, without doing themselves much mental or physical injury...It is manifest from this that Missionaries were expected to do all the virtue for the community...Secular things to secular men, piety and philanthropy to the priesthood. But such a distinction as this Protestantism utterly disowns. It claims for every individual of the community the privilege of laboring for the good of his fellow-men. It holds that every member of the Church has his peculiar gift, or gifts, for the proper exercise of which he is answerable to God. But, the parties to whom we are now replying do not profess to have any respect for priest craft... Missionaries in India have taken a prominent part in drawing attention to the actual evils of this country, and have been forward to exert themselves for their overthrow....Missionaries have not been idle on the subject of cruelty to animals. They have translated and published in the native languages, works bearing on this subject. The Bombay Tract and Book Society has in its list of publications, a book in the Marathi language, entitled *Kindness to Animals*. The original was written by Charlotte Elizabeth. It was translated by Rev. Mr. Wilder of Kolapoor and some 4 or 5 Missionaries in Bombay gave their best attention"

The issue of cruelty towards animals by buggywallas was interesting as it throws light on how the news readers expressed their opinions in Newspaper Columns and how the Missionaries reacted to it.

One more letter to the editor of *The Bombay Guardian* published in April 15, 1882 (pp. 229-230) goes... "Permit me to plead on behalf of our birds, squirrels and lizards. It is very sad and painful to see innocent creatures, some of them so beautiful and all so happy in the life that God has given them, wounded or killed by thoughtless boys. The midsummer holidays now give the youngsters full scope and opportunity for the use of stone and catapult, as they scour the countryside in pursuit of adventure.... Once and only once I believe, did I shoot a bird with a gun? It was many years ago, yet the memory of the poor thing's suffering- for I had only winged it- as it fluttered a bout in the thick bush into which it had fallen, is still fresh and painful. Thank God, for a tender heart, fourteen or fifteen years have not effaced the recollection of that act of thoughtless cruelty.... Boys, it is mean to be unkind to any creature kill scorpions and snakes, but do not unnecessary injury to any living thing. Jesus said, "Our Heavenly Father fed them and to be cruel to what are the subjects of His Special Care is a sin as well as a shame....Parents, Christian Fathers and Mothers, teach your Children to abstain from all cruelty of this nature particularly. If you do not befriend the poor birds, who will? ... Young Men, you who borrow guns to shoot on the Bombay flats, or in the country, crows, sparrows, cranes- anything almost you can have a shot at, and call it sport, let me say that it is a sad thing when a man finds his pleasure in that which involves the pain and death of other creatures...Verbum Sap".

Even today we find such environment related letters still in contemporary Newspapers.

5.3.4 Work of Other Societies

The twenty sixth report of the Calcutta Christian Tract and Book Society mentioned the appointment of the Rev. J. Wenger, as editor of Bengali works. Mention of one new Bengali work *Anecdotes of Social Life* and two new tracts, have been published. Works like *Life of Martin Luther, Wilson's Exposure of The Hindu Religion* were in press.

The Report of the Bangalore Tract and Book Society for 1854 and 1855, mentioned the following new publications - *Destroyer of superstition, A translation of Mr. Clarkson's Book; The True God and Idols; Paleys Horae Paulinae, The Way of Salvation, Identity of Popery and Heathenism, The Saviour of the World*; all in Canarese. It said "The Principle of circulating by sale only has been found to work well"[335].

Mention of Agra Tract and Book Society publishing *"The Testimony borne by the Coran to the Jewish and Christian Scriptures."* The work was in English with the quotations in Arabic and English.[336]

The Report of the Punjab Religious Book Society was published on front page of *BG*, March 30, 1878. It said... "no less than 71 new Books were published last year like '*A Life of Mohammad*' by Rev. Imad-ud-Din, '*A Life of Christ*' by H. Carre Tucker".

335 *BG*, May 31, 1856, front page
336 *BG*, June 7, 1856, front page

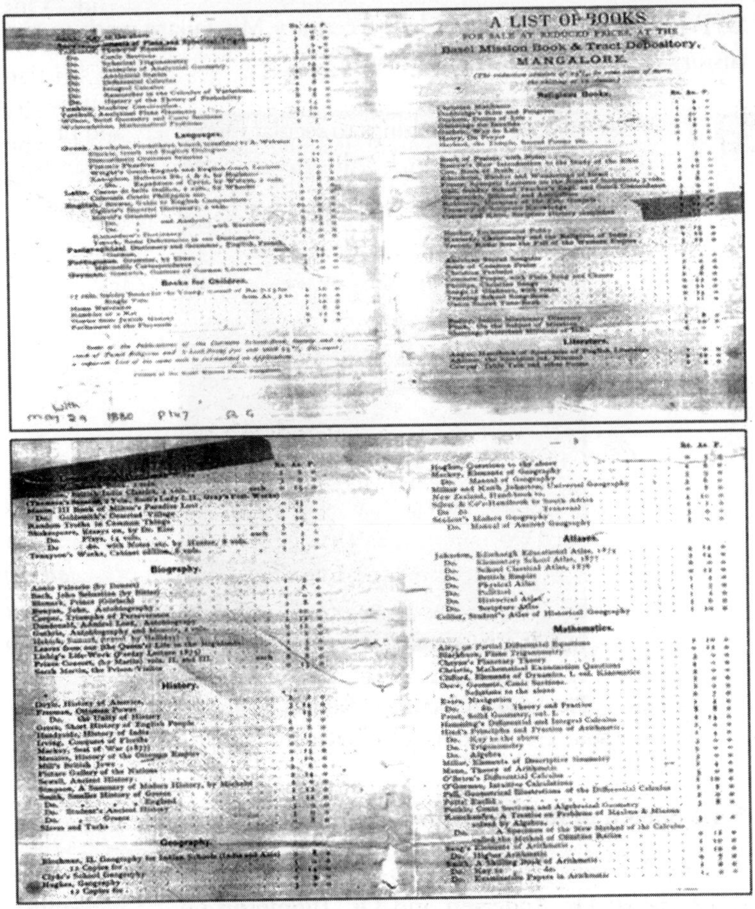

A LIST OF BOOKS
FOR SALE AT REDUCED PRICES, AT THE
Basel Mission Book & Tract Depository,
MANGALORE.

Religious Books.

Languages.

Books for Children.

Literature.

Biography.

History.

Geography.

Atlases.

Mathematics.

Slide 5.4: Basal Mission Book and Tract Depository List
(Source: BG, May 29, 1880, p.147)

5.4 Some Interesting Debates

Rufus Anderson, the greatest General Secretary of the American Boards of Commissions had come to India to lead the Deputation of 1854 which gave rise to some interesting debates. It began with Rev. Winslow's[337] speech followed by Rev. S. B. Fairbanks views…"Dr. S.

337 He was a Missionary at Madras

B. Fairbank, had completed half a century Missionary work in the history of American Marathi Mission".

Picture 5.1: Picture of Samuel B Fairbank
(**Source:** American Mission Report, March 1898)

5.4.1 Speech of Rev. Winslow

The speech covered the visit of the Deputation from Board in America consisting of Dr. Anderson and Dr. Thompson on 2nd November 1854. This deputation had reached Mumbai to personally see the local hurdles faced by Missionaries here. They toured Maharashtra for almost 72 days[338].

Mr. Winslow had been one of the educationists in Ceylon. He was speaking in front of deputation headed by Dr. Rufus Anderson the correspondent of the Indian Missions for many years. Anderson's deputation of 1854 had spoken against the Mission concentrating their works in urban centers and recommended that the Mission should move to the villages. The deputation in its report contended

338 S. R. Shirgaonkar, *Op.Cit*, p. 45

that the lowly and the neglected in the rural areas were more receptive to the Gospel than the upper caste and the Brahmins in cities and even in the villages[339]. Rev. Dr. Anderson wrote a tract entitled "*Labors and Hindarances of the Missionary*"[340].

Rev. Mr. Winslow said... "I can't say, sir, that I really have a voice; physically I have very little, for I have taken cold, ...morally I have none before an assemblage like this. The Lord has been pleased to spare me on Missionary ground for 36 years. I went out in 1819. It is said, I know that old men are conservative, slow to adopt changes, not prepared for the go-ahead system of Young America. I have however, some opinion in reference to the simple question before the Board, which may be of use to some who hear me. I desire to take and obey the commission of our Lord- " Go ye into all the world and preach the Gospel to every creature, but I would not restrict it to adults only, nor to oral preaching. I would do it by means of schools. I would have infant schools, Sabbath-schools, any schools, any method by which the Gospel can be preached. I would not have one system in antagonism with another. I would have them all. There are some places where oral preaching can't be done. A Missionary in South Africa told me that he had travelled a hundred miles more than once without meeting more than one or two persons. What is to be done in South Africa? You can't make known the Gospel merely by going from place to place. You must gather the people together and teach them".

He further said "if after 30 years you come to a sudden change, among a people like the Hindoos, the evil will be very great. You must not always change about like weather cocks. It will not do... The seed planted in the schools will nevertheless spring up afterward".

In the Report presented by the deputation, it was stated that the number of members of the schools who were converts was only thirty. Winslow said "thirty conversions is no small thing in India, though it may seem so in America. The conversion of a single one is a great thing. He further mentions that ... the results of Batticotta Seminary would have been more ratifying if there had been more native teachers...give us more. let us be generous, and god will be

339 M. D. David, Op. Cit, p. 123

340 *OCS*, August 1861, p. 361

generous. Do not say we can't support these schools because they are too expensive. I believe that many contribute to the Board for the support of schools, who would not otherwise contribute anything. When you say you will save the funds expended on schools and let the same amount go for the support of evangelists, you must remember that perhaps you can't get the same amount of funds for anything else. These funds are contributed to a considerable extent by the children in your Sabbath-schools. Look at the influence of the contributions on them. Does it not do them good? Undoubtedly, the only business of Missionaries should be the salvation of souls but when you hear the command, "Go ye and preach the Gospel to every creature," do not limit it to adults. We shall be entirely safe to do what the Lord Jesus commands us. Don't set one system against another, and among a people like the Hindoos, don't bring great and violent changes".

Winslow had a great opinion of Missionary wives and their influence, and he said, "Give them something to do beside taking care of their husbands. And beside this, do not suppose that all Missionaries are best suited for the same thing". Don't make any rule of this sort- a procrustes bed, on which they are stretched out if too short, and chooped off it too long. Don't make every man do the same thing. And let them manage their own details of business. Trust them to do that. If they are not worthy to do so, call them back, but trust them. If they feel that they can't be trusted to manage their own details of business, will so many laborers go into the field? Will they labor with so good a heart?... It is, of course, important that the Board would say what shall be done with the money contributed, and that they should lay down general principles for the government of Missionary operations. But don't limit the Missionaries in the detail, nor burden their consciences by making them suppose they are doing wrong in following their own judgement in minor matters. It is the privilege of the Board in every way to attempt the conversion of the Hindoos, and to get access to the native mind in every way. One way in which we can do this is by educating native teachers. It is necessary that such teachers should be educated. You can't give the natives a good translation of the Bible unless you do so. You must educate them in the English language, and give them thus the key to all that wide range of English literature, by reading English books. We cannot convey by the native language the essential ideas of the Christian faith" (Perhaps this method was adopted by the Free Church).

Winslow was against of giving up heathen schools. He said "I would not say to these Children, because you are heathen I reject you,' but because you were heathen I sought you out and gathered you into schools.' It would be like saying to all the Roman Catholics and Jews in your Sabbath Schools here, that the schools were not for them. Wasn't the Gospel sent to the heathen? Why, then should it not be preached to them?".

5.4.2 Speech of Mr. Fairbanks

Mr. Fairbanks of the Bombay Mission (who had been in India since 1847) was the next speaker. His speech thus read as follows:
"We are to make use of the converts from Heathenism as teachers- to instruct, to guide, to preach; but we must not labor to train young men in the mere hope that they will become our helpers hereafter. We must have schools to train only those who are to be our helpers, not those who are to be our enemies. In Fairbanks opinion, the oral preaching of the Gospel… is the best way for us to expand our strength. Now, it is said that you can't convey Christian ideas to a Hindoo mind through the Vernacular language. But the difficulty is not in the language. The difficulty is in the minds of the people. When their minds are capable of receiving the idea of sin, you can get the idea through the Mahratta language, as well as any other. There was cross-questioning of Missionaries by the audience[341].

In a nut shell, Rev. Mr. Winslow's speech on importance of schools and preaching Gospel through schools is significant. He was just not in favour of oral preaching to adults by Missionaries but he in fact was on the side of educating Indians by teaching 'English' as a language. While Mr. Fairbanks views were contradictory to that of the Winslow's, as he was for oral preaching and gave importance to teaching in vernacular medium.

---

341 *BG*, May 17, 1856, p.155

Some of the results of the deputations visit were as follows;

1. The employment of Non-Christian teachers were discontinued until almost 30 years later, they were employed in the High Schools in Bombay and Ahmednagar in teaching purely secular subjects.
2. The teaching of English was discouraged. Practically no English was taught in the Mission schools till the High Schools mentioned above were started, that at Bombay in 1877 and that at Ahmednagar in 1882.
3. Schools for Non-Christians were discouraged. The schools of the Mission were to be only for the instruction of the Christian children connected with the Mission, and for the training of Christian workers. This idea had been gradually modified, till the Mission recognized that schools were most valuable means of reaching those who were not Christians.
4. The Deputation gave most earnest thought to the establishment of churches served by Indian Christian pastors. Till 1854, there were only two churches, and Missionaries were invariably the pastors. The new churches had been organized wherever it was possible to and over these churches pastors were installed from among their own people. This led to the teaching of students for the ministry that in 1878 developed into a Theological Seminary.
5. Another recommendation of far-reaching importance was that new stations be opened in the rural districts. Four were opened and occupied at first in the Ahmednagar District.[342]

Anderson was opposed to appointing women as Missionaries throughout his entire long and effective career. As he was retiring in 1866 however he sensed a turning of the tide and said to his successor, "I cannot recommend bringing the women into this work; but you are a young man, go and do it if you can". It was the

342 Report of the AMM 1901-1910 (Marathi Mission Report) pp. 4-5

women themselves, however who turned the tide. Missionary wives in their letters home had long been movingly describing the tragedy of women in Asia, and particularly in India. One writer's capsule summary of the lot of Asian women was an unforgettable three phrases: "unwelcome at birth, unhonoured in life, unwept in death."

The greatest contribution of the Missions was in the field of education at grass roots level[343]. But, Western India proved to be a much harder ground for Missionary work than any other part of India. The loss of political independence of the Marathas coincided with the commencement of Missionary work and this made the government of Bombay hesitant to encourage the Missionaries lest the unsettled state of the country should further deteriorate.

One reason why the Missionaries did not make much headway was because of the attitude some of them had of condemning and confronting Hindu social practices which later changed to encouragement of bringing reforms in Hindu society.

Sir Bartle Frere, Governor of Bombay (1862-67) thus commenced his pamphlet on "Indian Missions". He has defined Missionary work and Missionary progress. He answered on what is real Missionary progress? As "Some would limit it to complete conversion and open profession of Christianity to such complete and sincere abandonment of another religion as would justify the strictest Missionary in admitting the convert by Baptism in to the congregation of professing Christian communicants. Any thing that tends to break up old beliefs aids in its degrees, the reception of a new creed. In this point of view, almost everything we do in India is more or less Missionary work. Not only railways and printing presses, education, commerce and the electric telegraph, our impartial course and inform systems of administration, but our misfortunes and our mistakes, our wars our famines and our mutinies"[344].

Frere's description of Christian Missions and their progress especially during the 35 years from 1834 to 1869 was historical and picturesque[345]. Bartle Frere being the Chancellor of University of

343 M. D. David, *Op. Cit*, p. xiv

344 Sir, Bartel Frere, *Indian Missions*, G.C.S.I & Co , London, 1873, pp. 8-9

345 Lt. General C. W. Tremenheere, *Missions in India: The System of Education in Government and Mission Schools contrasted*, Demy Svo. Sewed, London, 1876, p. 9

Bombay endeavored to promote the efficiency and independence of the University. He never missed the convocation function and from 1862-1867, he delivered regular convocation addressees on these occasions[346].

The first girl's school of the Bombay presidency established in 1824, by the American Mission in Bombay was named Salem school and it was for the.Jew Girls but the native girls were also enrolled in the school. Rev. Sheshadri gave an idea of the satisfactory progress of the schools on the basis of 1832 examination which appeared in the '*Bombay Hurkaru*' and Wurtaman, a Gujarati paper edited by a Parsi gentleman and which was translated in to English and Marathi in the '*Durpan*'...

"Last Thursday, there was as examination at the American Mission Chapel in Bhendy Bazar of the schools for Hindoo female children. Many European ladies and gentlemen were present and we also attended. At 11 O' Clock, the children were examined in Mahratta, which they read fluently. They answered questions promptly and sung a Christian hymn in a tone of pleasure seldom exceeded even by the English children. When the examination in the reading was concluded, the girls needle- work, the stockings they had knitted and embroidery work which they had made up, were exhibited and inspected. On examination, these appeared equal to work of the same description performed in England. There were children's woolen stockings finer than those made in England. The ladies present praised the children and also the lady who had instructed them".

The American Missionaries were therefore rightly called the pioneers in modern western education for girls in western Maharashtra. In the succeeding years the young native men highly influenced by the Missionaries worked for the promotion of women's education convinced of the necessity they started taking active interest in and formed groups or associations in league with the fellow workers to pursue the Mission with determination[347].

346 Rekha Ranade, *Sir Bartel Frere and his Times : A Study of its Bombay Years 1862-67*, Ph.D Thesis, Pune, 1988, p. 211

347 Sheela Patwarhan, *"History of Development of Women Education in the Central Division of the Bombay Presidency" 1818-1905,* Ph.D thesis November 1990,

Also, the first girls boarding school was founded in Bombay by the American Mission in 1836 and 13 girls were accommodated in it. The school progressed very rapidly under the guidance of Mrs. Hume from 1840. This was the first school in India, conducting co-education. The boys and girls were still learning together in this school. Many renowned ladies who became social workers had studied in this school e.g. Mrs. Bhor, Mrs. Navalkar etc. The period between the Charter Act of 1813 to the declaration of Wood's Despatch of education in 1856 was a period of experiments. The western education system and western knowledge was slowly replacing the indigenous educational system and indigenous subjects taught in schools so far. Among these experiments the Missionaries introduced the experiment of establishing the concept of women's education and educational institutions in Bombay and other areas. It was creditable to the Missionaries that when even the government, due to rigid social and religious restrictions imposed on women's education was doubtful about peoples reaction and hesitated to open schools for females with fear of incurring people's displeasure, disadvantageous on their political authority and stability ventured on the Mission of women's education. The *Bombay Guardian* of July 26, 1856 highlights bitter remarks made by *Chabook*[348] on teaching English morality and English manners to females (especially Parsees).

Inspite of various incentives provided by Missionaries to attract girls in their schools like free education, food, etc., many parents were not in favour of sending the girls to Mission schools for fear of religious influence and danger of conversion. When the indigenous girls schools were established by the middle of the nineteenth century, parents preference for these schools in comparison to Mission schools adversely affected the Mission schools. From 1856 onwards and

---

Pune, p. 91

348 *Chabook*, the Whip was a Paper Published in Bombay Presidency. The Bombay Times and Journal of Commerce of February 7th 1859 describes this paper some thing like What the *London Satirist* was before the clever scamp who edited that paper was extinguished by the duke of Brunswick. Nawrojee Dorabjee was its editor (mentioned in the *Calcutta Christian* Observer January to December 1839, p. 355)

especially after the event of 1857, the government policy changed and it also affected the working of the Mission schools.

The History of Post 1857 Indian education is the tale of a long struggle by the authorities to reverse Macaulayan trend and promote mass education, the ideal being a large pool of literatúre, skilled minor clerks and petty officials. To this end the Hunter Commission of 1882 headed by William Hunter championed the vernaculars over English as a medium, downgraded literary study, and promoted technical and vocational instructions[349].

5.5 News Papers, Bulletins and News Letters

Various aspects of the Missionary work were brought to light by the regular news bulletins / letters / magazines published in those times. The Chief ones include, *The Bombay Guardian, The Missionary Herald, The Oriental Christian Spectator, The Examiner, Western India Notes*. Together with these prominent English bulletins, news letters in vernacular medium were The *Bamdad* (chiefly Gujarati, periodical) and *Dyanodaya* (Marathi as well as English weekly). Their combination with publishing Societies like BTBS and Bombay Auxiliary formed an important tool in the hands of the Missionaries to spread the message of Gospel and related social issues. Interesting co-relations can be found in contemporary tract societies like The Bangalore Tract and Book Society, Calcutta Christian Tract and Book Society, Agra Tract and Book Society, Punjab Religious Book Society.

5.5.1 The Missionary Herald

The Missionary Herald was the oldest periodical in America established in 1818 succeeding the Panoplist established in 1805. It was a 50 page monthly which covered news from all over the world of the American Board of Commissioners for foreign Missions and was published from Boston. Later it was called the Missionary Herald at home and abroad. In Ahmednagar College Library in Maharashtra its issues from 1837-1939 are preserved.

349 Rimi Chatterjee, *Empires of the Mind, The History of OUP in India under the Raj*, New Delhi, 2006, p. 7

Table 5.3: List of articles published in Missionary Herald

Title of Article/ Illustration#	*Year*	*Vol/Page*
The Protestant Buddhists of Japan	Jan 1892	38/16
Village Schools in India (High Caste Girl School#)	Dec 1892	38/540
The need of Educational Work in India	Oct 1894	38/416
Samuel Beacon Fairbanks (Dr. Fairbank#)	1898	- /300
Industrial Training in India (Sir Dinshaw M Petit#)	Apr 1900	XCVI/168
Mid Winter foreign Mission study campaign (A new series of Charts on Japan#)	Jan 1905	- /22-23
The Marathi Mission in 1904 (with Map#)	Jul 1905	C1/335
America-India (1813-1913) (Hume Memorial Church, Bombay#)	Jan 1914	CX/09
A Student Conference in West India (The Alibag Student Camp#)	Apr 1916	CX/II/168
The triumph of India's Outcaste	Feb 1933	CXXIX/ 36-37
International Review of Missions (Map of the Madura Mission#)	Mar 1934	CXXX/96
The Sage of Bolpur (Rabindranath Tagore#)	Oct 1934	CXXX/432
The Witness of a Brahmin	Jun 1939	CXXXV/264
Tolands Memorial to Gordon Hall (Gordon Halls Great Grandson#)	Aug 1939	XXXV/ -

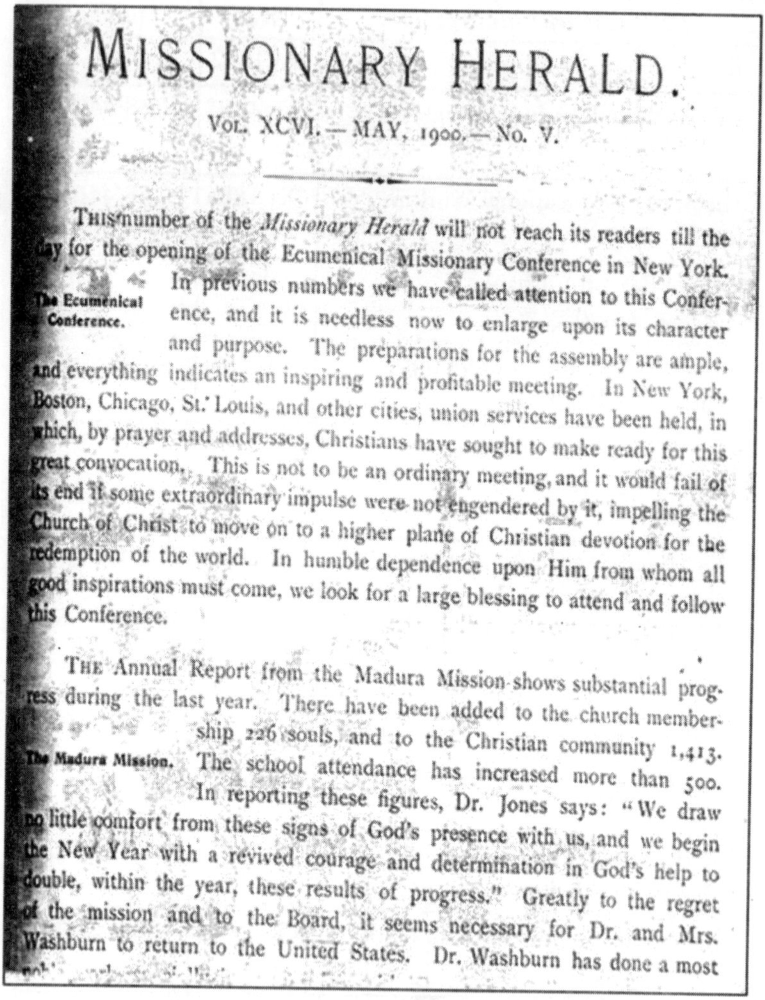

MISSIONARY HERALD.

VOL. XCVI. — MAY, 1900. — NO. V.

THIS number of the *Missionary Herald* will not reach its readers till the day for the opening of the Ecumenical Missionary Conference in New York.

The Ecumenical Conference.

In previous numbers we have called attention to this Conference, and it is needless now to enlarge upon its character and purpose. The preparations for the assembly are ample, and everything indicates an inspiring and profitable meeting. In New York, Boston, Chicago, St. Louis, and other cities, union services have been held, in which, by prayer and addresses, Christians have sought to make ready for this great convocation. This is not to be an ordinary meeting, and it would fail of its end if some extraordinary impulse were not engendered by it, impelling the Church of Christ to move on to a higher plane of Christian devotion for the redemption of the world. In humble dependence upon Him from whom all good inspirations must come, we look for a large blessing to attend and follow this Conference.

THE Annual Report from the Madura Mission shows substantial progress during the last year. There have been added to the church membership 226 souls, and to the Christian community 1,413.

The Madura Mission.

The school attendance has increased more than 500. In reporting these figures, Dr. Jones says: "We draw no little comfort from these signs of God's presence with us, and we begin the New Year with a revived courage and determination in God's help to double, within the year, these results of progress." Greatly to the regret of the mission and to the Board, it seems necessary for Dr. and Mrs. Washburn to return to the United States. Dr. Washburn has done a most

Slide 5.5: Front Page of Missionary Herald

The Missionary Herald

AMERICA-INDIA, 1813-1913

By WILLIAM E. STRONG, D.D.

Slide 5.6: Copy of Missionary Herald

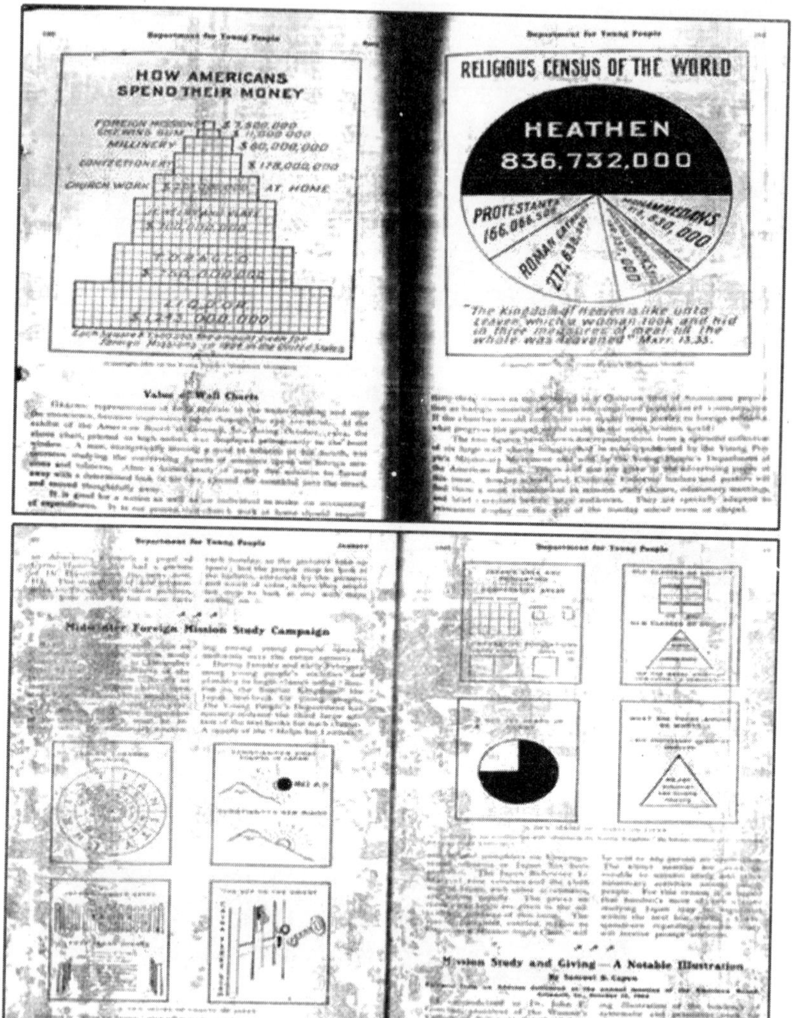

Slide 5.7: Copy of Missionary Herald

5.5.2 Oriental Christian Spectator

Oriental Christian Spectator was a magazine founded by the Missionaries. The paper has reproduced a number of letters from the other native news papers. Though the paper represented Missionary side, the facts mentioned therein are important.

THE
ORIENTAL
CHRISTIAN SPECTATOR.

NOVEMBER, M,DCCC,XLVIII.

I.—HISTORY OF THE CHURCH MISSIONARY SOCIETY'S MISSIONS IN THE BOMBAY PRESIDENCY.*

The agents for the Church Missionary Society in Bombay, desirous of acting upon the suggestions of the Parent Society respecting the approaching Jubilee, deem it advisable to lay before their friends a sketch of the history of the Society's operations in this Presidency. For they conceive that a considerable part of that indifference to, and prejudice against, the cause they promote, which still deprives them of the support of many who ought cordially to join them, is owing to mere ignorance; and that by removing this stumbling block by a plain statement of proceedings transacted on the spot, their assistance may be procured; or if not, one pretext for withholding it will, at least, be obviated. Besides this, the nature of the Jubilee requires that, wherever there are particular and local causes contributive to its general design, they should be especially remembered. Now in commemorating what God has done towards the Church Missionary Society, during the past history of its existence, all its friends who live in places where part of its work has been and is carried on, will naturally recur to that work; indeed the Society's particular history in such places will principally engage their attention. Whatever the past history of any of the Society's Missions may present, its prosperous and its adverse events, its successes and its disappointments, are to be viewed as a portion of those materials from which that praise, that humiliation, and those supplications and resolutions are to be prepared, which will constitute the song of our Jubilee. Our friends in Bombay then, being called upon to join in the Jubilee of the Church Missionary Society, are invited particularly to notice what has taken place in the Society's Mission in this Presidency. However, before we proceed to sketch this history of the Western India Mission of the C. M. S., we beg to lay before our friends a brief outline of the earlier history of the Society itself.

The formation of the Church Missionary Society took place in a period which formed a new Era in the Church of Christ. Towards the close of a century distinguished for intellectual progress not more than for moral and religious decline, during its last decade, when Europe was convulsed by the French Revolution, and began to witness its consequences, the Protestant Churches in Europe and America realised a remarkable visitation of mercy in the manifestation of a universal Missionary spirit. The Wesleyan Methodists, a body essentially Missionary, determined upon a Mission to India in 1792 (though they did not then carry out that resolution); the Baptist Missionary Society was instituted the same year. The London Missionary Society was formed in 1795, with a view to unite Christians of all denominations in Missionary efforts, and it was joined by many of the clergy and laity of the Church of England. In 1796 followed the Edinburgh, or as it was afterwards called,

* From a pamphlet printed in connexion with the Jubilee of the Society.

SECOND SERIES. VOL. IX. No. 11 43

Slide 5.8: **Front** page of *The Oriental Spectator*

Table 5.4: Topic covered in *OCS*

Title of Article	***Year***	***Vol/Page***
Report of Free Church of Scotland's Bombay Mission	1848	10/49

Bombay Guardian.

A CHRISTIAN WEEKLY NEWSPAPER CIRCULATING THROUGHOUT INDIA AND THE EAST

VOL. LI. New Series.—No. 7 SATURDAY, FEBRUARY 18, 1905.

WEEKLY REVIEW.

Parliament was opened on Tuesday by the King in person. The following is the telegraphic summary of the Speech from the Throne :—

"My relations with foreign Powers continue friendly.

"The war in the Far East unhappily continues and my Government has been careful to observe neutrality in the strictest manner.

"The condition of the Balkans occasions anxiety. ... radical reforms, especially financial ones, are still required, and his Majesty notes with satisfaction that Russia and Austria have lately addressed proposals to the Porte for this purpose.

"The Convention between Great Britain and France has been duly ratified and cannot fail to strengthen the friendly relations happily subsisting between them."

The speech then mentions the meeting of the Commission in Paris for the purpose of apportioning the responsibility for the deplorable incident in the North Sea.

"An agreement calculated to place the relations between Tibet and India on a satisfactory footing has been concluded at Lhasa. The great difficulties the Mission encountered were brilliantly surmounted by the Civil and Military authorities responsible for its conduct.

"China has sent a Commissioner to Calcutta to negotiate a Convention of adhesion to the Tibetan agreement.

"The Ameer has sent his son to pay a complimentary visit to the Viceroy, and a high officer of the Government of India has been deputed to Cabul to discuss with the Ameer questions affecting the relations between the two Governments.

...

the press, but failing health compelled him to leave the completion of this task to another. Dr. Murray Mitchell's volume is entitled "The Great Religions of India," or, as he says in the first Lecture, "it might almost have been called *the great religions of the world*; for all of these—with the exception of Confucianism—now exist in India." Yet Christianity is not the subject of either of the Lectures, nor would Dr. Mitchell have been the man to include it, for as his nephew, Dr. James Mitchell, says in the prefatory note :—

"He (Dr. Murray Mitchell) delighted in the comparative study of these religions, and in tracing the points of resemblance between Christianity and Buddhism and between the Bible and the Koran—yet never with the result, which some have arrived at, of regarding the Christian religion as but one of several systems, each of which has its distinctive excellence,—possibly the best of them all, but yet having no more right to be regarded as the one truth than any of the rest."

The Publishers, Messrs. Oliphant, Anderson and Ferrier, of Edinburgh and London, are to be congratulated on having presented these valuable lectures in a form particularly easy to read, a welcome contrast to the overcrowded pages of some other volumes whose valuable contents might as well be stored in a cellar as locked up in illegible print. Another charm of this volume is the beautiful frontispiece, a faithful reproduction of a recent photo of Dr. Mitchell. The volume is published at five shillings.

A high purpose and fervent missionary spirit sustained Dr. Murray Mitchell in this his last great contribution to the cause of missions. ...

...

Enough has been quoted to indicate the value of these lectures. A word as to their scope. The first lecture is a masterly review of the whole. Then follow four lectures, one each devoted to Hinduism, Zoroastrianism, Buddhism and Muhammadanism; the sixth and last lecture deals with the religion of the wilder races.

The place of honour in the *Church Missionary Intelligencer* for February is given to an incident which is likely to be remembered as memorable in the history of missions. This is the receipt by the Church Missionary Society in London of a letter from Lord Cromer inviting them to start missionary work, including simple forms of industrial and agricultural instruction, among pagan tribes in the Upper Nile Valley. The reply which the C.M.S. will give to this invitation cannot be determined at once; but previous calls elicited prompt offers of service from men remarkable alike for their natural gifts and devotion, and we trust it will be the same again.

The letter, which we reproduce below, is prefaced in the *Intelligencer* by a valuable sketch of the progress of missions in the great African continent. ...

Slide 5.9: Front page of the Bombay Guardian

5.5.3 The Bombay Guardian (*BG*)

The Bombay Guardian a weekly established in March 1851- the last issue of this weekly (July 22, 1905) is available in Maharashtra State Archives, Mumbai. Initially it was published every Friday and later every Saturday. It had circulation in India, Europe, America, Australia, China etc.

BG published letters from its readers dealing with various subjects.

Rev. George Bowen[350] was an associate editor of the *BG* in 1851. For many years he edited this weekly religious journal, which became distinguished under his direction for its evangelical tone and sagacious comments and suggestions on matters of Missionary and general interests. The editors of *BG* continued to work as an undenominational advocate of evangelical Christianity. This newspaper covered Baba Padmanji and Narayan Sheshadri[351] in many of its issues.

Interesting reports covered by *BG*

July 12, 1856 front page...In what light romanists are ready to review the honors rendered to Ms. Florence Nightingale' may be seen from the following passage in the charge of a French Bishop. "England scarcely knows what a sister of charity is. When a courageous women Ms. Nightingale offered her zeal and devotion to the soldiers in the Crimea. England thrown in to commotion by the advent of a single sister of Charity generated by the Anglican Faith.

The *BG* wanted to give the latest and the most accurate news of all movements for the spread of the Gospel. The reduction in international postage in 1892 made the circulation of this paper wide from Australia to China. In 1892, the premises of *BG* was close to the Ambroli Church of the Free Church Mission (Near Girgaum)[352].

---

350 He was a Minister of Fort American Methodist Church during 1887.

351 The details about him read in a paper entitled 'Missionary efforts of Narayan Sheshadri' at the 25th conference of Marathwada Itihas Parishad at Aurangabad in Nov 2005.

352 *BG*, January 23, 1892, p.12

Table 5.5: Articles published in *BG*

Title of Article	*Year*	*Page*
The Past Progress of Education, and the present crisis of the educated mind in western India	Oct 18, 1856	336
Rev. J. Murray Mitchell	Oct 23, 1886	681
Sketch of Mr. Bowen's Life	Feb 11, 1888	83
Pandita Ramabai's Widows Home	Sept 05, 1891	06
Industrial Training for Indian Widows	Oct 03, 1891	06
Return of Mr. Raju Naidu to India	Apr 22, 1893	3
An Island Mosque and the Hindu Festival	Sep 16, 1893	03
Pandita Ramabai's Farewell at Khedgaon	Jan 8, 1898	03
A Letter from Pandita Ramabai	Aug 27, 1898	03
German Missionaries in India	Sept 10, 1898	03
A Festival Day at Ramabai's farm	Oct 01, 1898	03
The Strength and Weakness of Indian Christian Community	Sept 20, 1902	09
Indian Christians and the Indian Customs- East Vs West	Feb 25, 1905	11,12
The Mahars of Western India	Apr 29, 1905	02
The Medical Art of Old India	May 27, 1905	11,12

Sometimes we see interesting letters especially in *BG*. A non-sporting Missionary wrote to the editor of *BG* "Is it right for a Missionary to go Shikaring? Published on (p. 11) August 5, 1893... "Sir- Is it right for a Missionary of the Cross to use a portion of his time in running after game when he himself has bread and meat enough and to space? ... During the past two years I have seen two men of the same Mission, who are in the receipt of good salaries, unblushingly shoulder their guns for the purpose. It is a fact that the heathen have very little respect for the Missionary who loves

Shikaring...Such men are stumbling blocks in the work of God, not only to the heathen, but also to nominal Christians. Let them use the hot shot of God's eternal truth knocking down sins and leading them to the Lamb of God".

5.5.4 Dyanodaya

Dyanodaya – Rise of knowledge has been a major source of the Missionary activities. It was published in Marathi and later also in English. It started in 1842, regularly appeared before the readers first as a fortnightly and then as weekly. The paper not only pleaded the Missionary cause but also the cause of reform in India. There were number of articles and letters discussing the weakness of Hinduism. It criticized evil practices and gave wide publicity to various views by reformers. It was critical of various Hindu customs and religion and articles published in it were often provocative[353].

Earlier in 1874 a very handsome *Dyanodaya* Almanac in Marathi (of 48pages) was published by the American Mission[354]. Dr. Fairbank of AMM was the editor of *Dyanodaya* from Bombay in 1850. Tukaram Nathoji was its marathi editor in 1906 and the English columns were edited by Dr. Abbot. and in 1947 Rev. Dr. B. P. Hivale was its English editor and Rev. S. L. Salvi was its marathi editor.

Dyanodaya also ran numerous articles to show that what the Brahmins described as divine and magic was natural phenomenon but could be scientifically explained. Thus, it explained the movements of planets as a part of natural order, involving no divine or magical powers[355].

---

353 Arun R. Joshi, *Renaissance in Western India 1823-1892,* Part I, Ph.D Thesis, Mumbai, 1976, p. 14

354 *BG,* January 10, 1874, p. 368

355 Adhi H. Doctor, 'Missionary teachings and social reformers in 19th Century India' in Toetonio D'Souza (ed), Discoveries, Missionary Expansion and Mission Cultures, Concept, New Delhi, 1994, p. 107

DNYANODAYA

Organ of the following seven organisations in the Marathi-speaking area:— American Marathi, American Presbyterian, Church of Scotland, Australian Churches of Christ, Joint Council of the Church of the Brethren, Methodist Church in Southern Asia, and (British) Methodist Missionary Society.

(Rise of Knowledge)
Established 1842

Editor: The Rev. Dr. B. P. Hivale, (on leave),
Advisory Editorial Board:
The Rev. Dr. J. Kellock,
The Rev. Roland W. Scott
The Rev. Miss Elizabeth Moreland
Church of Scotland Mission, Gowalia Tank Road, Bombay 7.

Marathi Editor: The Rev. S. L. Salvi
Agent. Mr. D. G. Gaikwad,

Vol. 106 | Poona : Thursday, November 20, 1947 | No. 47

PRESBYTERIAL SOCIETIES IN WESTERN INDIA

There has always been a band of devoted Indian women at work in remote villages as well as in larger centres, from the beginning of Christian work in this part of India, but it was not until 1923 that a Presbyterial Society was organized. From that time to the present, annually in February or March, from 5? to 100 woman have met together for fellowship and to report on their year's service for their Master. These women represent all the organized Churches of the Kolhapur Church Council area, two delegates from each being invited to be present. The annual meetings are planned largely by the Indian women, are held in a different Church each year, and are financed by the entertaining society. We see here a cross-section of the Indian Church in Western India, including illiterate but eager village women, teachers, pastors' and evangelists' wives, Bible women, College graduates, and [illegible] trades-men and workman.

The Annual Gathering

Although the following description of a Presbyterial meeting was written ten years ago, it might have been written of almost any one of the annual meetings:

"The program centered about the topic "The Church." The worship and teaching services of the Church, the sacraments, the festivals, the giving, the means of growth, were some of the subjects presented by the speakers, of whom two were missionaries, and the rest, including the presiding officers, were Indian women. There was opportunity to view the exhibit of articles contributed for sale by the various societies, to make the rounds of the farm and to admire the fine goats and chickens of the Boys' School, to inspect the practically new dormitory of the Girls' School, and to joy-ride in the Nipani bus to various points of interest in Sangli town.

"The evenings were well filled too. The first was the occasion of an impressive Communion service, at which nearly all the women were dressed in white, making a lovely sight as they came in groups to the front of the auditorium to be served by the Sangli pastor. The next evening the room was packed with women and babies to see in dramatic form how in each station "God works out His purposes in many different ways." these little plays proved so interesting that it was 10 : 30 before we knew it, with several skits still on the waiting list. The next evening a bountiful dinner of rice and curry, cooked by the Sangli women and served by them to the many guests seated in long rows on the ground of the bungalow yard, was a fitting introduction to the last session.

The Day by Day Activities

"One not familiar with such gatherings might ask if after all, such a group of women were accomplishing anything constructive in their home Churches, or if this were not just one more opportunity to get together to talk. To sit in on the meeting when one delegate representing each society gave the report of her group would prove enlightening and convincing. Some large societies had much activity and much money to report. Village groups showed a proportionate activity.

"We shall not soon forget one village woman who rose to report for her group. Apologetically she began, "I'm only a country woman and can't read, but I'll tell you about our society. We live in the country and there is no one to help us or show us how to do things. We don't even know how to pray properly as we've never had a real opportunity to learn anything much, but we met regularly anyhow and

Slide 5.10: Front Page of Dnyanodaya

5.5.5 Bamdad (Gujarati)

The *Bamdad* was the only Christian periodical in Gujarati. It started on July 1858 under the auspices of the Bombay Tract and Book Society[356](formed in 1828). This Society supplied regularly Vernacular Literature, and its object was to present to the natives of this country in language that they understand the truths of God's word in forms adopted to arrest their hearts. The Society had no regular sub-agencies of its own for selling books, but the work entirely rested on the co-operation of Missionaries. Rev. Narayan Sheshadri, Baba Padmanji, Mr. and Mrs. Murry Mitchell, Dr. Stevenson, Rev. R. G. Wilder and others regularly contributed their works in this society. Mr. and Mrs. Wilder were pioneers in Western India Mission[357] at Kolhapur. The friendship between Mr. Wilder and Sir Henry Bartle Frere proved a blessing to the people of Kolhapur[358].

Rev. Dhanjibhai Nawroji[359] (1820-1908) edited The *Bamdad,* i.e., *Dawn,* its issues of 1858,1859,1860,1861 are available at The K. R. Cama Oriental Institute, Mumbai. He also edited another Gujarati magazine *Gyan Dipika*[360]. In the third volume of 1859 issue its object to be useful to fellowmen-viewed as immortal beings have been highlighted. It said… "some readers of *Bamdad* wrote not to touch on religious subjects…." but the editor said "we do not mean to follow them, we shall not hesitate to state our thoughts and convictions on religious points". Sometimes, *Bamdad* carried articles in English with pictures and map.

356 The *Oriental Christian Spectator*, August 1861, p. 381

357 Later called American Presbyterian Missionaries

358 *WIN*, December 1932, p. 4

359 A Parsi converted to Christianity with Mr. Hormuzdi in 1839. Dhanjibhai was incharge of the Ambroli Native Church in 1878.

360 *BG*, December 11, 1886, p. 791

Table 5.6: List of articles in *Bamdad*

Title of Article	*Language*	*Year*	*Vol/ Page*
Visits to Britain by the Natives of India	English	1858	2/ cover
India Three Thousand years ago (Rev. John Wilson)	Gujarati	1858	4/ 66
A Flying Visit to the Caves of Karli	Gujarati	1858	7/127
Effects of Strong Drink	Gujarati	1858	9/163
Rationality	English	1858	10/
Dr. Bhau Daji's Lecture	Gujarati	1858	10/143
Promiscuous Bathing among the Hindus	Gujarati	1858	10/217
The Wonders of the Microscope	Gujarati	1859	1/11
The Maharajas of the Banyans	English	1859	1/59
Progress of Female Education among the Parsis	English	1859	4/81
Views of Public Men on Education in India in 1793	English		
A Word to the Slaves of Luxury	Gujarati	1859	10/185
The Population and Revenue of UK compared	Gujarati	1859	/237
Contrasted with the population and Revenue of India			12/
Death of The Hon'ble Mr. Wilson	English	1860	2/cover
Scotch System of Education	English	1860	/34-35
The Parsi Monopoly of Licenses in Bombay	Gujarati	1860	/36-37
The Late Discussion among the Hindus	English	1860	3/59-60
A Word to the lovers of Nautch	Gujarati	1860	4/117
Remarraige of Hindu Widow	English	1860	5/132-133
Travels in Great Britain (by Dosabhai Framji)	English	1860	1/cover
Correspondence Between Ourselves and Dr. Haug	English	1861	3/cover
Grammar in Rhyme for School Boys	English	1861	10/232
Bible in the Government Schools	English	1861	03/cover
The Bombay University and the Parsi Gujarati	English	1860	02/cover

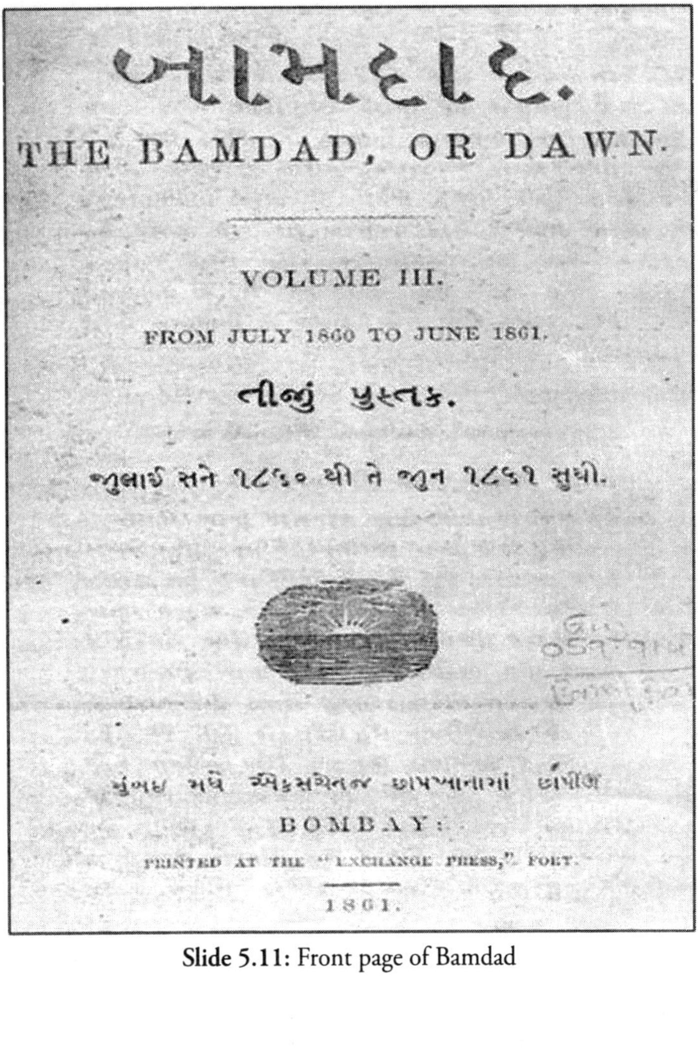

બામદાદ.

THE BAMDAD, OR DAWN.

VOLUME III.

FROM JULY 1860 TO JUNE 1861.

તીજું પુસ્તક.

જુલાઈ સને ૧૮૬૦ થી તે જુન ૧૮૬૧ સુધી.

મુંબઇ મધે એક્સચેન્જ છાપખાનામાં છાપીઓ

BOMBAY:

PRINTED AT THE "EXCHANGE PRESS," FORT.

1861.

Slide 5.11: Front page of Bamdad

GRAMMAR IN RHYME FOR SCHOOL BOYS[361]

Three little words you often see

Are Articles- a, an & the

A Noun's the name of anything as school, or garden, hoop or swing.

Adjectives tell the kind of noun,

As great, small, pretty, white or brown

Instead of nouns the pronouns stand –

her head, his face, your arm, my hand

Verbs tell of something to be done, To read, count, sing, laugh, jump or run

How things are done, the Adverbs tell, As slowly quickly, ill or well

Conjunctions join the words together

As men and women, wind or weather

The Prepositions stands before a noun, as in or through a door

The Interjection shows surprise

As Oh! how pretty; ah! How wise

The whole are called nine parts of speech, which reading writing speaking teaches.

361 *Bamdad,* 1861, Vol.10, p. 232

FOR THE CHILDREN[362]

. , : ; ? !

The Punctuation Points

Six little marks from school are we,
Very important, all agree,
Filled to the brim with mystery,
Six little marks from school.
One little mark is round and small, **.**
But where it stands the voice must fall;
At the close of a sentence, all

Place this little mark from school:
One little mark, with gown on trailing,
Holds up the voice, and, never failing,
Tells you not to pause when hailing

This little mark from school:
If out of breath you chance to meet,
Two little dots, both round and neat, **:**
Pause, and these tiny guardsmen greet-

These little mark from school:
When shorter pauses are your pleasure,
One trails his sword- takes half the measure,**;**
Then speeds you on to seek new treasure;

These little mark from school:
One little mark, ear shaped, implies, **?**
"Keep the voice away it replies",
Together information tries

This little mark from school:
One little mark with an exclamation, **!**
Presents itself to your observation,
And leaves the voice at an elevation

362 *The Vanguard* (An American Christian Newspaper in *BG*, January 18, 1896)

This little mark from school:
Six little marks! Be sure to heed us;
Carefully study, write and read us;
For you can never cease to need us;
Six little marks from school!

5.5.6 Western India Notes (WIN)

WIN was a quarterly paper of the Presbyterian Church, USA. Mrs. Ferris who came to Indian in 1880 was an abel and active correspondent with Missionary circles. She was keen to issues a small printed sheet given to American Friends information on Missions work, thus it was under her editorship that the first issue of WIN appeared for January 1893 (It was sanctioned without expense to the Mission). In 1895, then called *India Notes* was taken under the care of the Mission and the Mission agreed to pay one half the expenses of publishing the report number. The first six years of the publication of WIN was mainly due to the efforts of Mrs. Ferris who left the field in 1899. From 1st January 1899, publication of WIN was discontinued for a short time.

At the conference of the American Presbyterian Missionaries (AP) at Ludhiana, Punjab, a scheme was put forward to encourage local Missionary effort. The Board in America had agreed to give Rs 3 for every Re 1 contributed by Indian Christians of the AP Church, in order to support aggressive Missionary work of their own, the two funds being managed by the whole Presbytery in which Indians and foreigners sit side by side[363]. Till 1939 Mrs. Jane Goheen[364] was editor of WIN. In April 1939 issue (Front Page), the splendid service which Mrs. Goheen had rendered by ably attending to the editing of WIN amid the many fold and imperative duties of that busy Sangli station is mentioned. Later J. Evans was its editor. It carried articles along with lot of associated illustrations/pictures.

All the above news papers and magazines brought out information on European and American Missionary organizations.

---

363 *BG*, January 18, 1896, p. 4

364 Wife of John Goheen

In early 19th Century Missionary wrote about themselves and near ones for example Rev. John Wilson wrote about memories of his first wife Margret. Murry Mitchell wrote about Robert Nesbit.

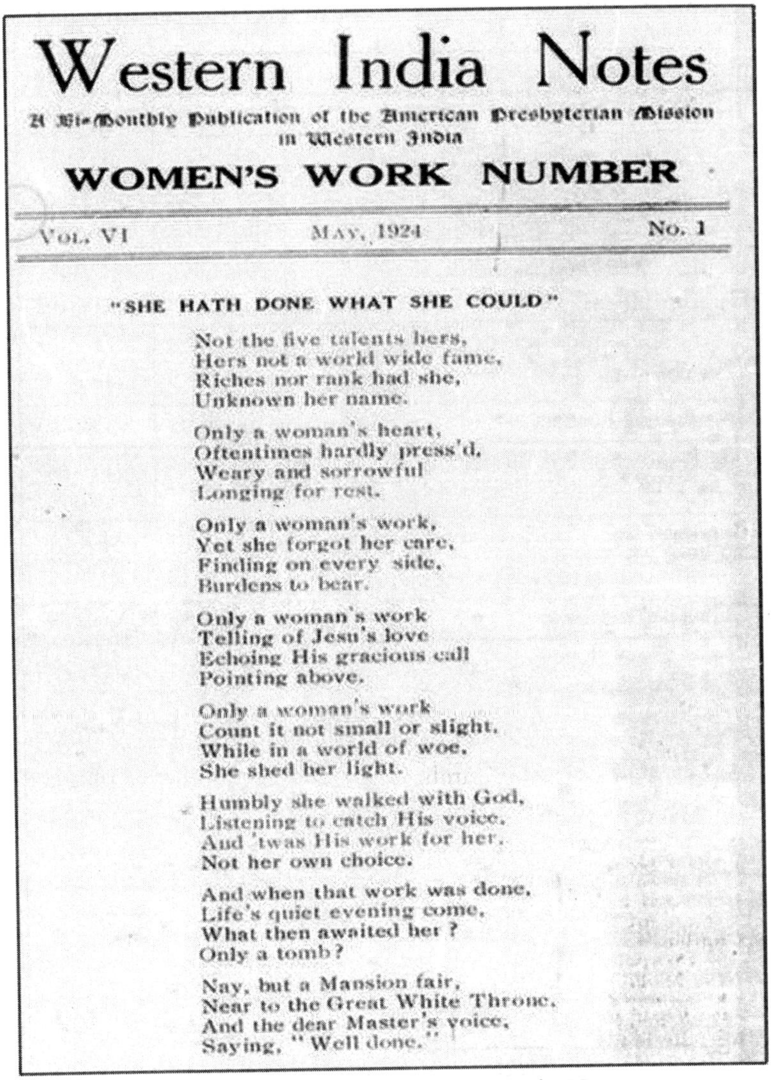

Western India Notes

A Bi-Monthly Publication of the American Presbyterian Mission in Western India

WOMEN'S WORK NUMBER

VOL. VI | MAY, 1924 | No. 1

"SHE HATH DONE WHAT SHE COULD"

Not the five talents hers,
Hers not a world wide fame,
Riches nor rank had she,
Unknown her name.

Only a woman's heart,
Oftentimes hardly press'd,
Weary and sorrowful
Longing for rest.

Only a woman's work,
Yet she forgot her care,
Finding on every side,
Burdens to bear.

Only a woman's work
Telling of Jesu's love
Echoing His gracious call
Pointing above.

Only a woman's work
Count it not small or slight,
While in a world of woe,
She shed her light.

Humbly she walked with God,
Listening to catch His voice,
And 'twas His work for her,
Not her own choice.

And when that work was done,
Life's quiet evening come,
What then awaited her ?
Only a tomb?

Nay, but a Mansion fair,
Near to the Great White Throne,
And the dear Master's voice,
Saying, "Well done."

Slide 5.12: Front page of Western India Notes

Table 5.7: List of articles published in *WIN*

Title of Article /Illustration#	*Year*	*Vol/ Page*
The Fragrant Memory of Ms Unsworth (with photograph#)	Jun 1927	09/cover
New Child Welfare Centre (Vengurla)	Jan 1939	20/08
The Rocky Konkan	Apr 1939	20/26
Shahu Chatrapati Maharaj#	Oct 1940	21/cover
G V Moses : Christian Gentlemen	Nov 1941	22/52
Dr. and Mrs. Servid Studying marathi with a pandit#	Jul 1951	34/19
What makes time fly in Vengurla	Jul 1953	36/37
Golden Celebrations- Golden Opportunities	Apr 1954	37/07
Morning devotions in the Vengurla Church#	Oct 1954	37/-
Tomorrow's Leaders	Jul 1956	39/08
The Beauty Spot of Western India - Vengurla	Apr 1957	XL /cover
Bombay 5 years later- Lester P Servid	Jan 1958	XLI/14
Our Interview (related to Vinoba Bhave)	Oct 1958	XLI/05
Farewell Sister Faye	Oct 1958	XLI/13

5.5.7 The Davidsonian

Davidsonian was a weekly News Paper of Davidson College of USA. It was a member of North Carolina Collegiate and Southern Collegiate Presbyterian Association. The digital archives of the College website contain the issues from 1914 to 2006. The 1922 issue covers the visit of Dr. R. H. H. Goheen who had spend 2 days at the College where he met the students, lectured and discussed his work and problems in India[365].

365 *The Davidsonian*, March 24, Vol. IX, 1922, pp. 1-6

5.5.8 The CMJI

The Christian Medical Journal of India was a news letter of the CMAI (initially it was known as Medical Missionary Association). Through these association the medical doctors shared information on medicines and new techniques / methods developed for treating diseases. The 2005-06 issue of CMJI was a special issue called 'The Heritage' which carried the photographs of the past presidents including Dr. William Wanless and Dr. R. H. H. Goheen. It also contains information and group photos of the meetings of CMAI, where in 1906 and in 1932, Dr. R. H. H. Goheen can be seen along with the other distinguished participants[366].

The literary works of Christian Missionaries was thus greatly influenced by the Indian counterparts who contributed to the advancement of Missionary activity which is discussed in detail in the following chapter.

---

366 *CMJI*, Vol. 20 & 21, No. 4 & 1, October - December 2005 and January - March 2006, issue. 1-17 and 18-25

Chapter 6

Indian Contribution to Missionary Work

Chapter 6

Indian Contribution to Missionary Work

6.1 Introduction

The Indian converts (Indian Missionaries) carried forward the work of original Christian Missions as social reformers. Their views and extensive writings brought out the impact of the Christian Missions in a big way.

The contribution of Indian personalities to Missionary work especially in nineteenth century includes writing of novels, books, extensive write-ups and poems. Baba Padmanji's literary works tried to change the attitude of society towards young widows and work for their overall moral and material uplift. Narayan Waman Tilak was called the herald of renaissance in Maharashtrian Christianity[367], both he and his wife Laxmibai helped to further elevate Marathi literature and more to the Marathi - Christian literature.

The needs of female education during early days were realized with the help of pioneer reformers of women's education most of whom were educated in the Mission schools. Female instruction was largely religious and oriented towards helping the girls become better mothers and housewives. The focus was on independent vocational

367 Samuel T. Sheppard, *Bombay*, 1922, Times of India Press, Bombay, p. 135

works which was deemed useful for the women widows of those times. Pandita Ramabai's distinguished contribution in this direction has been commendable.

The impact was also felt as many of them were either in Mission schools or were taught privately by the Missionaries like Jagannath Shankarshet, Dadoba P. Tarkhadkar, Bhaudaji Lad, Mahatma Phule etc[368]. The works of Baba Padmanji, Vishnu Bhaskar Karmarkar, Rev. Narayan Sheshadri, Pandita Ramabai, Rev. N. W. Tilak, Laksmibai Tilak, Nehemiah Gore and Gurubai Karmarkar have been highlighted. A brief account of the initial years of their conversion is included to have a complete view of the social situation.

6.2 Rev. Baba Padmanji

Baba Padmanji[369] (1831-1906) was a highly respected Marathi Christian Writer. He was one of Wilson's students who paid *glowing* tribute to the American Marathi Mission for the metamorphosis it brought about among the low castes after they had accepted Christ.[370] Padmanji had attended speeches and sermons of noted Missionaries and Englishmen such as John Wilson, James Murry, William Henderson and Major Candy. Through these dialogues he learnt much about Christian and humanitarian outlook of the Missionaries. He was baptised in 1854. In all he published around 92 Marathi books and articles of both religious and secular character. The Bombay Tract and Book society (BTBS) had published many of his works. On the occasion of 30th anniversary of BTBS, Narayan Vaman Tilak addressed to him as the "Founder of Marathi Christian Literature."

He became prominent after his marathi work "Wanderings of Yamunabai" (*Yamuna Paryatan*) written in 1857[371] . It was interesting to know that the first Marathi book was written and published not in Maharashtra but in far away Bengal at the Srerampur Mission, in the

368 Sheela Patwardhan, *Op.Cit*, p. 161

369 He wrote his autobiography Arunodaya (Sunrise)

370 M. D. David, *Missions; Cross-cultural encounter and changes in Western India*, Manohar, Delhi 2001, p. 61

371 This novel which propagated Christianity and conversion was written by Padmanji for getting over some personal monetary problems.

Picture 6.1: Rev. Baba Padmanji
(Source: M. D. David, *Missions: Cross Cultural Encounters and Change in Western India,* Manohar, Delhi, 2001)

first decade of the 19th century. The famous Missionary Willam Carey prepared and published the first marathi grammar and dictionary (1810). The cyclonic affect created by early newspapers in Bengal had its impact on Bombay too. The first social novel to have social reform (widow remarriage) as its theme was "*Yamuna Paryatan*". Certain observations made in this novel can be quoted....The novel depicts clearly the means Missionaries used to entice local people to send their children to Missionary schools. The novel mentions that the father of heroin Yamuna send her to the Mission school because the school offered clothes and money as enticement.... The hero of the novel Vinayakrao is shown advanced of his time. He was not irrational like other young men of his age, he provided freedom to his wife Yamuna to pursue her likes and she used to spend her time in her room reading books. Naturally, he also mentions that her being well read and well informed was not liked by her mother in law[372]. Later Yamuna and Vinayak went for a journey and while traveling they meet some Hindu widows who were sad and some of them got into bad habits. During their wandering her husband dies (before his death he was baptized by Yamuna) later she married a Christian. The journey of Yamuna is geographical as well as intellectual. Between 15th November 1856 and 22nd August 1857 many write ups and reviews on this novel were published in *BG* which are as follows:

New work of Baba Padmanjee was highlighted [373]on the front page of *BG*. It says "the small work in Marathi is on miseries that arise from the prohibition of the remarriage of widows of the higher classes of the Hindus.... the work will be printed on good paper and bound in embossed cloth. Its price to subscribers will be one rupees and eight annas. Parties willing to subscribe are requested to send their names to the undersigned at the Free Church Institution, Bombay-- Baba Padmanjee". The narrative he called' *The Wanderings of Yamuna bai*', the manuscript of which was given for inspection to the learned author of the Marathi Grammar, Dadoba Pandurang[374].

In June month the feedbacks to the above books started appearing in *The Bombay Guardian*[375] : The new Marathi work by Mr. Baba Padmanji deserved special notice on many accounts. "Nothing like it has appeared in the Marathi language. Its great aim is to exhibit the melancholy condition of the Hindu widow, and the necessity of doing away with the caste-law which prohibits her re-marriage: and as the author desired to affect the minds of his countrymen as extensively and as profoundly as possible he has chosen the medium of fiction. The work is episodical. It affords a rare insight into the domestic life of the Hindus. There is one thing which we cannot but regard as a defect in Mr. Padamanji's book. The principal character, Venayikrao, is represented as a Christian in

372 Neelima Bhave, *Social Change in Early 19th Century Maharashtra as reflected in contemporary literary output:* Project report of Asiatic Society Fellowship, Mumbai, Jan – Dec 2000 (not numbered)

373 *BG*, November 15, 1856

374 He wrote an introductory essay in Sanskrit in this book

375 See *BG* of June 13, 1857 (pp.186-187), June 27 (p. 204), August 22, 1857 (p. 266)

sentiment". The above two columns were written by a Missionary editor showing a favorable view of the convert's book.

But a correspondent *A Hindu* had criticised the above book, saying "it has found no credit elsewhere, but amongst the Christian circles. It is not denied that the book will suit well the purposes of the Christians and their converts, but the Hindu community, to whom alone a work on remarriage of widow could be recommended, have justly condemned the work not only on account of its being mixed up with Christianity, but on account of the obscenities it contains". Hindu press had condemned the work including the Hindu *Hittechu* and *Dhumketu.* It was said that "*Dhumketu* has proposed that the "Wanderings of Yamunabai should be publicly consigned to flames by the Hindu community".

At the meeting of the United Students Association some disapproved of Padmanji's work, for introducing the Christian element into a work for Hindus; and some for alleged exaggerations in the Pictures drawn. On the other hand some defended the author, saying that "if he was a Christian he could not be blamed for writing as one, and otherwise justifying him".

Padmanji's work *'Examination of the claims of Deism'* in marathi language was in press in April 1858. The Dakshina Prize Committee published *Nibandhmala* consisting of 40 original selected and translated article by Baba Padmanji[376].

The front page report of *BG* (August 15, 1863) read "Mr. Baba Padmanji has conferred a great boon upon the public, by his compendium of *Molesworth's Marathi and English Dictionary.* "A dictionary is now a days one of the necessaries of life and few persons that wish to write their own language correctly or to acquire the foreign language will be content to remain without one or more".

His *Shalan Karita Maharashtra Deshanca Sankshipta Itihas* in 1866 was a text book published by the Christian Vernacular Translation Society. It was a rapid survey of the History of Maharashtra from the ancient times to the establishment of British Rule. Baba Padmanji wrote introduction to Mahatma Jyotiba Phule's *Kavya Sangraha* work "*Brahmanache Kasab*". He also checked the

376 *OCS*, July 1860, p. 277

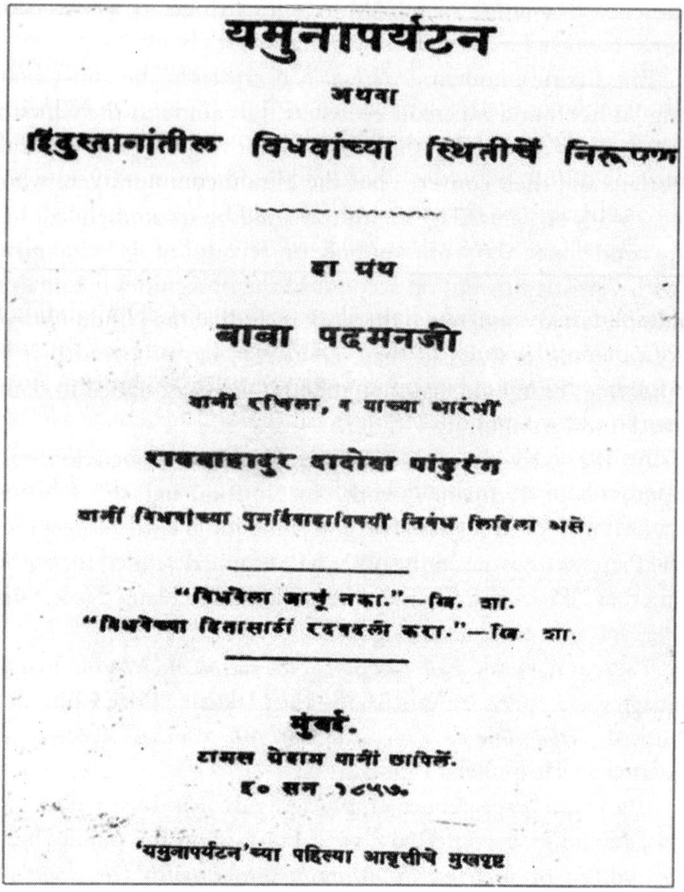

यमुनापर्यटन

अथवा

हिंदुस्थानांतील विधवांच्या स्थितीचें निरूपण

हा ग्रंथ

बाबा पद्मनजी

यांनीं रचिला, व याच्या आरंभीं

रावबाहादुर दादोबा पांडुरंग

यांनीं विधवांच्या पुनर्विवाहाविषयीं निबंध लिहिला असे.

"विधवेला जाचूं नका."—बि. शा.
"विधवेच्या हितासाठीं रदबदली करा."—बि. शा.

मुंबई.

टामस ग्रेहाम यांनीं छापिलें.

इ० सन १८५७.

'यमुनापर्यटन'च्या पहिल्या आवृत्तीचें मुखपृष्ठ

Plate 6.2: Baba Padmanji's work (Yamunparyatan)

proofs of his book "*Shivajicha Powada*" (1869)[377]. When Jyotibaji suffered illness in July 1888, it was Baba Padmanji who wrote of Maharaj Sayajirao Gaikwad to give financial help to ailing Mahatma Phule[378].

377 K. S. Karhadkar, *Baba Padmanji: Kal Va Kartutva (Marathi),* Maharashtra Rajya Sahitya ane Sanskriti Mandal, Mumbai,1979, p. 21

378 Veena Karhade, *Mahatma Jyotiba Phule* (Marathi), Lok Vanghmaya Graha, Mumbai, 2003, p. 33

A very interesting letter by "friends of the cause" in *BG* dated 29th May 1888 (p. 347) addressed to all Missionaries in Western India says Dear Sir, "It is with much sorrow we learn that the Bombay Tract and Book Society has had to stop all Vernacular Publications from lack of funds".

In the *BG* of November 24, 1888 the following suggestions had been given " that Baba Padmanji be sent by the society to all the churches – English and Native of Western India, Wherever Marathi is spoken – to take up the collections. A visit from him will not only help the society's cause, but will help us in our work, and will no doubt help some undecided seeker amongst the people to decide for Christ. And we are sure a great many Hindus who have read and are reading his works all over this land want to see and hear him. He will be able to plead the society's cause as no one else can.... that Bro. Baba Padmanjee be sent as the representative of the society and of the Marathi congregations of India to the home churches of England and America to plead for means to carry on the great and good work. A review was published in the Madras Christian College magazine of the life of Rev. Baba Padmanji which was compiled from his autobiography *Arunodaya*".

In 1880, Baba Padmanji wrote his book *What is in the Vedas?* Many interesting questions regarding the teaching and testimony of the Vedas are answered in this publication[379]. On January 8th Padmanji gave a very interesting lecture on the life of the Church in the first three centuries (wherein he spoke on in what way can the different churches of Bombay help one another). Later, it was published by BTBS in the form of a Marathi Pamphlet "*The Internal History of the Christian Church in some of its phases during the First Three Centuries*"[380].

The *BG* of September 17, 1904 (p. 2) carried a long letter by D. L. Joshi of Church Missionary Society written on 13th September 1904 to *BG* entitled "On the Attainment of Rev. Baba Padmanji's Baptismal Jubilee is published. It said "Padmanji was praised for his devotion for the production of Marathi Christian literature. When

379 *BG*, March 13, 1880, p. 14
380 *BG*, April 16, 1892, p. 8

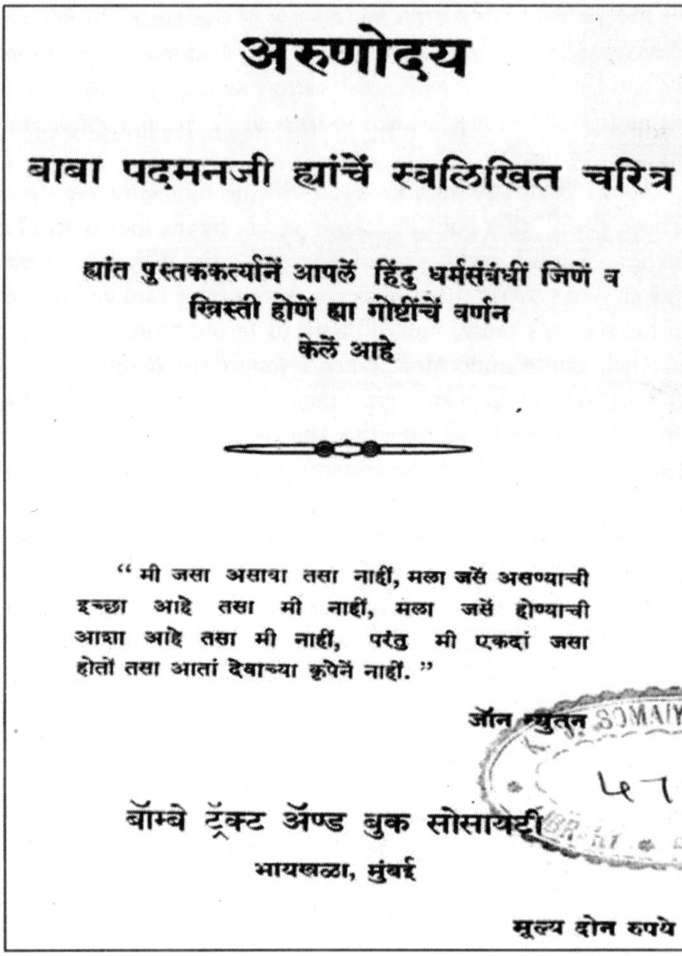

अरुणोदय

बाबा पद्मनजी ह्यांचें स्वलिखित चरित्र

ह्यांत पुस्तककर्त्यानें आपलें हिंदु धर्मसंबंधीं जिणें व
ख्रिस्ती होणें ह्या गोष्टींचें वर्णन
केलें आहे

“ मी जसा असावा तसा नाहीं, मला जसें असण्याची
इच्छा आहे तसा मी नाहीं, मला जसें होण्याची
आशा आहे तसा मी नाहीं, परंतु मी एकदां जसा
होतों तसा आतां देवाच्या कृपेनें नाहीं. ”

जॉन न्युटन

बॉम्बे ट्रॅक्ट ॲण्ड बुक सोसायटी
भायखळा, मुंबई

मूल्य दोन रुपये

Plate 6.1: Cover page of Baba Padmanji's Autobiography (*Arunodaya*)

the history of the Indian Church is written, your name will always figure as the chief Marathi Christian writer in its earliest stages….."

In *BG,* of October 02, 1905 (page 2), N. V. Tilak's wrote a letter from Rahuri to Baba Padmanji on the attainment of His Baptismal Jubilee. Tilak wrote his personal experience of Padmanji and his work. He says "my own conversion is due to the unknown European who put a copy of the New Testament in to my hands and next to you and none else.....You are the father of Christian - Marathi Literature and a greater author than any others whom I know in this presidency. Your writings are all useful but personally I love "*Arunodaya*[381]" and "*Anubhavasangraha*" very much". Baba Padmanji's reply to the above letter of N. V. Tilak said "I thank you very much for the letter you have addressed to me through *BG*".

6.3 Vishnu Bhaskar Karmarkar (Vishnupant)

Vishnu Bhaskar Karmarkar got converted in the year 1854 and by November 1857 he was licensed to preach[382]. In 1860 he was ordained as a pastor of the second Church in Ahmednagar. He had a great deal of poetic taste and musical ability and conducted Christian *Kirttans* in a most acceptable way[383]. He used to performed many *Kirtans* in the American Mission Church Bombay. The skill, with which he conducted them, drew a host of educated Hindus to the Church Hall and exalted their surprise[384]. He had established a printing press[385] partly with a view to relieve him and his family from dependence on Mission funds and partly to provide an industrial institution that might be helpful to converts. Some issues of *Bombay Guardian* were printed by him at this press[386]. Later his son Sumant Vishnu took over and was well known in the Bombay printing trade. At the Annual Subah at Ahmednagar in 1888 Vishnu Karmarkar spoke on 'Who is the Holy Spirit'[387].

Rev. Sumantrao and his wife Gurubai Karmarkar (also discussed separately) returned after their four year stay in United States in October 1893. At several public Missionary meetings it was expressed that the "Karmarkars had come as Missionaries". Mr. Karmarkar

381 Autobiography of Baba Padmanji (In English it was called Sunrise)
382 *OCS*, August 1858, p. 301
383 *BG*, April 26, 1884, p. 259
384 *BG*, August 27, 1881 p. 406
385 *BG* of January 07, 1882, last page mentions address as Sumant Vishnu Karmarkar, Anglo-Vernacular Printing Press, No. 36, Tank Street, New Nagpada, Bombay.
386 *BG*, August 13, 1881, front page
387 *BG*, November 3, 1888, p. 695

was of the view that he was a *Suwarttik* (an evangelist)[388] and not a Missionary of the foreign land.

6.4 Rev. Narayan Sheshadri

There were two Narayan's, who got converted to Christianity in the 19th Century., one Narayan Sheshadri and other Narayan Ramchandra Khisti[389]. Both were contemporary Brahmins but from different regions, one from Marathwada and the other from Ahmednagar.

Picture 6.2: Rev. Narayan Sheshadri
(**Source:** M. D. *David, Missions: Cross Cultural Encounters and Change in Western India,* Manohar, Delhi, 2001)

---

388 Though it is applied to anyone who preaches the Gospel it is peculiarly appropriate to one who has been chosen and ordained for the work.

389 Brother of Rev. Hari Pant Khisti, one of the first Indian Pastors of the American Marathi Mission in 1854.

In 1832, Due to John Wilson's (1804-1875) efforts the Missionaries of the General Assembly of the Church of Scotland[390] commenced their work with the establishment of the Ambroli School. The Indian convert teachers Dhanjibahi Nauroji, Hormasdji Pestonji[391] and Narayan Sheshadri taught at the school[392]. The baptism of Narayan Sheshadri had created much heat against the Missionaries in Maharashtra. Rev. Nesbit and J. Murry Mitchell's letter to Mr. Cook in *BG*, dated 22nd December 1843 talks about baptism of Narayan Shesahdri. It says Narayan had received his first lessons in English from Mr. Mitchell of Pune and for the last five years had been a diligent student of our English Education. The letter also mentions about his brother Shripat. Hormasdji and Narayan took lessons from Nesbit on systematic theology and scriptural interpretations. Mitchell taught them Church history, New Testament and Greek language. Hormasdji and Narayan were said to render valuable auxiliaries in the Missionary work. Hormasdji took charge of the superintendent of vernacular boy schools and Narayan had an important office in English institution.

In appcarancc Narayan Sheshadri was slightly below the average height with a full face, and weared no beard with the exception of a short heavy grey moustache. He wore a turban of snowy whiteness, which contrasted strongly with his swarthy complexion. His command on the English language was good and by 1881 a little foreign accent was noticeable (perhaps due to his visits abroad). He further mentions that "in a town (Bethel near Jalna) they had erected a Church and while constructing the building several trades were learned by his people who previous to the foundation of the Mission were pilferers and thieves. He further adds that the village had now masons, carpenters and gardeners and also a school which

390 It was the first non- governmental establishment to offer higher learning in Bombay that Wilson made his mark. It was the nucleus of the present day Wilson College.

391 Both these Parsis were Baptized by Dr. Wilson in 1839.

392 Mrudula Ramanna, *English Education and Social Change in Bombay City 1815-1858,* Ph.D Thesis, Bombay, 1985, p. 210

was called Bethany School in Philadelphia which contributed for this purpose" [393].

The two wonders of 1844[394] mentioned the native correspondent of the '*Bombay Times*' as

1. Shripat Sheshadri (discussed later) and
2. the appearance of the ganges in the island of Bombay

Narayan Shesadri was the first educated Brahmin who was received in to the bosom of the Christian Church in Bombay. While in Bombay he was often called '*Bombaika Padri*' by non christian natives, young and old. In September 29, 1856 he gave a discourse[395] at American Mission Chapel on "The past progress of education and the present crisis of the educated mind in Western India".

A *"Discourse on the past progress of Education and the Present crisis of the educated mind in Western India"* by Rev. Narayan Sheshadri at the American Mission Chapel, September 29, 1856 mentions the following.,

Table 6.1: Strength of Mission Schools (1856)
(Source : *BG*, October 18, 1856, pp. 336-337)

Year	*No. of Mission Schools*	*No. of Students*
1817	6	400 Boys
1820	21	1,050 Boys
1821	25	
1824	34	}about 2000 children
1826	39	

393 *BG*, January 01, 1881, p. 576

394 *Report of the Bombay Auxiliary Scottish Missionary Society*, 1844, pp. 6-7

395 *BG*, October 18, 1856 p. 336

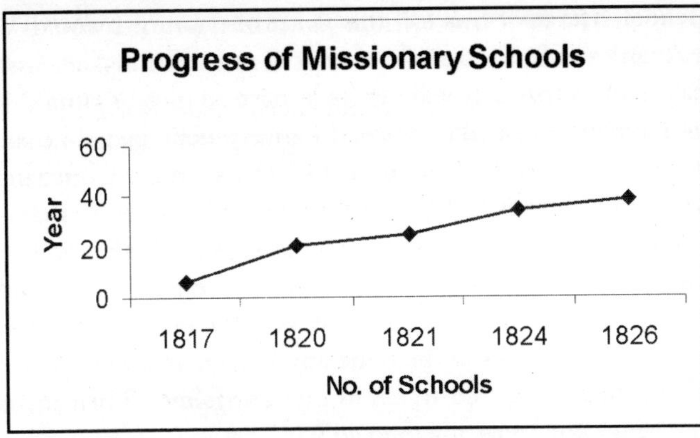

Chart 6.1: Chart showing the progress of Mission schools

6.4.1 Indapur-The First Missionary Station

The *BG* of January 24, 1863 (page 30) says "The Rev Narayan Sheshadri, a Native Missionary of the Free Church of Scotland, has founded a new Rural Mission in the Deccan.......the town of Indapur and the surrounding villages. Indapur is the largest town between Poona and Sholapore, and a good deal of inland trade is carried on their........It further mentions that thugges, dacoity, infanticide, suttee and merriah sacrifices have been put down, the civil rights of religious converts secured and the re-marriage of widows legalized (in the Indapur region).....

Though Indapur began well with a school, Church and a Mission station, it did not survive long. Sheshadri stayed at Indapur with his family. His presence as a learned man was fortunate for Indapur where he started 4 Marathi schools for children of all castes. He started an English school and taught in it, and also constructed a large hall to accommodate 500 people[396].

In August 1863, Narayan Sheshadri wrote from Indapur "Our quite labours for the last sixteen months have now fairly roused the higher classes of this town against us. They have threatened the Brahmin lads who attend our Anglo-vernacular school with excommunication and have succeeded in withdrawing them from

396 M. D. David, Missions.., *Op.Cit,* p. 288

the school. The poor lads feel this as act of tyranny. I would sooner have American Slavery than the slavery of caste. The higher classes are so jealous of us that they will not let us have an inch of ground in the town. If a house or site is to be sold by government, by public auction the common threat is "if you don't buy this soon the Christians will come and bid higher and thus get a footing in the town than what will you do?. Our most pressing want is a good Mission house with a number of outhouses for our Christian converts. We have hitherto lived through the kindness of the government in the travelers bungalow but this cannot be done any longer, and we expect every now and then to be told to vacate the bungalow. When the order comes we do not know where to go[397].

Dr. Sheshadri was a noble, monument of Dr. Wilson's spirit and work. The following paragraph contains the substance of a letter by ABC which appeared in *BG* of July 3, 1886 (pp.420 & 421). It talks of Rev. Narayan Sheshadri being honoured with the title and degree of Doctor of Divinity. "His energy in the propagation of his new faith by open preaching in the streets and on the sea-shore brought him prominently before all classes of people. He was the life and spirit of the Free Church Institution. He taught full 5 hours every day.......What was remarkable about him was that there was a sweetness about his way which charmed all. A happy, contented look always marked him and he seemed to be pleased with everybody".

The students, chiefly of the College Division[398], regarded him more as a friend than a teacher and spoke freely with him about their spiritual necessities. His house was an asylum for the poorer Native Christians[399] and a home for the educated converts of all Missions who met at his house, and his hospitality had been generous. Though his income was limited, his kindness had no limit. His style of living was simple and he stinted himself much with out any complain.

When Narayan first went to Indapur he lived in a mud house more fit for a cow-shed. He got up early in the morning and went

397 *BG*, August 22, 1863, front page

398 College division was started by Wilson in 1836.

399 As early as 1871 an indigenous Christian association called Native Christian Alliance was formed from all Christian denominations. Rev. Narayan Sheshadri was one member among the 16 Indian Pastors.

to the Maharwada, where he gathered the ragged, or rather naked children and catechised them under a tree.

Dr. Wilson's visit to Narayan at Indapur made an open remark "in the Mission Church from the pulpit, he never came across a more contented man than Narayan...while educated converts as a rule, are great grumblers and ambitious to equal the Europeans in the amount of their salaries[400].

6.4.2 Jalna[401] the Headquarter

A big one and a half page write-up "Account of a visit to Bethel[402] near Jalna"- talks of Rev. Narayan Sheshadri- Sabbath School. Sheshadri used to show the visitor houses, school, house, fields and wells in the village (the beautiful Mango tope cultivated was the source of revenue)[403].

A letter from Rev. Narayan Sheshadri appeared in *BG* of January 29, 1881 (pp.634 & 635) mentioning about his visit from San Francisco to Philadelphia and from Philadelphia to Boston to Lowell. He mentioned about 150th Anniversary of Presbyterianism at Oakville in Cumberland Valley. He recalled meeting Miss Emily Bissell and Miss Grace Wilder at Seminary at Mt. Holyoke. They both talked with him in Marathi, the language of their childhood. It said "...you will be glad to hear that these dear children of the Mission have given their hearts to the Lord, and mean to return to the land of their birth". Dr. Seelye who had a warm heart for India made enquiries about brethren Vishnu Pant and Shahu Rao. Narayan spoke of the late Dr. Bhau Daji with great admiration.

6.4.3 Writeups on his death

The *BG* of August 8, 1891 (front page) says that..... "the death of Dr. Narayan Sheshadri[404] will be deeply felt by the whole Native

400 An enclosed platform for preacher.

401 The *OCS* of October 1860 carries on pages 386-401 and again in November 1860, page 442 shows detailed information on Journal of Missionary Labour at Jalna by Mr. Ganpat Raghunath.

402 A Christian village established by Rev. Sheshadri

403 *BG*, January 7, 1882, pp. 5-6

404 He died in Glasgow while crossing the Atlantic Ocean from USA to Scotland.

Christian Community of Western India. Mr. Dhanjibhai Nauroji said " within a month he has lost two of his dearest friends, the late Rev. Hormasdji Pestonji and now Dr. Sheshadri. Dr. Sheshadri and Late George Bowen had a constant companionship. A correspondent says that in days past they were always together in open-air preaching, and together were assaulted, cow-dunged, abused, cursed".

Various American papers covered Sheshadri's recent visit there. One of his objects in visiting America appears to have been connected with his desire to study America's industrial enterprises with a view to introducing some of them among the Natives of India. The New York *Christian Advocate*[405] recalls his visit to that country as a delegate to the Evangelical Alliance in 1873, when his appearance was every-where greeted with the greatest interest and applause. On the same issue of *BG* on page 3 a special news (with signature of Dhanjibhai Nauroji dated August 4th, 1891) says "The Late Dr. Narayan Sheshadri - The First Brahmin Convert in Bombay". It says "Rev. Sheshadri was born in the territories of H. H. Nizam. In the Beginning of 1838 he came to Bombay for education, and then the whole process of his conversion is given..... Since at that time John Wilson was in Scotland he was baptised by late Rev. Missionary Robert Nesbit in September 1843. Besides, the scriptural instruction of the Missionaries, Sheshadri was most impressed by Nesbit's lecture on the holiness of God. His little brother, Shripat's case was tried in the Supreme Court, as the High Court was then called, and being found a minor he was delivered to the custody of his father. His case created a great excitement among the Hindus. He had broken caste by eating with his Christian brother, and the question arose whether he could be restored to caste. The matter was referred to a conclave of holy Brahmins at Benares, who decided that he could not be taken back into caste. He remained out of it up to the day of his death, a few years since[406]....Dr. Sheshadri was a born teacher....... But, he was pre-eminently a Missionary. Missionary work was a passion with him. Jesus Christ and Him crucified was the theme that lay nearest to his heart".

405 Name of a news paper

406 Some books say that Shripat was readmitted in to Hinduism after undergoing purification or *Shuddi* Ceremony (M. D. David, *Op Cit*, p. 276)

"…. Some 30 years ago he left Bombay on account of the climate of this city not agreeing with his wife. He went to the Deccan and took up Indapur as his first station. Labouring here for sometime, he went on a visit to Jaulna. He met with a considerable encouragement at that place. This led him to make it his 2nd Missionary station, dividing his time between it and the first, Indapur------ With wonderful energy and activity, he organised the Native Church at Jaulna, and was developing it, When an attack of sickness obliged him to leave the station. His medical adviser asked him to take a decided change, and with this object he went to Japan, America and Scotland. It was in the latter country, which he visited for the 3rd time (as also America) that this great Native Missionary finished his course. Thus passed away one of the most genial, sympathetic men, and a devoted servant of the Lord. May his mantle fall upon those who survive him". One of the front pages of *BG* of Saturday August 29, 1891 also covering the particulars on the death of Dr. Narayan Sheshadri.

6.5 Pandita Ramabai

Pandita Ramabai's (1857-1922) worked for the cause of upliftment of Indian women. Uma Chakravarty locates Pandita Ramabai's life and contribution as one of the first feminist of India. Ramabai's book *The High Caste Hindu Women*[407] (1887) is regarded as one of the earliest feminist writings in Western India (of which 10,000 copies were sold). During her two year sojourn in USA she undertook this work in order to marshall moral and financial support from the American public for her project to help widows[408]. In this way, the newly established Ramabai Association of Boston had collected

407 *BG,* November 26, 1887, p. 761

408 Meera Kosambi (ed), *Pandita Ramabai's feminists and Christian Conversions,* Research Centre for Women's Studies, S.N.D.T. Women's University, Bombay, 1995, p. 2

sufficient funds ($30,000 by May, 1888)[409] to support a secular widows home in India for a period of 10 years[410].

Ramabai's trip to England and America made her witness better gender relations between men and women.

Picture 6.3: Pandita Ramabai and stamp issued by India Post
(Source: American Mission Report of 1900, Vol. XXX, March 1900, No.3)

Isabel Hart, wrote about Pandita Ramabai in Christian Advocate which was published in *BG* of May 22, 1886 (p. 329). It goes as "The Presence of this remarkable Hindu woman in our country (Ramabai was in US from March, 1886 to Oct, 1888) has elicited a good deal of interest and inquiry concerning her history, religious views and expereince. As a confession of Christian faith, Ramabai sought baptism in the Church of England, but not as the door of entrance into that or any other denominational fold, nor as the profession of adoption of the formula of any council or Church of creed. She reminds one of the simple faith, distinct from all subtle ties and superfluities of doctrine. Ramabai insisted on the essential differences there must ever be between the type of Christianity peculiar to the East and West, to the Asiatic and European mind. The former is less doctriine and dogmatic. she said 'Me cannot be as jelly

409 Geraldine Forbes 'Education for Women' in *Women and Social Reform in Modern India* ed. Sumit Sarkar and Tanika Sarkar, CUP, New Delhi, 2007, p. 93

410 Meera Kosambi, *At the intersection of gender Reform and Religious Belief. Pandita Ramabai's contribution and the Age of Consent controversy,* RCWS Gender Series, Mumbai, 1993, p. 74

just to be cast into your moulds and stamped with your peculiarities and phraseology." Hart says the word Ramabai would speak to Missionaries would be something like this. "Go to my people with the simple desire to do them good as far as you can put yourselves in their place, study sympathetically their creed, their civilization, their customs. Don't too rashly disturb or too roughly oppose and abuse these. Show unto them the more excellent way, but don't be too anxious to make and mould and report converts at once. Love them, teach them, let the light of the Gospel shine, and that love shall win that teaching shall uplift, that light will purify and pervade".

Ramabai was instrumental in establishing Sharada Sadan near Wilson College in 1889 contributing towards so called industrial work of Missions. Various vocational courses served the widows to earn a living without leaving their homes.

Pandita Ramabai's write up on 'Child widows and their ill treatment and suffering' has been covered in many issues of *BG*. The year 1895 saw exclusive write-ups with a photograph in *BG* issues and the only Indian covered in these write-ups is Pandita Ramabai. In the annual gathering of the Bombay Bible Women Sabha which took place in rainy season in Bombay in 1895, many Marathi Christians and Bible women took part. The subject of the Jews was specially discussed with following bibliography:

1. History of the Jews from Abraham to the Captivity - Rev. Baba Padmanji.
2. History of the Jews in captivity - Rev. Tukaram Nathuji.
3. History of the Jews from the captivity to the coming of Christ - Rev. E. S. Hume.
4. Present condition of Jews in the World - Miss Campbell.
5. Full field prophecies concerning the Jews - Miss. Patterson
6. Unfulfilled prophecies concerning the Jews - Rev. M. B. Fuller
7. History of Bene Israelites, past and present- Miss Trott.
8. How to bring the Jews to Christ - Miss Campbell.
9. A recent trip to Palestine - Dr. Gurubai Karmarkar.
10. Is Jesus coming again ? - Pandita Ramabai.

In front page of *BG*, June 13,1891 an interview of Pandita Ramabai was published wherein she was asked "Are you satisfied with the results so far ?" to which Pandita replied "I should have rejoiced to see larger results, but considering the difficulties, I feel I have much cause for thankfulness. Take the one fact-out of these 30 widows I have the assurance from their own lips that their coming here has saved nearly 20 of them from suicide, starvation or a life of shame. This fact alone is an abundant reward for all our toil and expense".

PANDITA RAMABAI AND HER FAMILY OF WIDOWS

From a photograph by Mrs. Trimbak Canaran.]

Picture 6.4: Pandita Ramabai and her family of Widows
(Source: *BG*, September 5, 1891)

The *BG* of September 5, 1891 says "one by one thirty widows, varying in age from nine to twenty-three, were entrusted to her care. ......Her aim is to train the widows to earn their own living in an independent profession according to their capacities, as teachers, nurses, or any other suitable occupation......(an illustration showing Pandita Ramabai and her family of widows is also seen)". The *BG* of 3rd October 1891 (page 6) gave a write-up about the industrial training given to the widows at Sharada Sadan.

Pandita Ramabai supported Gokhale's allegations that two Poona women had been sexually molested by British troops during the plague in late 19th Century Poona[411].

INDIAN WIDOWS AT THE SHARADA SADAN

Picture 6.5: Indian Widows at the Sharada Sadan
(Source: *BG*, October 3, 1891)

"Ramabai was called the most unusual woman of her time. It is said for one thing she had an excellent knowledge of Sanskrit, supposedly the preserve of males. For another, she had become a Christian, something only a handful of Maharashtra's Brahmins had done. Thirdly, she believed that women had a right to their own opinions. She had no intention of exchanging the yoke of the Indian priestly tribe for that of male European clergy men ...Pandita Ramabai's conversion, her forcefulness in deed and word, and above all the seeming loneliness of her protest at this time might lead one to suppose that it would be folly to see her as representative of a great deal more than herself. Yet it is clear that there was much in Ramabai's background that was emphatically Indian. It is undeniable

411 Ramabai wrote a letter in May 1897 issue of *BG* (*BG* was a paper apparently sponsored by another contrapuntal element, a small group of European radicals, with Non conformist connections, in Bombay)

NATIVE GIRLS SCHOOL CHURCH OF SCOTLAND MISSION POONA.

Picture 6.6: Photograph of Native girls School at Pune
(Source : *BG* August 22, 1891)

that women had been and were in many respects in a position of real subordination in Maharashtra …To some extent, Ramabai's support of Gokhale's challenge to the Raj in 1897 may have reached across religion and caste, it is apparently still remembered today in a Marathi ballad[412].

"Certainly Pandita Ramabai's Plague protest, like that of Dr. Edith Pechey Phipson[413], had about it the ring of feminine assertiveness. But when Ramabai was asked how she differed from Pechey Phipson she pinched her arm and said 'you forget ……. She has a white skin which I have not.' As we see race is often part of the gender equation just as gender was part of the race equation"[414].

---

412 See Meera Kosambi's article Pandita Ramabai and Social Reform in Maharashtra in N. K. Wagle (ed) *Writers, Editors and Reformers: Social and Political transformations of Maharashtra* 1830-1930, Manohar, New Delhi, 1999.

413 She was one of the first women medical graduates in Britain, and was medical officer in charge of the first women's hospital in Bombay.

414 I. J. Catanach 'The Gendered Terrain of Disaster?' in *South Asia: Journal of South Asian Studies*, Vol. XXX, No. 2, August 2007, p. 250

Pandita Ramabai's work occurs in many issues of *BG*. A coverage on Pandita Ramabai's 'Widow Home'[415] starts with the 'Agitation on the Age of Consent Bill'. It highlights that every possible source of pleasure is cutoff from a widow's life. Moreover, she was blamed as a cause of her husbands death. An article[416] entitled Industrial training for Indian Widows shows the touch of livelihood given to Indian widows at Sharda Sadan. Special mention should be made of a write up entitled " Poilished Corner Stones from an Indian Curry"[417]. It highlights Pandita Ramabai's early career and later her role in Sharda Sadan, Pune. It also highlights her tussel with the advisory committee comprising of Hindu social reformers of the Sadan over liberal permission to girls who wish to attend her family worship which she called Christian liberty.

An Inspirational voice in an era when women in India did not have a voice, Ramabai's lectures, especially the one before the Hunter Commission[418] on September 5, 1881 moved even the empress Queen Victoria and inspired the establishing of women's hospitals and the training of the first woman doctors in India[419].

Sir William Hunter in a lecture delivered in Edinburg (1881) talked high of Pandita Ramabai. He mentioned about her early life and the three institutions (Sharda, Mukti and Kripa Sadan) as good places which are of use to the widows[420]. The Sharda Sadan (Home of Wisdom) introduced a structural change in the patriarchical social set-up by carving out a new space for women outside the private domain, though not quite with the public domain. It was a semi-public space where women were to be given education and skills towards economic self-reliance, hitherto unheard of concept in the upper castes. Godubai (renamed Anandibai after her marriage to Dr. D. K. Karve) stayed at Sharda Sadan.

---

415 *BG*, September 05,1891, p. 6

416 *BG*, October 03, 1891, p. 6

417 *BG*, March 02, 1895, p. 6

418 Before the Hunter Commission Ramabai stressed the urgent need for Women doctors and teachers.

419 Pandita Ramabai, *A Testimony of our inexhaustible Treasure*, Pandita Ramabai Mukti Mission, Pune, 2001.

420 *BG*, December 14, 1901, p. 9

Mukti was Ramabai's second school established 30 miles outside of Poona at Khedgaon due to famine of 1897. It became the home for girls who had experienced the horrors of famine. When Lord Sandhurst led Newspaper attacks upon Pandita Ramabai (since she had stated facts concerning the government Plague administration in Poona) the *BG* protected her by highlighting on its very front page of October 16, 1897. It said "There appears to be conspiracy of officials to destroy her reputation and to break up her admirable and unique Christian work.........The foremost Indian women of this age will not lack practical Christian sympathy. Nor will she lack the protection of an ALMIGHTY POWER".

A. B. Shah, who edited the letters and correspondence[421] of Pandita Ramabai, described Pandita Ramabai as 'the greatest woman produced by modern India and one of the greatest Indians in all history. Her achievements as a Champion of Women;s rights and as a pioneer in the fields of Women's education and social reform remain unrivalled even after a lapse of nearly a century since she first appeared on the scene... from her childhood Ramabai's life was an arduous one. Her father was persecuted for trying to educate his wife Laxmibai. To escape this persecution, the family set out on a long pilgrimage during which Laxmibai taught Ramabai Sanskrit. At 20 Ramabai was publicly honoured by the Shastris of Calcutta as a Pandita. In 1880, Ramabai married a Brahmo Lawyer, Bipin Behari Das Medhavi, but he died of Cholera two years later leaving Ramabai with her infant daughter Manorama. Ramabai traveled to England in June 1883 to Study Medicine. She traveled at her own expense but made arrangements to stay with the nuns of Wantage. She was to earn her living there by teaching Marathi to nuns who would be sent to Western India as Missionaries.... After three years in England, She went to the US where she was lionized. *The High Caste Hindu Widow* highlighted the Brahmanical Patriarchy that prevailed in all parts of India and specifically focused attention on Maharashtra. It shows Ramabai's capacity to present a coherent and convincing argument on the double standards of morality making distinctions between men and women. It also critiques the male

421 Published by Maharashtra State Board for Literature and Culture, Bombay, 1977.

reformers for their undue emphasis on remarriage of widows in a situation where most men were reluctant to marry widows and those who did faced obstracism.[422]

Picture 6.7: Pandita Ramabai's daughter (Manorama)
(Source : American Mission Report of 1900, Vol. XXX, March 1900, No. 3, p.99)

A write-up in *The Times Of India* February 8, 1888 (p.6) entitled 'The Cases of Rukhmabai and Ramabai' also quotes the above work of Ramabai. The write-up says Ramabai has witnessed the misery inflicted in India on Child-widows- i.e. on Children who have been betrothed and have been left husbandless even before they were married. She may have exaggerated the misery which these child-widows undergo. But facts are facts. The number of child-widows under 9 years of age is 78,976, from ten years of age is 207,388 from 15 to 19 years of age were 383,736[423]. Ramabai, herself a widow, though not a child-widow, wishes to open a home

422 Uma Chakravarti and Preeti Gill (Eds) *Shadow Lives: Writings on Widowhood, Zubaan,* Delhi 2001, p. 76

423 Pandita Ramabai, *The High Caste Hindoo Women*, Maharashtra State Board for Literature and Culture, reprint, 1981, Mumbai, p. 109

and a school for such child-widows as are willing to come to her. She wishes to educate them, to guard them from evil, and in time to make them useful members of society, it may be happy wives and intelligent mothers.

Ramabai wrote in Both English and Marathi

1. *Stree Dharma Neeti* (Morals for Women)
2. The Cry of Indian Women(1883)
3. An Autobiographical Account 1883
4. Indian Religion 1886
5. Famine Experience 1897
6. A Short History of Kripa Sadan or Home of Mercy 1903
7. A Testimonay of our Inexhaustible Treasure 1907
8. The word seed 1908.

Ramabai's greatest legacy was her effort, the first in India to educate widows and the pupils she left behind to carry her work.

"India has had some wonderful proofs of what Christ can do for women in Ramabai, in her tireless love and self denial for her Indian sisters... In the energetic Mrs. Sorabjee, with her Victoria night School; and in her accomplished daughter Cornelia, the first lady graduate of the Western College, the first lady professor in the Indian College whose students are men and the first lady law student; in the earnest quartette of sisters, Sunderbai[424], Manjubai, Shevantibai, Jaywantibai Powar in their evangelistic efforts for women in Toru Dutt "The Gentle Poetess" in Krupabai Sathianadhan[425], the Authoress in Chandrabose the esteemed lady Principal of the Bethune College, in Lilavanti Singh, the efficient teacher in the Lucknow College for Women. In Lakshmi Gorey, the sweet Hymn writer, in Dr. Gurubai Karmarkar the lady Physician; and in hundreds of other Christian women in equal or humbler ranks of life" [426].

---

424 Sunderbai translated into Marathi a little booklet containing a very remarkable narrative of Divine healing by Miss Hopwood (She was a Missionary in China)

425 Krupabai (1862-1894) wrote autobiographical novel '*Saguna* - A story of native Christian life' in 1886 and also her novel '*Kamala*: A story of Hindu life'

426 *BG*. April 15, 1899, p. 4

6.6 Rev. Narayan Vaman Tilak (1861-1919) and Laxmibai Tilak

N. V. Tilak (1861–1919) was the Marathi Church's greatest poet[427] and hymn composer. He was born in Ratnagiri district and he died in Bombay, his area of work had been Ahmednagar. He was baptised in February 1895, at American Marathi Mission, Bombay. The *BG* gave a detailed life history of Narayanrao and the process how he slowly became Christian in February 16, 1895 issue (p.10 & 11). He read Bible intently and was much impressed by the contents of 'Sermon on the Mount'.

Picture 6.8: Rev. Narayan Waman Tilak
(Source : Marathi Mission Report, 1908, p.6)

He accepted Christianity in 1895 for in the Christian religion he found the fatherhood of God and the brotherhood of man. After his conversion, Tilak tried to understand Christianity from Rev. Abbot, who had baptised him and also Dr. Hume at Ahmednagar. Upon this Tilak's composition had took a different turn. He started composing Kirtanas based on the life of Christ, keeping to the traditions of the saints of Maharashtra. His hymns were hence called '*ovi*' and *abhang chhandas*. He believed that doctrines of Christianity when explained through the musical forms which were popular in Maharashtra, which will help to remove the feeling of alienness of Christianity. In order to increase the number of Christian devotional

427 He inherited his love for writing poetry through his mother

hymns in Marathi, Tilak kept on publishing *Kirtans* and *Abhangas* through *Dnyanodaya,* Christian Weekly in Marathi of which he was the editor[428].

It was the contact with Reverend Narayan Vaman Tilak that instilled into famous Marathi poet Keshavsut a love for writing poetry. In 1895-96 Keshavsut was on the staff of the *Dnyanodaya.* Keshavsut's near relations were afraid that he, too might be converted into a Christian, as he was intimately connected with *Dyanodaya* and Rev. Tilak. Keshavsut loved reading the bible, and he once even told his younger brother Sitaram that he was inclined to embrace Christianity. Though Keshavsut and Tilak were friends, their poetry was very different. Keshavsut was more virile and had sudden flashes while Tilak was more somber and even. Tilak admired Keshavsut so much that he wrote a poem on the latter in his lifetime and he wrote two eleges on the death of Keshavsut in *Kavyaratnavali,* January 1906 and in *Manoranjan* , February 1906.

N. V. Tilak's name occurs as Instructor in Non-Christian Systems at the Theological Seminary on page 29 of American Marathi Mission Report 1898.

Narayan Vaman Tilak with his wife Laxmibai[429] (who became Christian in 1900) helped to elevate Marathi literature in general and Marathi Christian literature in particular. He also initiated the first Marathi Poets Conference in Jalgaon (2-3 March 1907). Laxmibai Tilak and Lady Ewing of Lahore were the two distinguished visitors at Annual Womens Conference held at Wai (near Mahabaleshwar) on February 17, 1932.

Pandita Ramabai and Narayan Vaman Tilak were first generation Christians, who were initially attracted to Christ intellectually and when they grew spiritually they accepted him as their saviour.

---

428 Santhasheela Sathianathan, *Contribution of Saints and Seers*, Vol. II, Kanishka Publication, New Delhi, 1996, p. 526

429 A Parallel can be seen with Govind Chander Dutt's family – one of the earliest in Calcutta to be radically influenced by British Colonialist and Missionary discourse. His wife Kshetramoni initially resisted to conversion but later became involved with the Oxford Mission in Calcutta (In Chandani Lokuge edited, Toru Dutt, *Collected Prose and Poetry,* OUP, New Delhi, 2006, p. viii)

"Rev. N. V. Tilak was also regarded the most gifted poet of the day, a born poet and thoroughly conversant with Sanskrit. He produced high class poetry, admired and appreciated even by non-Christians"[430]. In fact he was Marathi Church's greatest poet and hymn composer. He started with abhorrence of Christianity with also writing against it but one day on a railway journey a European or American gentleman got in to conversation with him and after a pleasant talk of some hours told Mr. Tilak that he was half a Christian already and gave him a copy of the New Testament. Reading this opened his eyes. He was particularly struck with the character of Jesus Christ and found many of his difficulties solved in the Bible. His first prayer was for some books that he wanted. The next day he found those very books in some waste paper in his office. It was all a miracle. He did nothing, God did it all.

He played a unique role in the revival of Marathi poetry that took place in the closing years of the 19th century. He wrote both secular and devotional poems and flourished as a poet of flowers and children. He became popularly known as the Wordsworth of Maharashtra or the Rabindranath Tagore of Western India[431]

Interestingly *BG* Tilak and N. Y. Tilak were contemporaries, but differed in political temperament. The latter always believed that a moderate nationalist programme would be a wiser path to follow. This is why the two Tilaks have been referred to as Tilak the 'lion' and Tilak the 'lamb'. Vaman Tilak won the confidence of the Christian community and urged them to become a force on the side of Indian Nationalism[432]. He also wrote *Khristayan*, the poetical life of Christ in Marathi Lyric verse, which was completed by his wife and son Devdatt. After his death in Bombay in May 9th 1918, Laxmibai added 64 chapters and died at Nasik on February 24, 1936. The preface editing and proof reading was done by a Non-Christian poet S. K. Kanetkar of the Fergusson college[433].

---

430 *BG*, November 26, 1904, p. 10

431 Louis D. Silva, *The Christian Community and the National Mainstream*, Spicer College Press, Poona, undated, p. 59

432 *Ibid*, p. 61

433 *Missionary Herald*, June 1939, Vol. C., XXXV, No. 6, p. 264

Laxmibai Tilak's marathi autobiography entitled *Smriti Chitre* remains a wonderful example of wifely loyalty[434] and became all time classic of Marathi literature. Laxmibai Tilak's autobiography 'I follow after' was translated by E Josephine (OUP, New Delhi).

6.7 Nehemiah Gore and Gurubhai Karmarkar

Nehemiah Gore (Neelkantha Shastri Gore) 1825- 1895, first joined CMS and later in 1865 he joined the Anglo-Catholic fold. He wrote a rational refutation of the Hindu Philosophical systems in 1862. This book discusses succinctly the six[435] philosophical systems of the Hindus (his work was confined more to the outside area of present study)

Gurubai took her M. D. from Women's Medical College, Philadelphia. The American Mission Report for 1894 talks about a new station opened at Bassein, in the Thana district by Rev. Sumantrao V. Karmarkar and his wife Dr. Gurubai Karmarkar. Mr. Kamarkar says "The work at Bassein commenced in February last year when houses for the dispensary and the reading room were rented without much difficulty". Dr. Gurubai's report says "about 1500 women and children and about 150 men were treated. This does not include those that were treated in the villages. People of 40 different castes attended the dispensary. The majority of the patients belong to the poor classes. The curse of drink and the oppression of the money lenders have reduced them to such an extent that they live from hand to mouth".

The American Mission Report for 1896, (p. 41), mentions a new school at Bassein where most of the boys belonged to the farmer, copper smith and gold smith caste. Dr. Karmarkar in 1896 writes "this is the third year of my dispensary for women and children at Bassein. Medical aid was given to a goodly number daily. The bible instruction was much more thorough in the dispensary this year owing to our new and energetic bible women Chandrabai, sister of Rev. Baba Padmanji[436]".

434 *Dyanodaya*, February 21, 1946, Vol.105, No. 8
435 *Nyaya, Vaishesika, Sankhya, Yog, Minmausa* and *Vedanta*
436 The American Mission Report for 1896, p. 69

The American Marathi Mission Report of 1917 (p.38) covers Dr. Gurubhai's departure for America. Her medical work in Bombay had been under the guidance of E. S. Picken. Rev. Gurubai's report on Baby Welfare Week in Vengurla[437] talks of child welfare and agriculture exhibition. Mrs. Evans was responsible for the baby welfare work. Several babies in batches of 5 or 6 in each of the three grades, were ready to be examines for a medal, irrespective of caste or creed. The Missionary spirit of equality for all women seemed very prominent. "It was beautiful to see women of all castes rubbing shoulders against each others. Even the shoemaker women freely mingled with the others".

The best considered baby by the judges in each group was to receive a dainty silver medal. One of the *bonnie mochi* babies was such a recipient and no one seemed to resent it. Mrs. Evans had very thoughtfully arranged for something for each child that appeared for the contest to avoid either the babies or the mother's disappointment. Mrs. Evans used to visit homes regularly every month and give advice on the care and feeding of babies[438].

The above Indian contributors made a gradual transition in Indian society which further paved a way for the process of inculturation which is discussed in Chapter 7.

437 *WIN*, March 1933, front page

438 *WIN*, January 1962, p. 8

Chapter 7

Inculturation Process

Chapter 7

Inculturation Process

7.1 Inculturation

7.1.1 The Process

The word "enculturation" is an anthropological expression that means the growth of the child into human society. The Louvin missiologists Pierie Charles S. J. used inculturation in this sense and meant by it the process of adaptation that a new convert or a "young Church" has to go through in order to become a full member of the group that is the Church[439].

What Ricci wanted to do in China and de Nobili in India was for those times revolutionary but those pioneers were concerned more with "adaptation" than "inculturation". The outward manifestations, the linguistic formulations, buildings, pictures, symbols, community life styles, laws liturgical forms etc in the churches in India need not be a carbon copy of the situation in Europe. As a human process, inculturation is a heart to heart encounter. It is not the colour of one's skin, or one's origin, one's language, one's activity or level of education that is the decisive factor. It has been described by St.

439 Karl Muller, Inculturation and Evangelization in *Indian Missiological Review*, Vol.12, No.1, April 1990, p. 30

Augustine as "Heart speaks to heart". Inculturation is a kind of encounter. Inculturation suggests transformation[440].

Since, human conditions differ from culture to culture. Missions too vary from one culture to another that is the nature of Christology's too differs for instance, for the blacks in USA, whoever contributes towards the removal of racial discrimination is a Christ. In erstwhile USSR whoever helped towards individual freedom was Christ. In Latin America whoever liberates the peasantry from economic exploitation and from repressions will be considered a messiah. The point is whether it is economic, social or political, all these Missions came at human emancipation. It is the human concern that constitutes the core of the universalisms of Jesus[441].

Prof Kellogg of Princeton's speaks three points to naturalise the Church in Heathen Countries. He said …

1. The standards of Doctrine and Polity must be adopted as closely as possible to the actual specific conditions of society in each country.
2. All churches, at one in their fundamental articles of Doctrine and Polity, Waiving minor distinctions, should be organically united.
3. Finally in due time and order there must be entire ecclesiastical severance from the parent churches in Indians and America[442].

Fred Field Goodsell in a full page article entitled 'The greatest thing in India, highlights about the Christian Church which is central from many angles of vision. He said "It is not an institution but a fellowship of which the Christ is the creative center. We may close schools and hospitals. We may retrench at innumerable points, or we may expand our lines of service. We do not close the Christian Church. It is a spirit that lives no matter what happens to budget.

440 Karl Muller, Inculturation and Evangelization in *Indian Missiological Review,* Vol. 12, No.1, Karl Muller, p. 37

441 K. Wilson, *The Twice Alienated Culture of Dalit Christians,* Booklinks, Hyderabad, 1982, p. 58

442 *BG,* January 31, 1880, p. 584

The Christian Church has begun to put its roots down in to the soils of India"[443].

Christianity entered upon a second stage of its history with the coming of the Portuguese in India in the beginning of the Sixteenth Century. Portuguese had established political domination in some parts of Konkan. One of the most famous Portuguese Governors in India was Alfonso de Albuquerque who encouraged intermarriage between Portuguese soldiers and native women which resulted in a strong consolidation of Portuguese rule in India. The offspring's of such marriage came to be known as Luso- Indians who obtained employment in factories and armouries and it was from these Luso-Indians that the European East India Companies recruited a large number of artillery men.

The descendents of the Luso - Indians are known today as Goanese, most of whom live in Goa, Bombay and the West Coast of India. Their Portuguese surnames D' Souza, Pinto, Pereira - together with some cultural characteristics are the sole reminders to the Goan's of their Portuguese heritage[444].

7.2 The Vasai Chapter

7.2.1 Introduction

Bassein is perhaps the most irritating name of all Anglo Indian corruptions for there are three towns in Indian Empire so named by Europeans (Bassein in Burma, Bassein in Bombay and Bassein in Berar).[445]

The converted Christians in and around Vasai namely the East Indians composed of wide variety of people including brahmins, Prabhus, Panchkalshi's, Chaukalshi's, Sonars, Khatris, Bhandaris, Kharpatil's, Kunbis, Kumbhar's, Nhavi's, Dhobi's, Kolis, Mahars and Chamar's. Since many of the above converts did not knew Portuguese they could not correctly pronounce the Portuguese names given to

443 *The Missionary Herald*, July 1935, p. 300

444 Evelyn Abel, *The Anglo Indian Community - Survival in India*,Chankya Pub, New Delhi, 1988, pp. 9-10

445 Major R. C. Temple, The Name "Bassein" in *The Indian Antiquary*, January 1893, p. 18

them, some names were thus pronounced with the oMission of either the middle or the last syllable and some with the substitution of some letters or syllables. Portuguese influence on surnames is visible.

Christianity in Mumbai associated with Western traditions and names, has gradually been Indianised, with a growing number of Christians in the city preferring to retain not just Indian names and attire but also their own culture whilte adopting Christ as their saviour. Many protestant churches have services in Indian languages ranging from Marathi to Malayalam and from Gujarati to Telugu.

Vasai was under the Archdiocese of Goa between 1535-1886 and later on under the Archdiocese of Damaun (Daman) between 1886-1928 and finally it came under the Archdiocese of Bombay in 1928 and today it has its own Diocese.

7.2.2 Role of various congregations in Vasai

The Chief congregations in Vasai are

- The Franciscans (spread of Christianity in North Vasai, Pali, Mulgaon area)
- The Jesuits (Sandor, Papdy and Manikpur)
- The Dominicans (Remedy, Tarapur, Palghar, Dahanu region)
- The Augustinians (Merces)
- Green Vasai- Save Vasai Campaign, Christian Priests had assumed Indian dress, learnt local languages.

Bassein had very few buildings before the coming of the Portuguese colonies. There was a Muslim fort which was the focus of the local administration. Most people lived in wattle and daub houses. Thus the architectural development of Bassein can be traced with the bulidings of the fort by the Portuguese. New buildings put up by the Portuguese at Bassein are documents of social change with thrust on Church buildings as an important item of construction activity. The rural areas also developed in to distinct parishes with the Church as its focal point. The building of Church complexes was supervised by Priests. With the help of books and their keen intellect these priests confidently used local building material and labour to put up new structures which were additions to their existing architectural models.

The vernacular style of architecture which subsequently developed was influenced to some extent by the colonisers. The Portuguese used to keep order and life and property fairly safe. Large areas of salt waste with reclaimed tillage were encouraged and new crops such as chilies, ginger and fruits like pineapple and figs were introduced.

In Portuguese times Mahim was the most important possessions of the Jesuits of Bandra who it is said, elevated palm growing in to a fine art[446].

Foreign traders and artisans were encouraged to settle in the Maratha State. '*Firangis*' (most probably the Portuguese, were experts in cane work and were given appointments such as those of gunners and the Christian artisans from Goa were employed on building work. Christian artisans were employed by Brahmendra Swami for the reconstruction of the Parshuram temple[447].

An order was issued on 27th June 1684 by Viceroy Francisco de Tavora which forbade the use of Konkani and ordered school teachers, priests and their parishioners to learn Portuguese within three years. This decision was quite opposite to that of Pope Pias -V who declared on 23rd March 1567 that no religious person should occupy the post of Parish priest unless he was conversant with the language of the place. This particular papal brief served as a boost for the Konkani language which flourished under the Franciscans and the Jesuits[448]. Jesuits[449] contribution to Konkani language is immense and they

446 Ernest Hull, *Bombay Mission History*, Vol. II, Examiner Press, Bombay, 1927-30, p. 272

447 P.L. Saswadkar, *Brahmendra Swami- His Life and Role in Maratha History*, Ph.D Thesis, Poona 1961, p. 421

448 Bailon De Sa, ' The Genesis of Portuguese Discoveries and their influence on Indian Culture' in T. R. D Souza (ed), Op. Cit, p. 74

449 The personality of Fr. Thomas Stephens stands out with considerable distinction. He is still reverenced among the Christians of the Konkan. In 1616 he published his life's great work the Christ Puran in the Konkani dialect of Marathi (reprint, Mumbai, 1996). Larry Rohter's article entitled "language born of Colonialism" thrives again in Amazon, published in *Times of India* 29th August 05, Mumbai highlights the Jesuit Priests accompanying the

even encouraged Konkani speaking priests. The epic *Christa Puran* known in Goa as *Konkani Puran,* of Fr. Thomas Stephens (1549-1619) was written with literary and religious motives. It contained about 10,000 Ovis and was divided into two parts based on the old and the new Testaments respectively. It was the most popular Jesuit Marathi work of the 17th Century. Fr. Stephens[450] was quite familiar with the medieval literature of Saint poets of Maharashtra like Mukundraj, Dyaneshwar, Mukteshwar, Eknath etc. Fr. Stephens describes Marathi in glowing terms:

"As the gem among Pebbles,
Or the blue diamond among gems,
Or the Mogari among flowers,
Or musk among perfumes,
Or the peacock among birds,
Or the Kalpataru among trees,
So is the pure, elegant and respected Marathi
Among all the languages."[451]

Santan Rodrigues[452] who died on 14 July 2006 was an important figure in poetry in the 70's. His poem *The Inquisition* deplores the forcible conversion of Goans in the 16th Century. Many of his poems were nostalgic about Goa.

Francis Xavier, the famous Missionary came to India at a time when Portuguese were at the zenith of political power. Printing in India owes its origin to Christian Missionaries from Portugal and the Netherlands (Holland) in Western Europe. The Jesuits brought the

---

Portuguese conquerors in Brazil concocted a mixture of Indian, Portuguese and African words which they called *Imnguageral* (general language). This language is recognized as an official language in one of the municipalities in Brazil.

450 A. R. Kulkarni, "Medieval Maharashtra: A Fusion Of Cultures" in *Indian Historical Review,* Vol.XXVIII, No. 1-2 (January & July 200, New Delhi, 2003), pp. 31-49

451 P. N. Paranjpe, Nishikant Mirajkar, Marathi Literature an Outline, Maharashtra Information Centre, Maharashtra, p. 15

452 Santan founded and edited the little poetry magazine Kavi

first Printing Press into India in 1550[453]. The activities of this press were restricted to print religious books, bilingual dictionaries and grammars, i.e., all that was required to carry on Missionary work[454] (there was a lithographic press at *Harnai* in Konkan where Dr. Wilson composed an elementary Catechism in Marathi in 1830[455]). The first Indian printed book - St. Francis Xavier's Catechism of Christian doctrine came out in 1557.

The 'Cosmos Award' for the year 1996 was conferred upon the noted writer and environmentalist Father Francis D'Britto for his yeoman contribution to the preservation of the environment in the Vasai region in Thane district. He ascribes the environmental degradation in the country to the adoption of the Western model[456]. In his book *Conversion and Indian Civil Law* by Fr. Julian Saldanha (Bangalore,1981, page 2), highlights that "when Christianity first came to India, at the dawn of the Christian era, it blended into the social patterns of the country and was accepted as part and parcel of India's religious set up. But during colonial era Christianity lost its original adaptability. It grew into a monolithic system in which faith,culture and social behaviour became a package deal which included besides the faith in Jesus Christ, the adoption of a different culture and the incorporation into a distinct society with its own personal law. Thus conversion was seen no longer as a spiritual personal decision".

Fr. Avellino Remedios belonged very much to the Jesuit tradition of dialogue and incluturation. His first encounters with the Warlis were as a boy growing up in Vasai, one of the more developed talukas of Thane district in the 1930's and 40's. Here the Warlis were out of their milieu, alienated from their natural habitat and at the bottom of the social ladder mostly they worked as bonded laborers. Later as a Jesuit Seminarian in Talasari and then as a priest there, his

453 Chummar Choondal, "*The Missionaries and Malayalam Journalism*", Minerva, Kerala, 1975, p. 28

454 Pia de Menezes Rodrigues, "Interactive relationship between Goa and Bombay Journalism" in P. P. Shirodkar (ed), *Goa's External Relations*, Other India Book Store, Goa, 1992, p. 91

455 Annual Report of Bombay Auxiliary Scottish Missionary Society, 1830, pp. 24 -25

456 *The Examiner*, 1st February, 1997, p. 21

encounters with them moved him deeply. Warli art practiced in the Warli villages dotting Dahanu, Palghar, Jawhar and Talasari Tribal areas in Thana. They are painted on austere brown surface with the use on only one colour: white occasionally using red and yellow dots. It was popularized in the 1970's. Today it is considered a norm for tribal art in India[457].

7.2.3 Inculturation of Vasai

Vasai at one end of coastal Maharashtra has been the prime center of Missionary activity during 16th and 17th Centuries. Today one can still find the impact of Missionary activities on the local structure of Vasai. Some of the important factors contributing to the Vasai culture are

1. The active Diocese of Vasai
2. Jeevan Darshan Kendra
3. The Churches and Schools in Vasai region.

Inculturation refers to the process by which a particular Church expresses its faith and life in and through the local culture. The word Inculturation has been in Missiological circles since the 1960's. The Asian bishops used it for the first time in their statement after the first plenary Assembly of the Federation of Asian Bishops' Conferences in 1974. The statement reads. "The local Church is a Church incarnate in a people, a Church indigenous and incultured".

Pope John Paul – II wrote through inculturation the Church, for her part became a more intelligible sign of what she is and a more effective instrument of Mission. This engagement with cultures has always been part of the Church's pilgrimage to history but it has a special urgency today in the multiethnic, multi-religious and multicultural situation of Asia where Christianity is still too often seen as foreign[458].

---

457 Ajay Dandekar ed. *Mythos and Logos of the Warlis A Tribal Worldview*, Concept, New Delhi,1998, p. 7

458 Kurian Kunnumpurum, Conversion: Christian Perspectives in *Journal of Religious Studies*, Vol. 3, No.1, January 2000, Pune, p. 154

"Christians all over the world have been accustomed to worshipping statues of a Western Christ (brown hair, blue eyes) without ever stopping to think that Christ - far from being a westerner - was a Asian who lived in the middle east". A statue of Jesus in Yogic Mudra at the Church of St. Francis Xavier, Girij (Bassein) was designed since inter-religious dialogue is the need of the hour. Bishop Thomas Dabre and Father Francis Britto have made major contribution in the process of inculturation and inter-religious harmony. Rev. Thomas Dabre's Doctoral Thesis is entitled *The God Experience of Sant Tukaram A Study in Religious Symbolism.*

When Pope John Paul-II visited Vasai in 1986, the monthly Suvarta published interesting articles on the late pope. When the pontiff landed in Vasai, he was greeted with the celebrated marathi anthem '*Jai Jai Maharashtra Mazha*'. The reason locals recall that the song was selected since they pray to god in their mother tongue (marathi), which the best medium to greet a distinguished visitor. Later the Pope also spoke a few words in Marathi[459].

Pushpanjali college of Education in Vasai was so named because Pushpa means Flower. Flowers are precious gift of God to Humanity. We see in them God's image, get perfume of God's love, smile and the beautiful colours. The very presence of flowers makes us happy and joyful

Saint Dyaneshwar sings in one of his Hymns –"The Jasmine buds start blooming as I go on plucking them". Saint Tukaram 'Our mind is like Jasmine flowers, which should be offered to God as we worship him' The institute Pushpanjali which serves people of all creeds and castes bears the name of St.Teresa –"Little flower of Jesus" The saint who lived her life as a fragrant flower. One can see the amalgamation of East and West Saintly ideas here.

459 *TOI*, 30th May, Mumbai, 2005

Picture 7.1: Jesus in Yogic Mudra, Girij, Vasai

Picture 7.2: Bishop Dabre and his work on St. Tukaram

Jeevan Darshan Kendra comes out with 12 issues of *Suvarta* (means Good News) in a year. This magazine has been in existence since 1955, earlier it was just 6 to 8 pages and now it has 64 pages and has 13600 subscribers throughout Maharashtra.

The main door of the Chapel near Jeevan Darchan Kendra depicts the symbol of all the major religions. One can see the sayings displayed in marathi outside St. Xaviers (Girij) Church.

Picture 7.3: Fr. Francis Britto of Jeevan Darshan Kendra, Girij

Picture 7.4: Jeevan Darshan Kendra, Vasai

Plate 7.1: Front Page of Suvarta Magazine published from Jeevandarshan Kendra, Vasai

Picture 7.5: The Marathi Prayers displayed outside the Church (Jeevan darshan Kendra)

Picture 7.6: The Door depicting symbols of all religions (Nr Girij Church)

In Vasai the local folklore had influenced Christian religious hymns especially on Mother Mary. Fr. Francis Correa wrote a *Bhakti* poem *Mauli Nau Mahine Garbar*, whih talks about Mother Mary giving birth to Jesus in a cow shed[460].

Picture 7.7: Jesus and Mary in Indian Outlook

११. मावली नऊ मयनं गरबार

ओळख : २००० वर्षापूर्वी बेथलेहेम गावी प्रभू येशू ख्रिस्ताचा जन्म गाईच्या गोठ्यात झाला. त्याचा वृतांत कथन करणारे हे गीत आहे.

'तू देवाची माता होशील' असा संदेश घेऊन गाब्रियल नावाचा एक स्वर्गीय दूत मरिया नावाच्या एका कुमारीकेकडे येतो. त्या विषयाने या गाण्याची सुरूवात होते. बाळंतपणासाठी वाटेतल्या घरात व पशू-पक्षाकडे मरिया गेली असता तिची अवहेलना होते. मात्र गाई सहानुभूती दाखवतात व जागा देतात.

भावार्थ : स्वर्गीचा देवदूत खाली उतरला, आणि त्याने पवित्र मरियेला खबर दिली. मावली, पवित्र आत्म्याच्या कृपेने गर्भवती झाली.'

नऊ महिन्यांची गर्भवती मावली, रात्रीसाठी एका स्त्रीच्या घरात गेली. परंतु त्या स्त्रीने घराचे दार जोराने दार बंद केले; मावली परत फिरली.

नंतर मावली चिमणीच्या घरट्याकडे गेली. परंतु तिनेसुद्धा आपले घरटे तिच्यापुढे झटकून टाकले.

तद्नंतर मावली म्हशीच्या गोठ्यात गेली. परंतु तिनेही लाथा झटकून टाकल्या.

शेवटी मावली गाईच्या गोठ्यात गेली. तिथे जागेची अडचण होती, तरीपण स्वतः तीन पायांवर उभी राहून गायीने मावलीसाठी जागा केली व तिथेच मावली प्रसूत झाली.

मध्यरात्री प्रभू येशू ख्रिस्त जन्मास आले आणि स्वर्गात घंटानिनाद झाला. बालकांसाठी गवताचे अंथरूण व पेंढ्याचे पांघरूण तयार करण्यात आले.

प्रभूसाठी सोन्याचे पाळणे केले नाहीत किंवा चांदीरूप्याचे सांखळदोर केले नाहीत. येशूरायाने स्वर्गातले पाळणे स्वर्गात ठेवले व स्वतः गवतात अडचणीच्या जागी जन्म घेतला.

Plate 7.2: The Local Folklore influenced by Christian Religious Hymns especially on Mother Mary

460 Fr. Francis Correa, Paul Rumao and B. Dabre, *Samvedi Boli Bhasa Lok Sahitya* (in marathi), Saptarshi Prakashan, Mumbai, 1992, p. 101

7.3 The Korlai Community (Raigad District)

Korlai is situated on the south of Chaul. It was considered to be one of the most interesting Portuguese fortification area in the Konkan. In 1521 the Portuguese factory was converted into a fort. With in the area of the fort and outside it many churches came to be built by the Portuguese Missionaries in the course of the 16th century.

Table 7.1: Various Missionary orders in Korlai[461]

Church	*Order*	*Estd. Year*
St. Barbara	Franciscan	before 1570
Mother of God Church and Friary	Franciscan	1584
Our Lady (OL) of the Sea	Secular	before 1523
OL of Guadalupe	Dominican	before 1581
OL of Grace	Augustinian	around 1585
College of Saints Peter and Paul	Jesuit	Before 1552
St. Sebastin	Secular	—
St. John	Secular	—

The Portuguese rule ended in Korlai in 1739. Most of the Catholics migrated to Goa but a small group of poorer classes remained. The Franciscans were in charge of Church of the Mother of God and OL of Carmel till 1839.This two later passed in to the care of secular clergy. The impact of the rulers is still visible in the language of the people called Portuguese Creole. Small, school going children speak this language as I could see while interacting with them. The agriculturists and fisherfolk still converse in this language which is a Marathi mix with Portuguese.

7.3.1 Community Museum

The community musuem refers to the project undertaken wherein the potentiality of the community can be understood. The concept of eco-museology or community – museology (individual and collective efforts) in Korlai of Fr. Rudolf Andrades welcomed surveys

461 Catholic Directory of the Archdiocese of Bombay, Ahura Printing Press, 3rd Edition, 1982, p. 82

and research on the Korlai community with a view to facilitating it's self – knowledge and empowerment in respect of development.

Fr. Rudolf Andrades (now incharge of Uran Church) tried to inculture individual and collective efforts for Korlai community museum in January 1999. The aim was to identify communities which are proud of their cultural heritage which they would not like to loose and to save it and they could join hands to build institutions. Fr. Rudolf welcomed surveys and research on the Korlai community with a view to facilitating its self knowledge and empowerment in respect of development. The Church of Lady of Mount Carmel has said to have motivated the people of Korlai to organise co-operative societies (it is called *Korlai Gramin Bigarsheti Sahkari Pathsanstha Maryadit*) with offices in the Mission building (its running into profit). An article entitled Co-operative Credit and the Indian Christian Community (*BG*, July 15th 1905, p. 3) dealt with the co-operative principle as applied to Poultry farming. The sketch shows how by perseverance, mutual trust and co-operation the financial prospects of a group of Christian families may be surely, if slowly improved. It is rightly said that "Once the principles of co-operation are grasped their application is a matter of comparative simplicity". Also the Bombay Tract and Book Society whose main work was to create English and Marathi Christian Literature worked entirely with the Co-operation[462] of Missionaries. (*BG*, March 4, 1905, p. 3). A very nice Mission hospital "Krupa Niwas" (Sisters of Helpers of Mary) was also established in Korlai where qualified doctors and nurses are permanently available not only for the local residents but for those living in the neighboring villages. One of the specialty of this hospital is effective treatment of Serpent bite (Average 400 Snake Bites cases per year are handled) With the joint collaboration of Church and community the infrastructure has been developed in Korlai.

462 One can see a beautiful write-up "A Model Co-operative Society" in Mahatma Gandhi's Paper *Young India* May 9, 1929, p. 148

Picture 7.8: Fr. Rudolph Andrades is Manager of St. Mary's Convent High School and Junior College, Uran. The old and present look of Uran Church (Shudhata Mata Church)

Our Lady of the Purification (Shudhata Mata Church) was rebuilt in 1852, on the ruins of the old Church of OL of the Assumption.

Picture 7.9: The Creole Speaking Children, typical house architecture and inside their home (standing from left to right) Montida Calmen Marthis, Nirmala Gavdayas Marthis, Clotilda Dangel Korea, Nitika Agostin Marthis

7.4 Heras Institute Contribution

Rev. Fr. Henry Heras came to India in 1922 from Barcelona and founded the Indian Historical Research Institute in 1926., presently known as the Heras Institute of Indian History and Culture. Fr. Heras collected antiquities from various excavation sites. He studied the Mohenjadaro Seals and the coins which he collected. Today, a seal for Mohenjadaro forms the logo of the Heras institute. He also encouraged Angelo da Fonseca in the Indian Christian art., especially in the field of painting. He became an eminent indologist.

HERAS INSTITUTE
OF
INDIAN HISTORY AND CULTURE

St. Xavier's College, 5, Mahapalika Marg, Mumbai 400 001. India.

Visit: www.herasinstitute.museum.com E-mail: herasinstitute@hotmail.com

Telephone: (022) 2262 0665 Ext. 321 / 320 Director: aubreyam@hotpop.com

Picture 7.10: Stamp issued and logo of Heras Institute, Mumbai

Fr. Heras himself had written 13 books along with over 200 scholarly articles. Some of his significant works include: *La Dinastia Manchu en Chine, The Writing of History, Notes on Historical Methodology for Indian students, The Aravidu Dynasty of Vijaynagara,*

The Pallava Geneology, Studies in Pallava History, The Beginnings of Vijayanagara History, Minkan, The Story of Magi and Studies in Proto-Indo-Mediterranean Culture.

Today the Heras Research Program (started in 1995) is a big hit among undergraduate students. It is held twice a year and is open to all students of the Mumbai city colleges. In the first part of the program the participants are expected to write research papers based on the artifacts in the Heras museum. The second part deals with the field study and on the spot research. Each student is assigned a research guide, after successful completion of the project; certificates are awarded to the participants. Students examine ancient artifacts like Mohenjadaro Seals, Buddhist Stupas, Gandhara's Culture, India Christian Paintings, Punch Mark Coins, Ivory Images, South Indian Bronzes, Wood Carvings and so on.

7.5 Fr. Julian Saldhana's Work

St. Pius Seminary in Goregoan (Mumbai) is a training center of Christain Fathers in India especially for the Diocese of Bombay. It enjoys a huge campus in the city surrounded by lush green trees. It has right ambience for study, prayer and play. It has been imparting training for laity and religions.

Fr. Julian Saldanha had majored in Philosophy and did his doctorate in Theology from Jnana Deepa Vidyapeeth, Pune. He had taught theology to several Christian scholars at St. Pius College and is associated with some other Institutes in India. He is a founder member of "Manavta" (Citizens' Forum of Goregaon East). As a researcher he has contributed number of articles in various journals across India. His chief work "Mission Today: Themes and Issues" covers systematic reflection on the Church's millennial Missionary activity and themes and issues of special relevance to India are discussed.

It houses a library which has rich collection of Journals relating to Missionary history across the world. Dr. Julian Saldhana has the credit of maintaining the library in its present state today.

Picture 7.11: St. Pius Seminary, Goregaon

Picture 7.12: Fr. Julian Saldhana at St. Pius Seminary Library, Goregaon and his work

7.6 Others

7.6.1 The Mission Festival

This was anniversary gathering of the AMM at Ahmednagar. It was a sort of feast of Tabernacles (in the Jewish feast the worshippers were gathered together form all parts of the land at Jerusalem, and had an opportunity to get acquainted with one another). In this festival Christians from all parts of Ahmednagar Collectorate and some from more distant places came together to mingle their testimonies for the lord.... Among the visitors were Rev. Narayan Sheshadri, Baba Padmanji, Dhanjibhai Nawroji and George Bowen. Rev. Mr. Barker of the SPG was also present ...At one of the sessions, Mr. Narayan Sheshadri gave a very interesting account of his visit to Rome, Oxford, Scotland and America. The meetings were held in the chapel of the American Mission which could accommodate about 750 persons. The native Christians of Ahmednagar felt it a great privilege to have with them the Revs. of the free Church Mission. There were a number of *Kirtan's*, Musical Performances of religious character[463].

7.6.2 Winslow's Mission in India

He had a twenty year Missionary career and was acclaimed as a "catholic–minded Sadhu Sundar Singh", a great Indo-Anglican mystic and a pioneer of indigenization. Yet, with the exception of two unpublished works on Christa Seva Sangh, the ashram community founded by Winslow, there is surprisingly little written about him. His early career was in England.

It is said John "Jack" Copley Winslow (1882-1974), the son of an Anglican clergyman, who was raised in a comfortable country rectory in the village of Hanworth in Middlesex, England. After graduating in 1905, and still preparing for ordination, Winslow visited India. In Delhi and Calcutta he was particularly impressed by the attempts of the Anglican Missionary brotherhoods to present Christianity in terms of Hindu culture to western educated elites through a lifestyle of austerity and good works. In Delhi he also met C. F. Andrews[464] (In *Young India* of August 11, 1927 (p. 252) ...Gandhiji supports the title of 'Dinabandhu' to Andrew) of the Cambridge Mission to Delhi, who later became his close friend and

463 *BG*, November 7, 1874, p. 283

464 He worked side by side with Gandhiji in the struggle for social reform and political independence.

guru. Winslow's friendship with Andrews was decisive for his future work, particularly in regard to developing the ashram ideal.

In 1914 Winslow returned to India as a Missionary with the Society for the Propagation of the Gospel. At first he was sent by Bishop Palmer to Dapoli in the Konkan 100 miles south of Bombay, where he devoted much of his time to the study of Marathi. Then from 1915 to 1919, he served as Principal of the Mission High school in Ahmednagar, where he began a close friendship with the distinguished Indian Christian poet Narayan Vaman Tilak. In his biography of Tilak in the Builders of Modern India Series, Winslow testifies to Tilak's influence. Tilak's life and example, he indicated, persuaded him of the importance of Indian ways and Indian ideals for Christian Mission. From Tilak he learned the value of bhakti (loving devotion) and the singing of bhajans (Indian devotional songs) for Christian worship and evangelism. It was also through Tilaks influence that he realized the valuable contribution the Church in India had to offer to the world. Winslow was fond of quoting Tilak's Prophecy:

> *...Yea, at the end of pregnant strife,*
> *Enthroned as Guru of the earth,*
> *This land of Hind shall teach the worth*
> *Of Christian faith and Christian life...*

Meanwhile, on furlough in England in August 1919, Winslow had "One of those mysterious experiences that he described in his autobiography as "divine guidance" or "revelation", which forcibly implanted upon his mind the importance of ashrams for the Indian Church. Three factors helped to shape this conviction. The first was the inspiration he had received from Andrews, Sundar Singh, Tilak and the Thomas Christians in Kerala. They had kindled within him a desire to enter more deeply into the spirit of India and to identify with its people. Secondly he was sensitive to the new stirrings of Indian nationalism and was conscious that a Church exclusive and remote could never win the heart of India. The Indian Church, in Winslow's view, had to show that it welcomed the desirable things of Indian religions and culture so that its message might be heard and its invitation accepted. Above all, however was the impact of the Jallianwalla Bagh Massacre in Amritsar in April 1919. The massacre in Winslow's view, gathered into one blazing point all the smouldering resentment awakened by a hundred lesser acts of cold superciliousness and cynical contempt, of callous indifference on the part of Englishmen to Indian susceptibilities.

7.6.3 The Christa Seva Sangh

Faced with the question as to how Missionaries could proceed after Amritsar, Winslow decided to establish a Christian ashram and to become a Christian Sanyasi in order "to try to contribute something towards the healing of inter-racial strife. Winslow's proposed model for a Christian community was to be truly Indian. The community must be patriotic and eager to promote India's freedom. The education of young children, Winslow envisaged, would follow a pattern similar to that in Tagore's ashram at Bolpur in Bengal, where children learned from the example of a revered guru. For worship, bhajans and other Indian devotional songs would be sung with Indian musical instruments. In terms of architecture, churches should follow the design of Hindu temples. On their walls would be frescoes of exemplary figures of different religious traditions:

Unlike the bulk of Missionaries working in India at the time, Winslow was sympathetic with Gandhi and other leaders of the Indian nationalist movement. He took on the Indian name Devdatta. He wore Khadi (homespun), a potent symbol of Indian nationalism and hosted lectures at the ashram on Gandhi's philosophy of nonviolence.

In his final work written in India the dawn of Indian Freedom co-authored with Elwin, he opposed the governments bullying tactics of Missionaries[465], he sang the praises of Gandhi Satyagraha Campaign, and he went as far as to depict Christ as the fulfillment of India's national aspirations.

465 Winslow opposed the governments actions in extracting pledges from non-British Missionaries not to engage in political matters, and in bringing pressure upon British Missionaries who took an independent line.

In his poem[466] "Hail to the Mother", written during the civil disobedience campaign of 1930-31, Winslow is quite lyrical about the nationalist movement.

> *....India, My India! Mother beloved!*
> *Shatter the chains of thy thralldom Past!*
> *Ransom they captives and raise they fallen!*
> *Fold to thy bosom thy sons outcast!*
> *Rise in the might of thine ancient splendour!*
> *Shout for thy great Release, at last !*

The Thuma Bhagats[467] were the most extraordinary and interesting class of *fakirs.* These people found similarity in Sermon on the Mount and teaching of Guru Nanak. Their belief is garbled Christianity mingled with the Sikkhism of Nanak. They said they had two gurus one was called 'Thuma' and lived a very long time ago and the other was 'Nanak'. They had two sacred books. Granth of Nanak and Book of Thuma . 'Thuma' is the urdu form of Thomas and Bhagat means simply saint. Can these people be descendants of the converts of the Apostle Thomas? Just as the combination of the positive and the negative wires produced sparks of electricity so out of the junction of the past and the present great events were bound to follow.

In a town square in Germany stands a statue of Christ, its hands blown off during the bombing of World War II. Though the towns people could have restored the statue which read "Christ hath no hands but yours' lend your hands and create your own destiny![468]. The Abhay Mudra shows right hands up raised is means 'have no fear I'm here' or *Main hoon na mudra,* one of the most necessary gestures in the history of humankind. Its universal handspeak for protection.

---

466 Willam W. Emilson, The Legacy of John Copey Winslow in *International Bulletin* Vol. 21, No. 1, January 1997, pp. 26-28

467 The Thuma Bhagats (from the Punjab Mission News) *BG*, December 17,1887, p. 813

468 T. G. L. Iyer 'Everything we want is Beyond the Comfort Zone' in *Bhavan's Journal*, December, Chennai, 2007, p. 91

Roby D'Silva of Papdy (Vasai) a suburb of Mumbai, studying in J. J. School of Arts (1954) secured a scholarship (prize) in national competition for postage stamps on occasion of Buddha Jayanti which paved a way for his further study in England and received several distinguished awards. The School by his name stood up in Vasai in his honour. She studied in Sir. J. J. School of Arts in Bombay and started painting holy pictures in the Indian style. She was famous for her indianization of her paintings. She was inspired by Gandhi to represent Christ as "one who loved all and who taught us to live in peace and harmony. Her Best Painting was the 'Assumption" and "Coronation of our Lady." They were influenced by the Ajanta Frescoes[469].

Mr. Raul D'souza a renowned Bharat Natyam dancer performed with well known actress cum dancer Hema Malini in the lead-role of Krishna in a dance ballet Meera and Radhakrishna.' He danced before Pope John Paul II on the occasion of Gen Fest 90. He has won awards in competitions. He got the title of *Singar Mani* title.[470]

Mumbai based publishing house, St. Pauls has come out with an Indianised version of the bible which has references to Mirabai, Mahatma Gandhi and Rabindranath Tagore[471].

The modern Indian Church is responding with courage to the challenge of the contemporary scene. The cultural gap has been tackled with imagination and varying degrees of Indigenisation. Church architecture no longer follows the old western pattern, hymns and bhajans set to indigenous tunes are replacing the sometimes ludicrous translations from the English. Todays Missionaries are specialists in agriculture, technology, medicine and education[472].

A number of Christian Priests strictly follow the ancient union ashram system of monastic life such as those at the Beathany Ved Vijanan Peeth, Pune., Sachitananda Ashram, Trichy., Purusumala Ashram and Samikshana Ashram at Kerala[473].

469 *Indica*, 1953, pp. 142-143

470 St. Xavier's College (Annual Magazine) Mumbai, 1999, p. 137

471 DNA, 6th August, Mumbai, 2009, p. 9

472 Jamila Verghese, "Christians" in the *Illustrated weekly of India*, 1972, p. 96

473 *Times of India*, 25th October, Mumbai, 2005, p. 13

The study of de Nobili's awakening coupled with the national awakening consequent on the freedom movement headed by Mahatma Gandhi convinced Fr. Heras of the need of indinigenization of the Church to remove the wrong impression the few western elements in the Christian Worship might convey of Christianity having entered India as a hand made of European imperialism. This indigenization might as well start with Church architecture taking its inspiration from temple architecture found in the country. What Fr. Heras meant was that we should enter in to the spirit of Hindu architecture and infuse with a new Christian life[474].

Even Carey conceived the idea of a 'Christian Benares' where Christian Scholars would be steeped in Oriental and Western learning, and Indians of all caste would have access to the best that east and west could jointly provide[475].

Thus, the Chapter covers earlier phase of impact of Catholic form of Christianity on the daily life, architecture and language of the people of Konkan. Moreover this work tries to cover the Nineteenth Century Bombay where with the entry of Protestant form of Christianity a slow inculturation process began between the Christian Missionaries and the locals from all castes. The present work also brings out the prominent role played by the Christian Missionaries in shaping the overall life style of people in Konkan region from near past to present. The efforts of Missionaries to bring people of various castes together through their activities before independent India are visible. Missionary activity is said to mirror the Church's theological position.

The major issues affecting the society which became the matter of concern for the Missionaries forms the basis of further discussion.

474 G. M. Moraes, "Henry Heras, the scholar and his work, The Historian "in the *Heras Memorial Lectures*, 1976 (ed. John Correia Afonso)

475 Arthur May Hew, *Christianity and the Government of India*, Faber and Gwyer, London, 1929, p. 139

Chapter 8

Major Social Issues of 19th Century

Chapter 8

Major Social Issues of 19th Century

8.1 Introduction

In the second half of the nineteenth century four major issues became a centre of concern for the Missionaries. This chapter highlights the interesting ways they followed to make society aware about these issues namely drinking habit, Anglo-Asiatic opium traffic, famine and plague. Temperance societies had been established by Missionaries to stop drinking habit in the mid-nineteenth century. Thomas Evans and Canon Wilberforce's views on alcoholic drinks had been very forceful.

Interest in the opium question was revived in the 1880's and 1890's, when a large-number of Missionaries began to participate actively in the anti-opium crusade. The opium trade was a growing industry, for opium extracted from the Poppy was the only Indian commodity that the merchants of Bombay traded with China in return for tea[476]. The role played by these two commodities in the rise of Bombay and its capitalist's class is generally recognized, but the centrality of opium has not been sufficiently emphasized[477]. The splendor of Victorian buildings in the fort area, or the posh

476 Aruna Narayanan, *Op.Cit*, p.115

477 Amar Farooqui, *Opium City: The Making of early Victorian Bombay*, October 2006, Three Essays Press, New Delhi, p. XI

bungalows of Malabar hill were made possibly by earnings from the opium trade. The nerve center of opium trade in Mumbai was the old custom house where opium was auctioned during 1920's.

Narayan Shesahadri, Soonderbai Pawar along with Manshukhlal and Raja Naidu strongly supported the anti-opium drive. The write-up[478] 'Opium from the Missionary standpoint' says "the Missionary cannot remain neutral on the opium question". Rev. Sheshadri brought face to face 'the drug' and its consequences regularly and he further said "I am bold to say that every true Missionary, whether he be in India, straits settlements, or China, condemns it from his heart, and fearlessly declares it to be one of the greatest obstacles to the spread of the Gospel of the Lord Jesus Christ".

The major famines and debilitating disease 'plague' of the 19th Century has been briefly dealt with.

8.2 Temperance Movement

The vice of drinking was widely spreading in Maharashtra after the advent of the British rule. Lokahitavadi Gopal Hari Deshmukh held the Government policy responsible for the spread of this vice. Govind Narayan Madgaonkar (1815-1865) wrote a small book on the subject entitled '*Daru Pasoon Anartha*' in 1855. Upon this, Mama Parmanand the editor of the *Native Opinion* paid attention to this problem. Temperance societies were formed at various places in Maharashtra. Lokahitavadi was the chairman of Aryan Temperance Society[479].

Temperance was mainly based in Britain and North America[480], being brought to India by Protestant Missionaries from those areas[481]. The Temperance Movement[482] in the Konkan was discussed in *BG* as... "when the Government revenue from this source alone amounts to 'more than half a crore of rupees', and besides this contractors

478 *BG*, June 25,1892, p. 10

479 Arun R. Joshi, *Op.Cit*, pp.176-177

480 Rev. Marcus Ormund D. D., a prominent clergy men of Pennsylvania was a leading lecturer on temperance (*BG*, March 13, 1880, p. 21)

481 Frederick S. Downs, *History of Christianity in India*, Vol. V, part 5, CHAI, Bangalore,1992, p. 227

482 *BG*, January 08,1887, p. 24

become very wealthy, and shopkeepers grow rich, owing to the excessive drinking habits of people, the great mass of whom are very poor and who receive only a few *annas* per day as their daily wage for toil, there must be a vast amount of untold suffering and misery".

Blue ribbon was a symbol of the Temperance movement. Before 1850, Thomas Carre was concerned with the consumption of strong spirits that led to the untimely demise of nine tenth of European soldiers[483]. Rev. R. A. Hume, one of the American members, founded the Bombay Temperance Union, perhaps the earliest and certainly one of the most stable and influential temperance organizations in India[484].

A big letter by Wallace J. Gladwin titled "The Bombay Tract Society Favouring the Deadly Liqour Traffic" was published[485]… "it is a shame and a public wrong for the Tract society to encourage liquor-selling, and hence drunkenness, by advertising strong drink in their Almanacs. In their Almanac for the current year were advertisements dealing Brandy, Whisky, Beer, Old Tom, Gin, Port, Sherry, Champagne, Stout etc. Dr. Palmer and other of England record "Religious" periodicals taming with advertisements of all sorts of damning drinks….all because their cruel traffic is so terribly successful that they can pay well for such leading notices. The cup of the Lord and the cup of devils form a strange mixture…The Bombay Tract Society represent not only all the evangelical Christian Churches and ministers of Bombay, but also the great Religious Tract Society of England. Hence, it very authoritatively represents the whole protestant Christianity and must be looked upon as representing Christ. Alas, in this it has crucified him afresh".

Christian Bombay applauded the poor Hindu labourers of Guzarat and the Konkan who were giving up drink by thousands. It said "yet the society which represented nearly all our Missionaries published 15 alcoholic poisons to destroy the homes, and blast the

483 M. D. David, *Missions: Cross Cultural Encounters and Change in Western India*, Manohar, Delhi, 2001, p. 249

484 G. A. Oddie, *Social Protest in India British Protestant Missionaries and Social Reforms 1850-1900*, Manohar, New Delhi, 1979, p. 200

485 *BG*, January 15,1887, pp. 36-37

lives, and ruin the souls of the people! It says poisonous pages of (Almanac) well paid advertisements".

Thomas Evans had for many years labored in the cause of temperance reform and was considered one of the best authorities on the subject. His letter[486] to Samuel Smith of Liverpool from Ootacamund dated 20th November 1886 said "the liquor trade is the curse of the country.. After highlighting the large revenue from drink trade he says native drinking has two facts…

1. Natives of India have no idea of moderation in the use of strong drinks; they drink to get drunk, therefore, they imbibe by the bottle and not by the glass. No less than some half a dozen of the Native Rajahs have died, at a comparatively young age, within the last few years, from indulging freely in pegs of Champagne and brandy.
2. Another feature of native drinking is, once a native becomes a hard drinker, he seldom or never can give up".

Thomas Evans wrote a big write-up "In Britain after 20 years" where Thomas was given a cordial reception by The Temperance and Anti-Opium friends in London in the year 1896. Also Mansukhlal, an Indian Anti-Opium delegate visited Scotland in the same year and spoke on ever increasing opium curse[487]. A big full page article by Mansukhlal with a photo of audience listening to horrors of the Opium traffic in Glasgow can be seen in April 1896 issue of *BG*.

Samuel's letter dated 14th January, 1887 (*BG*) was published[488]. It said "Thomas Evans[489] (calling him old Missionary) who has for many years laboured in the cause of temperance reform, and is believed to be one of the best authorities on the subject". While addressing a gathering of native Christians at Madras on January 14th, Mr. Thomas Evans urged the natives "to be vegetarian in diet (not to accustom to flesh eating and not to drink). He said he had

486 *BG*, March 12, 1887, p. 170

487 *BG*, January 4, 1896, p. 9

488 *BG*, Op. Cit, March 12 issue.

489 Thomas Evans was requested by Baptist Mission to compile a Mission Hand Book in Welsh for the use of Welsh Church (*BG*, January 4,1896, p. 9)

lived in India 36 years without the help of brandy or whisky, or gin or beer and he did not think he was a bad specimen of a teetotaler. He said the great evil of alcohol was that it gained insidiously upon people and created a crave in them"[490].

A big article entitled 'The Christian Church and the Temperance Cause' mentions Mr. Tomlinson's views on the subject of temperance[491]. He gave an interesting sketch of the spread of the movement in Scotland and England. The journey of temperance movement from America to England and back to America as a total abstinence movement has been discussed at length.

Front page of *BG*, May 30, 1863 mentioned about a four page marathi metrical tract on the subject of ardent spirits. It was in popular form of a *lawani*, a class of poems, the subjects of which are generally of a very objectionable character. A faithful wife here addresses her husband on the evils of intemperance and dissuades him from the use of *daru*.

BG of February 22, 1890 (p. 9) carried a report Canon Wilberforce at the Money School, Bombay. Wilberforce[492] gave an address on total Abstinence from alcoholic drinks. This address was attended by a mixed religious audience and was presided over by Hon. Justice K. T. Telang. He uttered a few weighty words upon the fact that there is "no sex in citizenship" and urged India to develop the intelligence of her women. "No nation can possibly attain strength that is afraid to educate its women." He said that "there were several aspects under which the subject of alcohol was treated, as the political, the social and the physiological aspect. But there was one aspect which embraced all the others, the aspect that he should take up this evening, the religious aspect...". He added "all social movements thrive by opposition. Just as a man grows stronger by temptation manfully resisted, so do these great movements. Let no one say that they are not their brother's keeper in this temperance work. To be self-centred is to be an unconverted man, whatever our

490 *BG*, January 30, 1892, front page

491 *BG*, July 4,1891, p. 3

492 Relative of William Wilberforce the great anti-slavery pioneer. The following issues of *Bombay Guardian* (*BG*), Weekly News Paper has been used: 1863, 1890, 1899

professions of religion might be. The difference between a man who is a true man and a man who is not a true man, between a man who is converted and a man who is not converted is similar to that of the ideas of astronomy before and after the times of Copernicus. Before Copernicus men believed that the earth was the centre of everything and that everything revolved round the earth. Now men know that the sun is the centre of the solar system and that this little earth revolves round that. Just so the true man, the converted man is a God centred man, whilst the man who is not true, the unconverted man, is a self-centered man. "If you are an unconverted man all the world revolves round you, you think that your Children, your wife, the British Government itself is all for you. But, if you are a God-Centered man you know that there is not an opium eater or a drunkard in all Bombay that has not a claim on you, as far as your influence can go to raise them from the gutter of sin in which they lie."

In speaking upon the drink question, he always took three heads

1. Drunkenness is ruinous
2. that moderation is dangerous
3. Teetotalism is safe.

In 1879, the Blue Ribbon Movement reached Britain after sweeping America. Its members were ardent teetotalers who wore a blue or some times red or white ribbon to advertise their opinions, and held fervent evangelistic meetings. Soon blue ribbons were spouted on jackets and dresses all over the country and also appearing on post men's uniforms, the post master general having ruled when appealed to, that his staff could 'wear… all the colours of the rainbow so long as they were kept from the drink'[493].

A letter published in *BG* of August 11, 1883, talks of the Blue Ribbon Movement in Nagpur. It talks of distribution of regular blue ribbon pledge card whose motto said "I can do all things through

493 Norman Longmate *The Water Drinkers: A History of Temperance*, 1968, Hamilton, Great Britain, p. 216

Christ which strengthen me … Curse of strong drink is to be overcome".

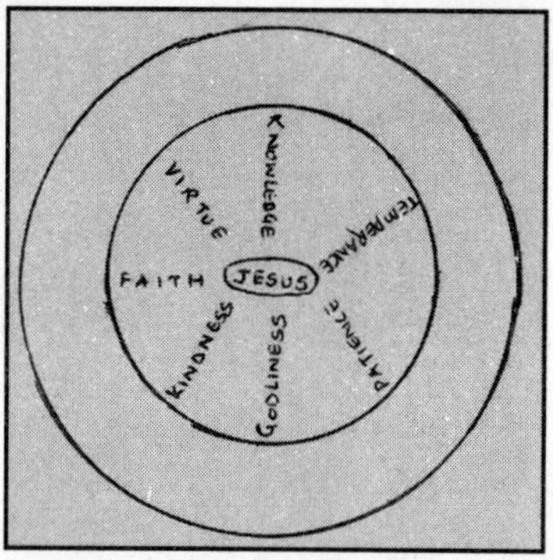

Figure 8.1: The Christian Wheel by Uncle Robin (reproduced from *BG*, February 29, 1896, p. 7)

Whisky Bottle[494]

Whisk'y bottle Whisk'y bottle
Where have you been ?
I'e been to the slum district to visit a friend.
Whisk'y bottle Whisk'y bottle
What did you do there?
I ruined a life I killed a wife
I left a table bare

– M. Elizabeth Ohdborn

In the Robert Money School of the Church Missionary Society most of the meetings of the Indian Temperance Association were held[495].

A poem on temperance appears in Bombay Guardian[496] where the poet describes a drink shop as a 'bar'

494 *Dyanodaya*, November 27, 1947, p. 197
495 *BG*, May 13, 1893, p. 3
496 *BG*, July 26, 1902, p. II

Picture 8.1: Temperace Orators urging their audience to clench the nails and renounce drink (Source : Norman Longmate *The Water Drinkers: A History of Temperance*, 1968, Great Britain)

A bar to heaven, a door to hell;
Whoever named it named it well;
A bar to manliness and wealth,
A door to want and broken health,
A bar to honour, pride and fame,
A door to sin and grief and shame;
A bar to hope, a bar to prayer,
A door to darkness and despair;
A bar to honoured, useful life,
A door to brawling, senseless strife;
A bar to all that's true and brave,
A door to every drunkard's grave;
A bar to joy that home imparts,
A door to tears and aching hearts;
A bar to heaven, a door to hell,
Whoever named it, named it well.

8.3 The Opium Problem

One of the most important articles of export from Bombay was opium. When opium was first officially noticed in 1886-87 in Bombay, it was attributed chiefly to the effect of the 'Chefoo Convention' of September 1876 which added to the increased consumption in China of locally grown opium[497].

A big article entitled 'The Unchangeableness of Sin' talks about the slave trade a century ago , and the opium traffic in the 19th Century. On Opium certain joke like information can be seen[498]. *Bombay Kamgar Newspaper* was quoted by a wife of a newspaper editor Jankibai telling her servant Rama to buy some opium for her "When her husband Rambhaoo came to know Jankibai replied "you printed in your newspaper that a doctor says that opium if harmless". On next page of same issue of *BG* (p.9), a big write-up entitled 'Fourteen Questions on the opium Traffic' answered by Dr. James L Maxwell was published.

Thomas Evans had collected a lot of information during his tour in India with regard to the present status of the opium dens which government professed to have closed[499]. A big article 'The Opium Future of India' with a big map showing the consumption of opium in the Indian Empire is shown[500]. Also an advertisement of a book was published[501].It came with an attached preparatory note by Benjamin Broomhall who was the secretary, China inland Mission for many as under...

OPIUM AND VICE

Recent Personal Investigations
By
Mrs. Elizabeth Andrew
And
Dr. Kate Bushnell

497 Aruna Narayanan, *Op.Cit*, p. 114
498 *BG*, June 4, 1892, p. 8
499 *BG*, April 02,1892, p. 2
500 *BG*, August 01,1891, p. 9
501 *BG*, March 21,1896, p. 15

The Thief Tobacco[502]
STEALS
Our health
Our good looks
Our liking for play
Our strength
Our memory

A very interesting letter in 1891 by a Eurasian to the editor of the *BG* entitled 'Opium Shops in Bombay' shows two signboards of shops shown as below.

Table 8.1: (Source: *BG* May 30, 1891, p. 11)

Jadawjee Khodidas – No. 4 Farmer – Antaji Vinayak Mandvi Bhikoo Bunder Licensed Opium Vendor Price 5 annas per tola	Cullianjee Lukmichand Farmer- Kurimchina No.2 Chundool Vendor Price 5 annas a tola

In 1889, the *Bombay Guardian*, which had formerly been controlled and edited by Missionaries of the Bombay Missionary Conference, passed into the hands of the English Quaker reformer, Alfred S. Dyer. Supported from England by the Friends' Association for the Abolition of the Regulation of Vice and others, he purchased the press and paper, which he himself edited from 1889 until 1899. A trust was formed in England to hold the *Bombay Guardian* property for the stated purpose of spreading the Gospel in Asia and extinguishing the traffic in vice, opium and intoxicating liquor[503]. The January 1891 *BG* had special supplement of four pages entitled 'Chinese Statesmen on the Great Britain and the Opium Curse' written by Alfred S. Dyer[504]. Another supplement entitled 'Is India to be ruined by Opium?' talks of opium plague in Bengal and Bombay.

502 *BG*, November 27,1897, p. 7

503 G. D. Oddie, *Op. Cit*, p. 232

504 Alfred Dyer took lead at the anti-opium movement in the start of 1891 in England.

THE ANTIOPIUM CRISIS
DEVASTATION
OF
INDIA'S MILLIONS
BY
OPIUM UNDER BRITISH RULE
By A Resident in India
32 page pamphlet giving valuable information on the vast evil caused by the consumption of opium in India and other countries under the British flag and plainly setting forth which lies at the door of the British nation for the part they have taken in the matter.
Should be read by all who wish to see the evil stopped and the British nation freed of participation in the traffic.
Source : BG April 18, 1891, p. 13

In August-September 1880, When Rev. Narayan Sheshadri was touring to Singapore and Hongkong, he wrote a letter from Hongkong highlighting how many have taken to opium Smoking in China[505]. It said "the Christian Missionaries, who were unhappy eye-witnesses of the dire distress, disease and degradation directly attributable to the policy pursued by the British Government on opium revenue, were very bitter in their complaints to their friends in England"[506].

On May 9th 1892, a crowded public meeting was held in the American Mission School room, at Roha, Kolaba district, in the Konkan addressed by Miss Soonderbai Powar, and several local Indian gentlemen. A petition to parliament was unanimously passed praying for the abolition of the injurious traffic in opium, which as loyal subjects the petitioners could not but feel to be out of harmony with the general character of the benign reign of the Queen empress. Another petition to parliament was passed on May 12th by the Chrisitan Church of Astami near Roha, signed by the pastor, deacon

505 *BG*, September 4, 1880, p. 315

506 R. P. Masani, *Dadabhai Naoroji*, George Allen & Unwin Ltd, New Delhi, 1975, p. 116

and secretary of the Church. A letter (a bit exaggerated) entitled Anti-Opium Meeting at Roha was published on page 12 of May 28, 1892 of *BG* which said "Sunderbai Powar was the first woman who ever spoke at Roha since the world was created, she spoke for about three-quarters of an hour".

8.3.1 Soonderbai Pawar's visit to England

BG of 1895 speaks of her as ... "to proclaim the evils of Opium traffic[507] in India, she opened her campaign in Sheffield before a large and sympathetic audience". Her style of oratory is described simple and direct. She said "I have left my sunny India and come to this foggy England to tell you sad news, I know that the Christian people of Great Britain knew nothing of what is going on in India, and unless they know it they cannot help us so I thought I will go myself and tell them what I have seen with my own eyes. She gave many distressing details of misery and degradation brought upon the people of India by the sale of Opium under the direct sanction and encouragement of the government"[508]. She happened to take with her two soul stirring Christian Hymns on the subject. These Hymns have since been sung by scores of thousands of Englishmen and women in public meetings...

1. Stand Up Stand Up for Jesus !
2. Onward Christian Soldiers ! Marching as to War.

She also wrote a Hymn based on an incident occurred in the streets of Bombay entitled "The cry of an Opium victims widow..."

Blighted, crushed, forlorn, heartbroken,
Hungry, weak and sore;
From my life all brightness taken;
Sad and Poor, Poor, bereaved my Children crying,
Naught have I to give, Tears flow fast, while living, dying sad to Live[509].

507 In 1895 issue of *BG* articles like Opium Conflict (July 20, p. 9) The Narcotic Weed (Tobacco) and Christianity (August 24, p. 3) can be seen

508 *BG*, February 20, 1892, p. 5

509 *BG*, September 17, 1892, p. 9

She had again been to England as Anti-Opium Missioner in early 1893 where she pleaded the devastating plague of opium in India and China[510]. When she returned to India, a welcome meeting was held for her at Pune. In her speech Ms. Pawar spoke of her parents early dedicating her to god to work for Indian women. She gave a number of instances of Opium wrecks that had come under her own observation and urged the necessity of immediately stopping the evil[511]. The *Young India* dated April 23rd 1925 carried a four page supplement on opium… 'Memorandus on Opium'. It said "the rapidly growing consumption of opium with its alkaloids, morphia and heroin is now becoming a menace to the world".

However, inspite of increasingly outspoken attacks on the 'evils' of Government policy and opium smoking, especially in the pages of the *Bombay Guardian*, many other Missionaries were still reluctant to embark on a public crusade. The split within the Missionary ranks over the opium issue was clearly revealed during the proceedings of the 3rd Decennial Missionary Conference held in Bombay in 1892-93. Although a resolution condemning the Government's connection with the opium traffic was put forward at one of the regular sessions, it had to be withdrawn on the technical grounds that, in accordance with previous practice, no resolutions could be passed at these gatherings, which were held simply for conference. An opportunity for proposing such resolutions was, however, provided for at the closing business session. The Business Committee specifically invited resolutions on which there was 'practical unanimity' and, although a resolution on opium was actually moved and seconded, a member of the Committee intervened saying that the Committee had decided that no resolution should be submitted to the Conference.' After some confusion and further discussion, the Chairman eventually ruled that the resolution would not be proceeded with 'in face of the opposition.

At the above conference of 1892-93, an article 'A Missionary manifesto on moral questions in India' highlighted "We Missionaries

510 A very beautiful long poem by Martin K. Tupper " The Opium Trade" published in *BG*, October 11, 1856, p. 328 talks about opium poison in China.

511 *BG*, June 17, 1893, p. 11

are unalterably opposed to the participation by the government in the demoralizing traffic in opium and intoxicating liquors, and we record our conviction that these are sins against god and wrongs to humanity[512]. Oddie in his book, *Social protest in India* has dealt in detail about how some Missionary order came openly in signing manifesto against opium and some were silent.

Also a small pamphlet entitled the Bombay anti opium alliance asked for members to join it saying no religious qualification is required for membership[513]. Following this a cartoon from Pekin the capital of China where family of a mandarin is shown of becoming a slave to the opium pipe.

Figure 8.2: Britain's guilt and gods judgments in relation to the Anglo Asiatic opium traffic[514]

Mr. Mansukhlal from Gujarat and Raju Naidu from Madras also were active in the anti opium drive in the late nineteenth century. Mansukhlal and his wife Phulbai were invited in Glasgow where they spoke against the evil.

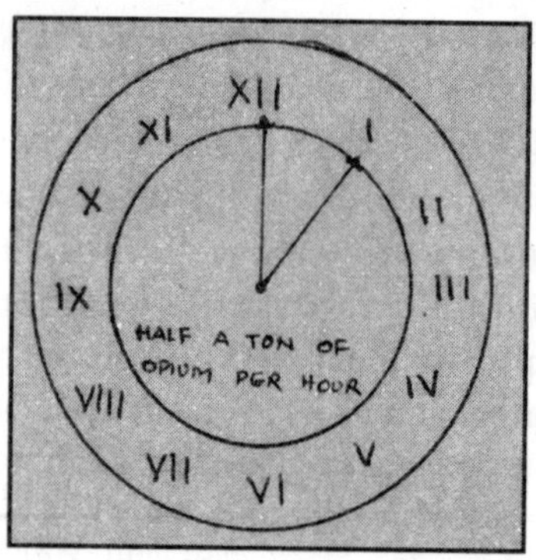

The Christian doctors, nurses and social workers had successfully organized a door to door complain against the then existing obnoxious practice of mixing opium in infants milk which

512 *BG*, April 29, 1893, p. 11

513 *BG*, June 20, 1891, Opposite p. 8

514 *BG*, January 01, 1898, p. 3

was in vogue to keep children sleeping and thereby freeing mothers and *ayas*.[515]

8.4 The Famine issue

Two major famines in the last quarter of the 19th Century lead to starving people flocking to Mission houses[516]. In the famine of 1877-78, Dr. Fairbank was invited by Government to engage in special "famine work". He prepared a monograph on the peculiar rat which suddenly swarmed in vast multitudes over some parts of the Deccan. He was familiar with the flora of the Deccan[517].

The famine of 1896-97 was more wide spread than any other famine[518], India has experienced hitherto. It was officially described at that time as the most disastrous famine of the country[519]. Pandita Ramabai had herself suffered terrible privations from famine during her wander years. She had begged food for her dying mother and had lived with her brother on roots and wild berries. She departed now for the stricken area. The first site of three little famished skeleton like forms determined her in her resolve to admit into her institution all the destitute girls who needed refuge. She organized at Khedgaon near Poona, the *Mukti Sadan* or the house of salvation[520]. The mention of pathetic communication[521] from Pandita Ramabai concerning her experiences in the famine districts in quest of starving child-widows is mentioned. It states there are now over 70 famine child widows in Pandita Ramabai's Home, and many more are expected soon. Many issues of *BG* of January and February month of 1897 covered Pandita Ramabai's famine experiences and these issues soon got exhausted.

515 Nalini Keller, *Women under the Cross changing Gender roles in Christian families*, Cosmos, New Delhi,1997, p. 9

516 M. D. David, *Asia and Christianity*, Himalaya Publication, Bombay,1985, p.169

517 *BG*, June 8, 1878, p. 117

518 Between 1866 and 1900 there were four major famines in India. In all 9 million people died of starvation, hardly any part of India was free from this curse.

519 N. Benjamin, "Great Famine of 1896-97, The Missionary factor" in Indian Church History Review, June 2006, p. 1

520 Eunice D. Souza and Lindsay Pereira, *Womens Voices*, OUP, New Delhi, 2002, p. 60

521 *BG*, January 1897, p. 8

In the Financial Report of Mukti school and Mission Pandita Ramabai writes of the sad lack of rain which has been felt through the Bombay Presidency and other parts of India.....she says, "The girls had scarcely any vegetables during the past 6 months, and as the grains were growing dearer and dearer we had to give up eating rice, wheat and other such nourishing things and lived on Jwari, the coarsest and cheapest grain we could get. This *Jwari* even is to be had at a high price now. Our cows and buffaloes yield very little milk as they have no green grass. All but 30 very little children have to go without milk and butter[522].

The Indian Messenger (Calcutta)[523] entitled Christian Missionaries and the famine, "Famine work must not close without a word of recognition of the valuable services rendered by Christian Missionaries towards mitigating its horrors. All honour to these ambassadors of Christ. They have proved themselves to be worthy followers of Him whose heart bled for the sorrows of men. For the last 6 months every Mission station in the central provinces, amongst the santhals, in central India, in Guzerat and in many parts of the Western Presidency, was converted into a relief camp. The Missionary workers did not know rest, but were out day and night relieving distress and saving lives. The strain was so severe that one of these workers writes: "every Mission in these parts has lost at least one European worker by death and ours one each month for the last 4 months." Not only did these workers offer themselves as sacrifice, but money also flowed freely for the relief of distress from Christian centers in the country and abroad. Verily at this threshold of the 20th century Christian philanthropy comes to us with a healing balm for the many afflictions of mankind—Let all classes of Indian society accord their admiration to these worthy servants of Christ in unstinted measure.

A write up by Helen S. Dyer entitled the "Sharada Sadan" in Camp talks about 160 inmates of Sharada Sadan, "the new comers from the famine districts were accommodated in eight tents under the care of Ms. Soonderabai Pawar". When Helen asked Pawar,

522 *BG*, September 16, 1899, FrontPage

523 *BG*, November 10, 1900, p. 2

"How did you come to get this little ones? They are not widows? Oh! in various ways was the reply. " This one Pandita found by herself in a Jungle, deserted, and in an apparently dying state...[524]

Mansukhlal's writeup's of famine in The Panch Mahals can be seen in May 1900 issues of *BG*

Picture 8.2: Famine affected family
(Source: Missionary Herald, January 1906, p.6)

Mansukhlal's writeup's of famine in The Panch Mahals, can be seen in May 1900 issues of *BG*.

524 *BG*, April 3, 1897, p. 9

Picture 8.3: Famine affected children at Roha (Source: Roha Famine Children (1900), American Mission Report of 1900, p. 36)

Picture 8.4: Family affected by famine (before and after shelter) (Source: Famine Children before and after they received care (1900), American Mission Report of 1900, p. 49)

Picture 8.5: Group of Famine widows moved to Ms. Abott's Home (Mumbai) (Source : American Mission Report of 1900, p. 55)

8.5 The Plague issue

One of the most debilitating diseases in this period was plague[525]. In December 1896, a terrible plague broke out in Pune, which led to the assassination of Plague commissioner Rand in June 1897. In 1898 the Plague[526] continued low in Poona, but owing to its increase in Bombay, so much quarantine was imposed that traveling was made very difficult for Natives. Seven days detention was ordered at Kalyan of all leaving Bombay and 10 days detention at Poona of those arriving from the other side.

8.5.1 Dr. Goheen's initiative during Plague

From 1918 for a decade plague was raging in Vengurla town. Dr. Goheen started a rat-killing campaign by dividing the whole town

525 Plague and Famine issues were widely covered in American Marathi Mission report for 1897. Also Plague and Riots in Bombay is discussed by Dr. Karmarkar on page 19 of the American Marathi Mission Report for 1898.

526 *BG*, January 1898, p. 5

into wards. With the help of the medical staff, municipal staff and volunteers, poisoned baits were placed in every house on the same day, dead rats were destroyed to uproot plague. Again in August 1930, Dr. Goheen called a meeting of official and private medical men of Vengurla and vicinity. This body made recommendations for a thorough health campaign in the whole town, including rat destruction (rat destruction battle heed Dr. Goheen as general) sanitation, inoculation etc.

Thus we see the issues and debates on drinking, opium addiction, famine, plague epidemic, taken up by the Missionaries and its information brought to limelight by the weekly *BG* which attended longetivity amongst the members of literary common wealth. The pictures charts and poems provide glimpses into the contemporary situation.

The Christian voluntary movements also contributed in some way in highlighting the above issues and are separately dealt with.

Chapter 9

Christian Voluntary Movements

Chapter 9

Christian Voluntary Movements

9.1 Introduction

The Christian Voluntary Movements like the YWCA, YMCA and the Salvation Army took birth around 19th century. The YWCA was one of the oldest and largest multicultural women's organisation throughout the world. It was basically started to eliminate racism and empower women. With its roots in the Christian faith and strengthened by diversity, the YWCA brings together members striving to create various opportunities for growth of women. The focus was on leadership and power to attain peace, justice, freedom, and dignity for all concerned. The YMCA Movement was formed to overcome the unhealthy conditions after the historical industrial revolution including those like helping servicemen and noncombatants during national wars.

The Salvation Army was a Christian movement, international, multiracial and non political. It combined a fervent, joyous, religious, faith with a practical and a world wide social service. It had identified itself aggressively with the imperial aims of England of the time. Born in the 1870's it catched on the popular image of romanticised imperialism by adopting marches, flags, brass bands and uniforms for its employees[527]. General Booth had spelt out his plans to salvage the English poor in his detailed work, *In Darkest England and the Way Out* in 1890.

The United Service Organizations (USO, 1940) brought together YMCA, YWCA and Salvation Army along with various supporting associations. Today YWCA and YMCA centers address to the critical social needs of the people including children and adults of all ages, races, faiths, backgrounds, abilities and income levels. They have gone a long way in imbibing positive values, commitment to service and motivation to learn amongst youth and children alike. The organizations have played a prominent role in improving family and hence community relations besides helping for the overall development of an individual. The help and support needed by the youth during the crucial beginning years of earning a living is clearly visible through their activities. This chapter highlights the 19th century important issues in connection with YWCA, YMCA and the Salvation Army.

9.2 Young Women's Christian Association (YWCA)

YWCA was started in 1851 in London by Lady Kinnaird[528] its an organization in the service of women, by women, with women and for women[529]. It is the oldest institution which conducts courses in continuing education (non-formal). It is a well known organization working mainly for the weaker section of the society.

Picture 9.1: Symbol of YWCA

527 Meena Radhakrishna, *Missionaries and Myth Making: Salvation Army and Itinerant Communities in Madras Presidency*, May 1997, Teen Murti, New Delhi, p. 23

528 *BG*, January 13, 1900, p. 12

529 Roy Kinikar (ed) *International Women Years Book*, Bombay, 1975, p. 256

A profile of YWCA In India

In 1987, YWCA in Mumbai completed its 100 years to the community at large. Their motto is by love serve one another. The "Blue Triangle" symbol of the association seeks to unify the three aspects of a perfect personality, body, mind and spirit. It is a endeavor of the association to promote the full development of women and girls and to develop a responsive membership through service to the changing needs of the whole community, in a changing world. YWCA started the first hostel for working women at Dhobi Talao in 1887[530]. YWCA has its branches all over the world. For overall management and coordination there is general board of management.

The name Young Women's Christian Association and the institute women originated in the union of two associations[531] (open to young women of all denominations and all classes of society) for the benefit of young women.

Table 9.1: The associations of YWCA

The Friendly Union	*The Prayer Union*
It consists of members of Bible classes and any young women who may desire to place themselves under Christian influence.	The members are those who desire distinctly and avowedly to be on the side of Christ and to unite in prayer on Friday, Saturday or Sunday evening.

The monthly magazine of the association was entitled *"Home Friend".* Dowager Lady Kinnard was associated with the formation of YWCA, she died in 1888[532]. In *BG* of May 30, 1891 in an article entitled 'Is the YWCA suited for India', Hon. Emily Kinnard[533]

530 Joshi Sulabha, "An evaluative Study a few selected continuing education programmes for women for weaker section, run by YWCA, Bombay", *Masters Diploma in Adult and Continuing Education of SNDT,* May 1987, Bombay, p. 22

531 *BG,* February 7, 1880, p. 591

532 *BG,* December 29, 1888, front page.

533 *BG,* March 1898, p. 12 mentions Lord and Lady Kinnaird's 3 months visit to the Mission stations of the Z. B. and M. M. and the Presidency cities (Calcutta,

writes "as an organised means of helping you g women of all classes, the YWCA has proved itself to be most powerful instrument. It has the advantage over the other organizations of being world wide in its character, Catholic in its working, simple in its constitution. Its aim is a very high one ... to bring every girl to realize the high ideal of Christian womanhood : Its rules are most adaptable for they are meant for women of every land, its method are simple and vary according to the needs of different countries". Founded in 1855 its different departments have helped thousands of girls to a better life for this world and the next.

Alice Andrews of the Zenana Mission House, Ludhiana wrote .... "Dear, Miss Kinniard, I feel it a matter of deep thankfulness that you are devoting yourself to encouraging , developing and consolidating the YWCA throughout India". She pressed the great need for the spread of YWCA amongst native Christian girls.

Emily Kinniard describes two forms of YWCA work found specially adapted in India.

Table 9.2: Forms of YWCA work

Branches in hill stations for Bible study as a means of banding English girls of different classes together.	Branches in native Christian Villages and Compounds which will help band the women together in Christian fellowship.

Emily further exclaims "looked at from a Missionary point of view the YWCA had already done good. In Bombay the members have met fortnightly ever since April 1891 to work for the Missionary hospital which sorely needed many articles the Mission was unable to afford and they met one day at the hospital to see the patients enjoying and benefiting by the fruits of their labor....

The need of YWCA in India is so great that volume might be written upon the missing links...

Madras and Bombay)

I. All classes of young women have been drawn together thus breaking down to some extent the caste feeling, which even in own land has often hindered the lords work.

II. The gatherings held in the rooms of the Association have been instrumental in bringing many souls to Christ and leading others to a fuller consecration of themselves to his service.

The boarding houses have saved many young women from evil influences who have been (and sometimes suddenly so) thrown out of situations when far from home and friends".

BG of May 2 1896 (page 4) carries a report 'opening of a Home in Bombay for the Young Women's Chrisitan Association.' It says "for several years the Bombay YWCA have had in view the desirablility of a place where central meetings could be held, and where a Home for Young women in business and unprotected girls passing through the city could find shelter. This was one need, a permanent secretary was the other". Miss Wardlaw Ramsay rented a house in Nesbit Road, Mazgaon Mumbai and had volunteered for its secretary ship.

On Tuesday 26th September 1893, the Grant Road YMCA[534] had an interesting debate on " Would the amalgamation of the YMCA and YWCA be mutually beneficial ?" Mr. W. Lane, Mr. E. J. Harrison and Mr. T. T. Wright spoke on the negative side. It brought forward that there were certain lines of work which alone women could do, and the other lines which only men could perform and it was argued that amalgamation would tend to weaken all such specialist work. On the positive side it highlighted the fact that "the best work in the world is done by the joint efforts of men and women"[535],[536]. The girl guide movement was taken up in Bombay in 1912 by the Bombay YWCA.

---

534 YMCA is composed of members from all churches, *BG*, March 10, 1888, p. 147

535 *BG*, September 30, 1893, p. 8

536 M. D. David, *How Much We can do for Others (brief history of YMCA)*, Ebenezer Printing House, Mumbai, 2005, p. 2

9.3 Young Men's Christian Association (YMCA)

The YMCA was founded in London by George William on 6th June 1844. Later it spread to the other parts of the globe.

Picture 9.2: Symbol of YMCA

While Christianity remains divided the YMCA came to symbolise the spirit of Christian unity and reconciliation. By 1888, YMCA became a Missionary movement. Luther L. Gulick invented the Symbol of YMCA, the Red inverted equilateral Triangle[537] in 1891. The triangle indicates the three fold nature of man, mind, body and spirit.

The YMCA National Convention was held at Bombay in December 1899 to January 01, 1900. Forth six earnest men from all parts of India met together with one accord to discuss the one great question of YMCA life - how to help and save the young men of India whether European, Anglo-Indian or Pure Natives of the soil. Such was the soul of the convention.[538]

YMCA work had two objects[539] firstly to bring non-Christian students into Christian atmosphere as a means to a knowledge of the truth as it is in Jesus and secondly to build up life of the Christian members. One of the most interesting parts of the work of YMCA

---

537 Represents harmonious development of women's personality namely body - mind - spirit.

538 *BG,* January 6, 1900, p. 10

539 *BG,* May 20, 1899, p. 3

was among sailors[540]. *Bombay Young Men* (1905) was the official organ of the Bombay Young Men's Christian Association.

Earlier the roles of YMCA were focused on providing Hostel accommodation in different areas and encourage sports today. It also carries community activity especially running *Balwadi's* in slums in Mumbai and mobilizes youth for preservation of peace, equality and harmony to build a just society and also for preservation of nature.

In January 9th 1896, YMCA, Apollo Bunder, Bombay hosted the student voluntary movement conference, where in the Christian Masters of the Indore College had spoken about YMCA work to the Hindu Students who had begged for the formation of the YMCA.

Mr. A. C. Owen was a warm supporter of YMCA. Mr. A. E. B. Gordon's suggestive paper on the duty of YMCA[541] has been published, It said " in 1905 the YMCA in Bombay completed 30 years. It had a membership of 500 then, with four religious meetings weekly, literary, social, athletic and games departments, reading room, library and restaurant".[542]

To mark the 150th birth anniversary of YMCA (1855-2005) Dr. M. D. David wrote a brief History of the YMCA entitled *How Much Can We Do For Others.*

9.4 Salvation Army

The movement was founded by William Booth and his wife Catherine in 1865. There first meetings were conducted in a dilapidated tent. William Booth renamed the Christian Mission to the Salvation Army in 1878. A military plan of organization was adopted, Mission stations became corps, members became soldiers, and evangelists became officers. Other distinctive features included uniforms, ranks, the designing of a flag and a crest.

This Crest was designed in 1878 by Captain William H. Ebden. The 'S" stands for salvation and the swords for its warfare: the cross represents the Cross of Jesus and the shots, the truth of the Gospel. The surround the sun is the sun of Righteousness and speaks of the

540 *BG*, April 23, 1881, p. 123
541 *BG*, April 30, 1904, p. 11
542 *BG*, January 21, 1905, front page.

Picture 9.3: The Crest of Salvation Army

fire and light of the Holy Spirit. The whole is surmounted by a crown of glory which god will give to all His Soldiers who are faithful to the end.

Salvation Army was the largest and most well known of the organizations that operated in the American Cities. In 1880, the first official Salvation Army contingent arrived in the US[543]. Evangeline Booth daughter of the founder of the Salvation Army William Booth[544] was in US[545].

One of the favorite hymns of the Salvation Army commences thus – Elijah was a Jolly old man, and was carried up to heaven in a fiery van. The moral of this interesting specimen of fervent psalmody

543 *BG*, February 28, 1880, front page reports that the Salvation Army has made its appearance in Philadelphia and many persons of the lowest classes were being converted.

544 His evangelistic efforts in the slums of East London in mid -1860's was the origin of the Salvation Army.

545 Mark A. Knoll and others (ed), *Eerdmans Handbook to Christianity in America*, Grand Rapids, Michigan 1980, p. 350

is: - "Let us every one be a jolly old man and be carried up to heaven in a fiery van" [546].

A letter by T. Glover in *Bombay Guardian* of January 26, 1884 (p. 53) talks of Salvation Army's arrival in Bombay. The Salvation Army adopted certain measures and modes which other bodies of Christians had not thought suited to a Gospel Ministry. The members of the Salvation Army were expected to glorify god by giving the whole strength to the Army and treating other religious bodies as of comparatively little accounts[547]. In 1885, the head quarters of the Salvation Army was removed from Bombay to Kanery Caves (Salsette Island)[548].

Salvation Army chose to draw people to their services by means of music, banners and sensational handbills[549]. According to *BG* of September 3, 1887 (p. 567), some of the Salvation Army members shaved their heads and painted their foreheads to seek converts from high caste natives in south India.

The salvation army arrived in the Travancore area in 1891. Centers were established in Nagercoil, Trivandrum, Mavelikara and Tiruvalla. Membership included converts from *Parayas* of Southern Travancore and *Pulayas* of Northerm Travancore[550]. Salvation army in Travancore is also covered in April 18, 1896 issue of *BG* (p. 11)

Many of the salvation army have given up home and business and good worldly prospects for a mere maintenance allowance and the joy of being engaged in what they believe with their whole hearts to be gods purpose for saving the world. An article on Mrs. Booth Tucker[551] reads... "Tucker had come with 50 new workers from England and stated that after six years of waiting the salvation army had got permission to play music to the native streets, as the

546 *BG*, September 11, 1882, p. 3
547 *BG*, May 24, 1884, p. 323
548 *BG*, July 25, 1885, p. 467
549 *BG*, September 2, 1882, p. 554
550 K. C. Zakariah, *The Syrian Christains of Kerala*, Orient Longman, New Delhi, 2006, p. 68
551 *BG*, September 29, 1888, p. 617

Hindus and Mohammedans are already allowed to do". She sang the following[552]...

All I have I'm bringing to thee
In thy steps I will follow
Come Joy or Come Sorrow
Dear Savoir I will follow thee !"

A salvation Army song by Commissioner Booth Clibborn of Paris...

TUNE- "Life's morn will soon be wanning"
See the Army comes to bless you,
Comes to set your spirit free;
For their Master to possess you
That you too with Christ may be.
Then your happy life outflowing
In this saving course shall run,
Ever good on, all bestowing,
Holy, radiant like the sun

The article[553] "The Christian Church and the Temperance Cause" mentions Mr. Tomlinson's views on the subject of temperance. He gave an interesting sketch of the spread of the movement in Scotland and England and showed how the temperance movement came from America to England and was sent back to America as a total abstinence movement. The oldest and the youngest of the Christian Churches- the Roman Catholics and the Salvation Army- were doing much for the temperance cause. In the youngest they found total abstinence was made an absolute basis for all its officers of which there are over 2000 and the oldest Church has formed a temperance society called the league of the cross under Archbishop Manning.

The Criminal law Amendment Act following the demonstrations of 1886 rose the age of protection for young girls thereby providing for more effectual punishment of the flesh trade.

552 *BG*, January 25, 1896, p. 10
553 *BG*, July 04, 1891, p. 3

The rescue and Preventive work in this direction by Mrs. Bramwell Booth[554] of the Salvation Army received Universal sympathy. They established "Rescue Home" in Bombay and were open to receive cases from all parts of India. The article[555] illustrates the portraits of the staff devoted at the "Rescue Home". Moreover the Rescue staff used to visit women in the worst part of the city and had set up a small rented house at Camathipura. It is reported that in 3 months period, 243 houses of Infamy had been visited thereby rescuing 13 women. The Staff walked along the streets inviting the people to support the cause. The open air meetings were held sometimes. The women in the Home did all kinds of needle work like plain sewing or as the need may be. Captain Dayabai says "this work of salvation though slow and needs patience but is surely encouraging".

About the Salvation Army Pandita Ramabai in her writeup 'To the Friends of the Mukti School and Mission' writes "There are some among the girls brought from Central India who could not be safely placed among the Mukti girls. The dear servant of God, major Yuddhabai, of the Salvation Army, took care of over 25 of them in her home for women. As she is now about to leave for England, it was thought advisable to bring some of them back to be placed in a separate home at Kedgaum. Several of the girls are still in the Salvation Army's Home for women to be trained as Christian workers, I am thankful to know that they have given their hearts to God and are willing to do His work......... Many people have the idea that the officers of the Army are entirely recruited from the lower classes in India. It is true that some of their brightest gems have been gathered from the gutter, but the majority of the staff officers are persons of education and good position in life."

A big full page write up "Salvation Army in India and its Critics" can be seen on page 9 of *BG* of February 29,1896. The state of Salvation Army in Gujarat was widely covered in the March issue of the above paper. Also the role of Major's Hira Singh and Amrit

554 In 1898 Pandita Ramabai in London shared platform with one Mrs. Bollington Booth who spoke about her work in America Prisons (*BG*, June 11, 1898, p. 12)

555 *BG*, February 15, 1896, p. 3

Bai related to Salvation Army in Madras can be seen in *BG* of March 21, 1896.

In 1988, Rotary's highest honour for world understanding, good will and peace through selfless service was given to the Salvation Army.

Picture 9.4: Salvation Army run Hostel at Colaba (more than 75 years old)

Picture 9.5: Shield of the Salvation Army

In the 21st Century these voluntary organizations have to take greater challenges for the overall development of the society. New programmes involving youth towards international co-operation and goodwill is the need of the present day.

Chapter 10

Conclusion

"The American Missionaries especially aimed at preparing Indians to take over and carry forward the Missionary work which they had started"
.... R. F. Goheen

10.1 Conclusion

Coastal Maharashtra popularly known as Konkan is geographically separated from the Deccan (*Desh*) by the Sahyadri range in the east and by the Arabian sea on the west which has influenced its history, politics, economy and culture. The topography of coastal Maharashtra has always been congenial to settlement. In this region; bays, peninsulas, estuaries and capes coexist. From first century till fourteenth century AD the Missionary work was sporadic. It has gained momentum only after the arrival of Vasco da Gama via the sea route. The patches which were most influenced by the Missionaries include Bassein (Vasai), Korlai and later Bombay (now Mumbai) during the initial stages to be followed by places like Kalyan, Roha and Vengurla.

The arrival of European powers, especially the Portuguese led to mass scale conversions to Christianity along the coastal belt of Maharashtra. With the aim of spreading the 'Word of Gospel', the initial Missionary efforts aimed at contacting local crowd through varied means. Consistent efforts were made by Missionaries in the sixteenth century to learn the local language. There were also efforts to spread the Portuguese language among the local people. There is a mention of the Jesuits, learning Konkani (also called *Canorimor Lingua Brahmana*) from 1540's. A parallel can be found with Rev. Savidge and J. H. Lorrain learning Lushai language of Mizos in the late nineteenth century and codifying the first Mizo alphabets.

Even after conversions most indigenous Christians of the region retained their former traditional patterns. William Carey, a radical Missionary sought to arouse public opinion against several evils like infanticide and sati. He was instrumental in planting teak trees as well as setting up the Agri-Horticultural Society to practically improve India's agricultural economy and supply of food for the people. The Missionary efforts brought interaction among various castes especially before independent India. There was remarkable progress in the arena of education.

The educational and medical work of Missionaries in different regions of India during the British period has been discussed by many writers. A more complete and in-depth analysis of the coastal belt of Maharashtra, supported by equal number of primary sources, from a completely different viewpoint forms the basis of this dissertation. The seeds the Missionaries laid in spreading female and vernacular education especially after 1850 bore fruits later. The work of the powerful Trio of the Scottish Mission in Maharashtra namely Murray Mitchell, Robert Nesbit and John Wilson reveal the importance of education. Wilson was closely connected with the University of Bombay from its foundation (1868) and during his term of office as Vice Chancellor (October1868 to March 1870), the foundation stone of the University Library and the Clock tower was laid. He always stressed the importance of Indian languages.

The Missionaries made a timely beginning in the spread of liberal education in our country. The progress of education among the women and the untouchables triggered the general awakening and were slowly freed of general restrictions imposed on them by the Indian society. Female education helped in changing the outlook of women towards their family and instilled in them a new desire for economic independence. A different social setup stated to evolve and the torch was further carried by the Indian converts like Pandita

Rambai, Naryan Waman Tilak and others who got converted to Christianity and were nationalist to the core of their heart. They strengthened the foundation of Missionary activity initiated by the Missionaries for the betterment of our country.

The most challenging work of printing textbooks, story books, essays and prayers in various languages by the Missionaries in nineteenth century has today culminated into the curriculum development and its review from time to time by the NCERT and various State Boards in India. The progress in this line has realized new heights leading to the child-centred system (CCS) of education outlined in the National policy of Education (1986). In CCS system children's get lot of space to explore rather than compelling them to learn by rote method. The focus of the presentation of the content in the textbook is on development of processes and skills with a view to sustain the interest of the children, dialogues, indoor and outdoor activities, dramatization etc. The aim is to develop imaginative activities and questions amongst children. The two poems composed on learning Grammar in 'Rhyme for School Boys' and The 'Punctuation Points' are so relevant even today.

The Mission schools have produced distinguished citizens through their educational institutions like Sunil Gavaskar, Ismail Merchant, Pankaj Udhas, Michael Fereira, Morarji Desai (former PM), Poet Nissim Ezekiel, Journalist R. K. Karanjia, B. K. Karanjia, Rajdeep Sardesai and Cricketer Dilip Sardesai etc. The 'discipline factor 'in schools as well as their community meetings has been maintained to date. A vide variety of institutions catering to the technical, vocational, medical, female education, handicapped and the home for the aged have been successfully run through out our country. St. Xavier's group of Institutions has put strong footing in technical, vocational and management education at all levels. Fr. Agnelo Technical Complex has made its mark in twin city of Mumbai (New Bombay). The Nirmala Niketan College is devoted to study of social work and home science. Sophia College, in Mumbai city is an exclusive women's College run by the Missionaries. An attached polytechnic and *Sadhana* school for mentally retarded children adds to its glory. Mar Thoma school for the disabled children, Shantivan home for the aged and holy cross hospital have become important land marks of Kalyan City.

The Missionary families were emotionally attached with the places of their work. Missionary children have reached great heights which go clearly against the notion that Missionary children average up fairly well. The best example is of that of Late Dr. Robert F Goheen born to Dr. R. H. H. Goheen and Ewing Goheen, the medical Presbyterian Missionaries at Vengurla who later had an opportunity to visit our country as an Indian Ambassador (1977). The medical doctors of the Mission were active and kept themselves updated from time to time through the bodies like Christian Medical Association of India. The new techniques and methods employed to treat the prevalent diseases of those times were discussed in their meetings. They used to share their experience and information in their mother countries thus influencing youth to take part in the Missionary activities. Their work was not only was confined to medicine but their Missionary's wives used to dedicate their time in educational and vocational activities. There are Missionaries like Dr. Ron Seaton and Edith Seaton and Dr. Lester Servid, who had liberally donated money for the cause of Charity.

The nineteenth Century Bengal and Maharashtra can be compared on the basis of synonymous issues like conversions, widow remarriage and intellectual communities. The Serampore Missionaries brought vernacular education to the villages around Serampore. The first printing of Marathi was in Dr. Carey's, *Grammar of the Mahratta Language* (marathi) printed at the Baptist Mission Press at Serampore (1805). Later many tracts were written as well as translated on widow remarriage.

The Methodists, the Evangelical's, the Priest's were most active Christian sects of 19th Century Bengal. The Calcutta Tract Society was functional in Bengal while the Bombay Tract and Book Society were popular in Bombay. The Missionary habit of maintaining systematic records of their experiences which they got during women's education, field trips, medical conferences and lectures have been well preserved. A host of news bulletins like The *Missionary Herald, Oriental Christian Spectator, Bombay Guardian, Dnyanodaya, Bamdad and Western India Notes* brought out information on

American and European Missionary organizations. The Davidsonian and Church Missionary Journal of India carried the real experiences of the Missionaries. All these publications have served as potential primary source materials in shaping the dissertation in its present form. It is felt that an independent study on regions other than Maharashtra can be attempted using these sources. Similarly the work of American Marathi Missionaries in rural areas of Bombay Presidency in the *Ghat* region of Maharashtra calls for an independent study. The Missionary records during natural calamities like plague and famine in late nineteenth century may be explored from economic point of view. It contains sufficient data for statistical analysis of the areas and people affected during these calamities. The Orphan children affected by the famine of 1901 were taken care by Laxmibai Tilak and later passed on to Soonderabai Pawar at Pune for further training. The environmental concern, establishment of temperance societies, fearless appeal against Opium- drug addiction and women's emancipation are of much relevance even today. Due to global nature of Christian voluntary organizations like YWCA and YMCA, a sought of attachment and good will between the countries have been developed. The dreams of young generation are realized by a host of activities carried out world over by these organizations. Cardinal Oswald Gracias, the Archbishop of Bombay recently exclaimed 'India is leading figure in the world now, even the Vatican is internationalizing with its recognition to Asian contribution.

The faith of local community in the Church (Diocese) and the spread of Gospel in local vernacular language reflect the process of Inculturation. We see Fathers not only serving Mass or tending to his Parishioners but also to art for e.g. father Peter Drego has formed a museum in the Choir loft of St. Andrews Church., Bandra. It includes wooden and silver artifacts and ornate crosses rosary and candle stands. The recent Indianised version of the Bible with reference to the Upanishads and the Bhagvad Gita and drawings of a turbaned Joseph and a sari-clad Mother Mary with baby Jesus in her arms has been published by St. Pauls Mumbai (Appendix-5). It also has reference to Meerabai, Mahatma Gandhi and Rabindranath Tagore. It brings the Christian message in an Indian context. This project was inspired by the Christian Community Bible in Spanish in the Philippines, the brainchild of Berbard Hurault, a Chilean Priest. The Heras Institute Musuem, Community Musuem of Korlai and many others have contributed to the preservation of our heritage.

The Jesuit community fathers are well qualified and distinguished in their respective fields of study. Fr. Aubrey Masceranas holds a doctorate in Sanskrit, was director of Heras Institute and editor of Indica Journal from Mumbai. Fr. Saldhana is attached to St. Pius Seminary at Mumbai includes teaching of Dogmatic Theology and Missiology and has authored several books. The other names in this direction include Bishop Thomas Dabre and Fr. Francis Britto of Vasai. Late Fr. Aloysius Schlegel was called an ordinary man with an extraordinary life, who established Jnandeepa Vidyapeeth Library in Pune based on his study on the library systems in USA and UK.

The author would like to emphasize the fact-often ignored-that in spite of their blind faith in the exclusive truth of their own religion and the activities to which it led, one should not look upon the Missionaries as devoid of many good qualities which we appreciate in men. For this would prepare the ground for the object the author has in view in writing this dissertation, namely a proper appreciation of their contribution to the intellectual and moral progress of the people of Konkan.

Thus we see direct and indirect changes being brought by the efforts of various Missionary works. The present work helps to define Christian Missions and to highlight the motive behind their works. It provides a systematic and in-depth study of work of Christian institutions (educational, medical, vocational and evangelical) since their advent in India with reference to Coastal belt of Maharashtra. The Impact of Christian Influence on the local populace has been dealt with. The devotion of the Missionaries towards the social work (see questionnaire Survey) has been highlighted. A detailed list of primary and secondary sources available for the study of Missionary history has been prepared. Interaction with Christian Institutions imparting training of various kinds and with the priests associated therewith has been thus brought out. An overall review and progress of Missionary activities with an insight into how the Christian Institutions were developed, maintained and its relevance to the present day society has been covered.

Some of the prime issues still faced by our country are education for the deprived class, women education and medicine and health care. A systematic approach to the education system, dedication and hard work is needed for this purpose. Generation of funds, generous grants from the public, sense of brotherhood among countrymen, dedication to Mission, empowerment of women and measures for good health of the local population is called for. The Missionary help and guidance in this direction will surely go a long way in achieving the above goals.

Appendix-1

List of Libraries & their Collection

S. No.	*Library*	*Content*
1	Maharashtra State Archives (Elphinstone College)	19th Century News Papers - Bombay Guardian, Telegraph and Courier News Paper, Poona Observer, Times of India
2	Kolhapur Archives (branch of Maharashtra Archives)	*Rumals* during the time of Shahu Maharaj
3	Balasheb Khardekar Library, Shivaji University, Kolhapur	Ph.D Thesis
4	Asiatic Society, Mumbai	Indian Antiquary, Oriental Christian Spectator, Bombay Guardian
5	Ahmednagar College Library	Missionary Herald, Dyanodaya, International Bulletin, Annual Report of the American Board of Commissions for Foreign Missions, Report of the American Marathi Mission, Indian Missionary Directory and Memorial Volume

6	Mumbai University Fort Library and JNU Library, Kalina.	*Bhartiya Vidya*, Voice of India, Oriental Christian Spectator, Calcutta Review, Annual Report of the Bombay Auxiliary Scottish Missionary Society, A Short History of the Elphinstone High School
7	SNDT University Library, Mumbai	Ph.D Thesis
8	Wilson College Library, Mumbai	OCS, Dyanodaya
9	Sophia College Library, Mumbai	Secondary Sources
10	Xaviers College Library (Heras Institute)	The Examiner, Indian Antiquary
11	Pius Seminary Library, Mumbai	The Examiner
12	Baisinger Library, Miraj	Western India Notes
13	American Information Resource Centre (AIRC), Churchgate	Secondary resources
14	Goa Archives, Goa	Some Primary and Secondary Sources
15	Central Library, Panaji	*O Heraldo* (in portuguse)
16	Jnandeep Vidyapeeth Library – Papal Seminary, Pune	Secondary Sources
17	Jaykar Library, Pune University	Ph.D Thesis
18	United Theological College Library, Bangalore	Secondary Sources
19	Presbyterian Historical Society, Philadelphia, USA	Original R. H. H. Goheen Family Papers

20	Topiwala Library, Kudal	Local History of Konkan region
21	Sarvajanik Vachnalaya, Vengurla	Local History of Konkan region, old books
22	Jeevan Darshan Kendra, Vasai	Suvarta Magazine
23	Marathi Granth Sanghralaya, Dadar, Mumbai.	Secondary Sources
24	K. R. Cama Oriental Institute Library, Mumbai	*Bamdad*
25	K. J. Somaiya College of Arts and Commerce Library, Mumbai	Secondary Sources
26	Nehru Science Centre Library, Mumbai	Secondary Sources
27	Khem Sawant College, Sawantwadi	*Vainateya* News Paper
28	Sophia Center for Women, Mumbai	Secondary Sources
29	Nirmala Niketan Library	Books on Social Work

Appendix-2

Letters of Private Correspondences

I. **Dr. Robert F. Goheen,** rfgoheen@princeton.edu
Former President Emeritus, Princeton University
U.S. (Ambassador to India, 1977-1980)

13th April 2008

Dear Dr. Khandpekar,

I am sorry to have to inform you that my father died on March 31st.

Stephen Goheen

8th October 2007

Dear Dr.Khandpekar;

I have your aerogramme of Sept 21and must apologize for my recent silence. I have been under the weather for some weeks and am still quite short of energy. If you wish to call me by 'phone, toward the middle of the day, any weekday, would probably do. My number here is 609.-924-2751

Best regards --- R. F. Goheen.

23rd January 2007

The Co-ordinator
Research Fellowship Program
Presbyterian Historical Society
415 Lombard St. Philadelphia , PA 19147 -1516

Dear Coordinator:

I am writing to recommend again consideration of Dr. Neeta Khandpekar, of Mumbai, India, for one of the Society's research fellowships. Over the past two years she has shared with me the written results of her investigations into the work of the Christian Missions in western India, with particular reference to the Konkan region and the former Western India Mission of the Presbyterian Church. In my judgement she is an industrious. and sound researcher working in a field that merits wider attention.

As I indicated a year ago, I do have a special interest in this case. My parents served in the then Western India Mission for forty years and worked in Konkan region during much of that time. Their efforts and those of their colleagues have been recorded and analyzed only in a most fragmentary way so far as I have been able to discover. Naturally

I am interested in encouraging more serious research and writing that may illuminate that phase of the Presbyterian Church's engagement in the development of what was to become an independent India .

Access to the records in your files of the work on my parents (Robert H. H. and Anne E.), my grandparents (Joseph M. and Amanda), and Uncle and Aunt (John L. and Jane) and of their dedicated colleagues would do much to fill out the account that Dr. Khandpekar is developing . I do hope you can grant her that opportunity.

November 13, 2006

Neeta wrote :

Respected Dr. Robert Goheen,

Following information on Page 135 of India Missionary Directory, 1876 says J. M. Goheen born in February 1847 at Rock Spring , Pennsylvania , USA . Converted in 1865, Graduated at Princeton College in 1872, and at Princeton Theological Seminary in 1875...

What does the above Converted means ?

regards,
Dr. Mrs. Neeta Khandpekar, Mumbai

Reply :

I expect it means accepted baptism and membership in the Church, probably as a Presbyterian, after having rejected those ties earlier in his life.

Thank you for the picture of the Carters.

Best regards., Bob Goheen

17th October, 2006

Your letter arrived today following your e-mail inquiry of yesterday. A corrected genealogical chart follows

Joseph Milliken Goheen & Amanda McGuines [Kolhapur]

Robert H. H. Goheen & Anne Ewing John Lawrence Goheen & Jane Corbett

[Vengurla and Miraj] [Sangli and Allahabad]

Nancy Sherrard John L., Jr. [Jack] Alice Ewing Mary [May]
Richard R. P. [Dick]
Hunter Robert F.[Bob]
Patricia [Patsy]
Andrew C.[Andy]
Good luck on Oct. 17. R. F. Goheen

6th June 2006

Dear Dr. Khandpekar - ... I look forward to seeing it fleshed out as you continue your investigations.

You ask for a copy of Dr. Fletcher's book. Unfortunately I gave my Copy away sometime ago. You will surely have a chance to read the book when you visit the Presbyterian Historical Society. You also ask for a photograph of me. I have never collected them but shall see if I can turn one up. Finally, you ask for the title of my PhD dissertation. It was THE IMAGERY OF SOPHOCLES' ANTIGONE and obviously reflects a very different set on interests than those that relate me to India

With best regards -R. F. Goheen

23rd April 2006

Dear Dr. Khandpekar—I'm glad that the Bassinger Library has proved so fruitful.

In reply to your questions, Dick and Bob must refer to my older brother (IRichard R. P. Goheen) and me. Jane Corbett Goheen was the wife of one of my father's younger brothers, John Lawrence Goheen. She and her husband served as Missionaries in Sangli for many years. He established a vocational school there and later he headed the Allahabad Agricultural Institute. An unusual phase in his career that for a number of years he served as Diwan of the then princely state of Itchelcurenji (sp ?).

I don't have family pictures from India days in hand but shall try to dig some out for you.

Namaskar – R. F. Goheen

13th March 2006

The Co-Ordinator
Research Fellowship Program
Presbyterian Historical Society
415 Lombard St. Philadelphia, PA 1914 7-1516

I am writing to join in supporting the application of Dr. Neeta Khandpekar of Mumbai, India for a short term research fellowship at Presbyterian Historical Society. I have been in touch with her forseveral months over her investigations into the work of the Christian Missions in western India, with particular reference recently to the Konkan region, just north of Goa. Having read a couple of papers that she has written on this subject,I judge her to be a careful and competent historian. As my parents, Dr. R. H. H. and Anne Ewing Goheen, served in the then Western India Mission from 1905 to.1944 and worked in the Konkan from 1907 to 1936 at Vengurla, where my father established St. Luke's Hospital and my mother taught English to generations of young Indians in the Mission High School, I am naturally interested in seeing more research and writing may illuminate that area and phase of the Presbyterian Church's activity in India. The records you hold on their work and that of other members of the Western India Mission (including my grandfather, Joseph Milliken Goheen, and my uncle, John Lawrence Goheen) should be an invaluable resource for Dr. Khandpekar. I do hope you can help her take advantage of them.

Sincerely,

Robert F. Goheen

11th March 2006

Dr. Seaton's 'phone number is 304-466-1365.. I do not have Dr. Servid's. Good luck. –R. F. Goheen

8th November 2005

Dear Dr. Khandpekar -- I cannot bring up your power point presentation on my computer, but I have read your paper with much interest. I had hoped to see more about the work of the American Missionaries in Vengurla and Ratnagiri, but you have a large theme and lengthy span of years under your lens, and I can understand the need for compression.

Incidentally, two small suggestions. A) On p.14 the J. M. Goheen at the top of the page and the American Missionary in Kohlapur who fathered my father was the same person, my grandfather, Joseph Milliken Goheen B.) On p.16 where you mention the Vengurla Mission High School, it would have been nice if you had mentioned my mother, Anne Ewing Goheen, who taught English to generations of young Vengurlakars there. She too was a child of American Presybetarian Missionaries who served in India, in her case in the Punjab…

Best regards, R. F. Goheen

6th October 2005

Dear Dr. Khandpekar …

First I wanted to let you know that I had mailed to you yesterday the two mysteriously missing obituaries.

More importantly, I wanted to report that I had been in touch by 'phone with Dr. Ronald Seaton about your interest in the work of American Missionaries in western India including my father. Dr. Seaton was in charge of the work at St. Luke's Hospital in Vengurla in the 1960s and 1970s.

He has a history of that hospital that he would be glad to share with you, and I am sure he has much more information that you might find helpful.. I think very highly of Dr. Seaton and his wife, Edith and when I visited Vengurla was much impressed by how well and widely they were respected in the local community. If you wish to reach them, the e-mail address is ajiaja_seaton@yahoo.com.

With best regards -- R. F. Goheen

20th September 2005

Dear Dr. Khandpekar-- I sent you two pictures of my father taken at the height of his career as a physician in the 1930s a week ago by first class airmail post. Please let me know if you receive them. Best wishes -- R. F. Goheen

10th July 2005

Dear Miss Khandpekar:

I am very pleased to hear from you and learn of your postgraduate thesis project. Unfortunately, however, I am away from my home and office,and shall not return to Princeton until September. So, I cannot send you the photo of my father that you ask for or provide much other information thtt might be of use to you until I return there.

Here are just a few items. My father was born in Kohlapur, where

His father Rev. Joseph Milliken Goheen, was a pastor and teacher from 1874 to 1909 in the Presbyterian Western India Mission. My father was sent to the U.S. at age eight for health reasons and an American style education. After gaining his MD degree in 1904, he and my mother, Anne Ewing Goheen,who was a school teacher, returned to India to serve initially at the Mission Hospital at Miraj. In 1906 they were sent by the Mission to open a medical clinic on the coast at Vengurla. In 1915 after raising enough funds in this country,my my father established St. Luke's Hospital and went on to develop a TB Sanitorium and Leprosy Center.He served in Vengurla until 1936,when he was called back by the Mission to be Director of the much larger Miraj Medical Center, and he worked there until retirement age in 1944 when he returned to this country where he died in 1968 at age 88.

A fairly good source of information on Presbyterian Missionaries like my my father and others who served in the Konkan region is the Presbyterian Historical Society in Philadelphia, Pennsylvania, USA. I am sorry I do not have its address but I expect you can turn it up on the web.

If you will send me your postal address, I'll send you the photo and Some written materials on my father's life when I get back to Princeton.

With best wishes -- Robert F. Goheen

2. Dr. Ron and Edith Seaton, ajiaja_seaton@yahoo.com

14th July 2008

Dear Friends,

Pl. note our new address: P. O. Box 523 Penney Farms FL 32079 USA Phone : 904-529-9007

Peace and Joy

Edith and Ron Seaton

15th March 2008

Dear Ms. Khandpekar, We are busy working on a family-initiated move to an assisted living facility in Florida and came across Western India Notes from 1957 to 1966. Have you seen them? They contain quite a bit of Western India Mission history. If you need them we can send them to you. We will let you know our address when we know it. Respectfully, Ron Seaton

7th February 2008

Dear Dr. Khandpekar,

Here is the photo you requested. I hope it comes through. Sincerely, Edith Seaton

3rd July 2007

Dear Dr. Khandpekar, Thank you for sending us the December issue of the Indian Church History Review. Your paper is most interesting and exciting to read. We will try to get off to you something about our Vengurla experiences, but it will take a bit of time to get it together. Again thanks for your interest in the work of our colleagues. in India, a land and people we have learned to love very much. Peace. Edith and Ron Seaton

29th October 2006

Dr. Khandpekar, Thank you for the Diwali wishes. We enjoyed and appreciated your power point presentation and narrative. With warmest regards, peace, Edith and Ron Seaton

13th March 2006

Dear Dr. Khandpekar:

I think Dr. Servid's phone number is 360-354-4370. Edith Seaton

25th October 2005

Dear Ms. Khandpekar, We are happy that you are going to visit Vengurla. Please do not be surprised by how rundown and dammaged the hospital has become especially since the last monsoon. If you can, please contact Mrs. Dorothy Dhanawade up at the old Leprosy Hospital, Pastor Mcwan of the Goheen Memorial Church, and Mrs. Seelam, the founder of the Nursing School there. We would love to hear from you. Cordially, Edith and Ron Seaton

8th October 2005

Dear Ms. Khandpekar, We are interested in your studies and will help you all we can. Today I will send you a Golden Jubilee booklet covering the history of St. Luke's Hospital from 1915-1965. I hope this will be very helpful fo your research. My wife, Edith, who edited this will answer your specific questions in a day or two. We wish you all the very best. Cordialy, Ron Seaton

8th October 2005

Dear Ms. Khandpekar,

We are mailing to you a copy of the Golden Jubilee booklet of St. Luke's Hospital, Vengurla. One thing left out of the history in this booklet was the important work of Dr. Lester and Mrs. Harriet Servid between the early 1950s and 1964. You could get this information from them. They live in Seattle. Their e-mail address is: servid@juno.com. It would be good if you sent them the letter you sent to us.

For several years Dr. Seaton had a clinic every two weeks in Mapuca, Goa.

We were in Vengurla from 1958 to 1970 (except for two trips back to the U.S.), from 1974 to 1976, and later for a short term. You asked how the locals reacted. Dr. Seaton was loved and respected by the entire community, and our family quickly became part of the Vengurla community -- to the extent that our children (now in their 50s and away from India for many years) still think of Vengurla as "home." We were welcomed in the homes of rich and poor, Hindu and Muslim. Vengurla was a wonderful place to live because there was no friction that we perceived between Hindus and Muslims.

There are some photos, not too clear I'm afraid, in the booklet. If you go to Vengurla, you will find St. Luke's Hospital pretty run-down. Do try to talk with Mrs. Kumudini Seelam, who was the Nursing Superintendent and Director of the A. N. M. School. She's retired. She still lives in Vengurla, but may be in Nipani teaching student nurses. You could also talk with Mrs. Dorothy Dhanawade (she lives in the Vengurla Camp area -- anyone at the hospital could direct you -- or ask her to meet you at the hospital). She is a nurse who ran Bal Niketan -- a home for children of leprosy patients from Miraj, Sangli, Kolhapur, etc., who lived there so that they could attend school. (They were not welcome in schools where they were known to live in "leper colonies").

The central office of the Mission was and is in Kolhapur.

We hope this information is helpful.

Sincerely, Edith Seaton

3. Lester P. Servid servid@juno.com

12th October 2005
1001 East Front St.
Lynden, WA. 98264
10/12/05

Dear Dr. Khandpekar,

Because we had recently talked with Ron Seaton via phone, and he had told us of your interest in the history of St. Luke's Hospital, we checked the e-mail, and sure enough your letter had arrived. I trust that the following facts will be of interest. We have been home since June, 1966, and it is not easy to come up with the right names sometimes. We had good relations with merchants and townspeople.

Before we embarked on the ship to India, we had the pleasure of visiting Dr. and Mrs. R. H. H. Goheen in their apartment in New York. We were assigned to Vengurla after language study, and we were really glad to meet the Goheens. Our language study was done mostly in Miraj in early 1951, and we shared meals with Dr. and Mrs. Gene Evans, who had worked for a number of years in Vengurla before being called Miraj.

On taking up residence in Vengurla (Nov, 1951), I worked with Dr. Daulet Saltralkar, who was the only doctor in the hospital at that time. There were patients in the TB San, mostly under government contract.

The leprosarium was closed, and was being cared for by two leper caretakers.

Hospital days began with the night nurse's report at 7:00 a.m. Daily chapel services were held in the Christian Church across the road from the Hospital. Chapel was for all staff, and was led by Christian staff members taking turns. Hospital staff included Goanese Christians (Catholics) Hindhu, Muslim, and Christians. Rounds were made on the men's ward and women's ward, private rooms, and maternity. Out patient clinics and scheduled surgery were tended to during the morning hours,with additional out-patient persons being seen at 3:00 p.m. after the lunch break. Rounds were made at the TB San daily.

Dr. Saltralkar left to carry on a private practice in Belgaum. For some time I was the only Doctor in the hospital. I requested the Presbyterian Board of Foreign Missions in New York to send us another doctor. When we went to Vengurla we were joined by Betty Hilty, R. N. who was subsequently moved to Miraj.

The basic rock and foundation of the hospital was Nursing Superintendent Irene DeSouza . who had been at the hospital since Dr. Goheen was Medical Superintendent. The hospital also had a dental department headed by Dr. Albert Amanna, who did fillings, pulled infected teeth, and made dentures. When he was on vacation, the task of pulling teeth fell to me. Mrs. Servid spent time working in the laboratory during our years in Vengurla.

Soon after taking up work at St. Luke.s Hospital John Weir and others from the Presbyterian office in Delhivisited us and were instrumental in helpint us get funds for improving buildings and equipment. For example: window air conditioning units for the O. R.; new X-ray unit; construction of a dharmashala for the families of ward patients, giving them a roof and walls with protection from the weather, andcupboards for storing supplies plus cooking facilities. Most patients were fed by their family, and ward patients did not have cooking space that private room patients had.

Due to Sister Irene failing health, the hospital sent Sister Kumudini Sheik to Vellore for the Sister Tutor training, and she returned after successfully completing the course to work for several years with

Sister Irene before she died. Then Sister Kumudini stepped into the place of Nursing Superintendent. Meanwhile, her sister, Rohini Sheik, joined the staff at St. Luke's as O. R. Superviso

Dr. and Mrs. Seaton joined the staff in the late 1950s. Dr. Seaton came with speciality training in surgery and brought many referred patients. We were transferred to the Wanless Chest Hospital in the early 1960's.

Trust that this may be of some use to you.

Sincerely,

Lester P. Servid, M. D.

Note: The hospital also had a dental department headed by Dr. Albert Amanna, who did fillings, pulled teeth, and made dentures. When he was on vacation the task of pulling infected teeth fell to me. There were also clinic visits to villages once or twice a week dispensing medicine that we took with us.

Prof. Robert Goheen's Letter to Mr. Shri Ram Mantri

ROBERT F. GOHEEN

12-viii-03

Dear Mr. Mantri

Some time ago one of your grandsons reported that you would like a picture of my father to include in your memoir of Vengurla.

Two are enclosed for you to choose from. The larger and more formal one is dated 1936 and marks his retirement as President of the Christian Medical Association of India, of which he had been the founder a decade or more earlier. The somewhat smaller photo probably dates from about that same time. It shows him in his normal daily garb as a working physician. I think the location is in front of our house in Vengurla, but it may have been taken in Miraj after he had been moved there to head the larger Wanless Hospital and Medical Centre.

(PTO)

1 Orchard Circle, Princeton, NJ 08540
(609) 924-2751

I hope these pictures are not too late to be useful. I have been away from Princeton the past six weeks. I should apologize too, for my poor penmanship. I am temporarily without a typewriter and my hand is not as steady as it once was.

With best wishes.

Robert F. Goheen

Prof. Robert Goheen's letter to Ms. Neeta Khandpekar

ROBERT F.GOHEEN
1Orchard Circle
Princeton, NJ 08540
rfgoheen@princeton.edu.,

9-ix-05

Prof. Neeta M. Khandpekar
B-1- 11 Garnet CHS
Godrej Hill, Kalyan 421 304
INDIA

Dear Dr. Khanpekar;

Thank you for your reminder, but on my return to Princeton I had very much in mind my promise to send you more information about my father's career. Unfortunately one document I especially wanted to send seems to have disappeared. It was, as I recall from some years back, a memorial minute published in WESTERN INDIA NOTES, a publication of the then Presbyterian Western India Mission.. Perhaps the Miraj Medical Centre might have a record of it in its library.

Lacking that, I enclose an obituary issued upon my father's death by Princeton University and a reminiscent tribute to my father written by Renato De Sa in a Goan publication, HARPA GOESA. in 1979. The latter seems particularly relevant in light of the venue of the conference where you are to speak. The fact has probably not escaped you, but I might point out that Goa was an important source of revenue for my father's medical work in and around Vengurla. As one of the very few, if not the only, western trained physician in that part of the Konkan, he attracted educated Portuguese and Goan patients, and what they could be charged let him treat many indigent fishermen and farmers in need of medical attention..

Also enclosed are two pictures dating from the 1930s. In the one where he is standing, he is in the garden fronting the bungalow he designed and had built at the edge of the hospital compound in Vengurla. It's where I was born. The more formal picture (dated 1936) records his retiring as President of the Christian Medical Association of India, of which he was I believe a founder.

I regret that my records on my father's life and work are so poor and that my memories are so fragmentary and scattered that I cannot provide you more useful information about him. I do hope you will send me a copy of your talk. I expect to earn much.

With best regards,

Sincerely,

Prof. Robert Goheen's correspondence with Ms. Neeta Khandpekar

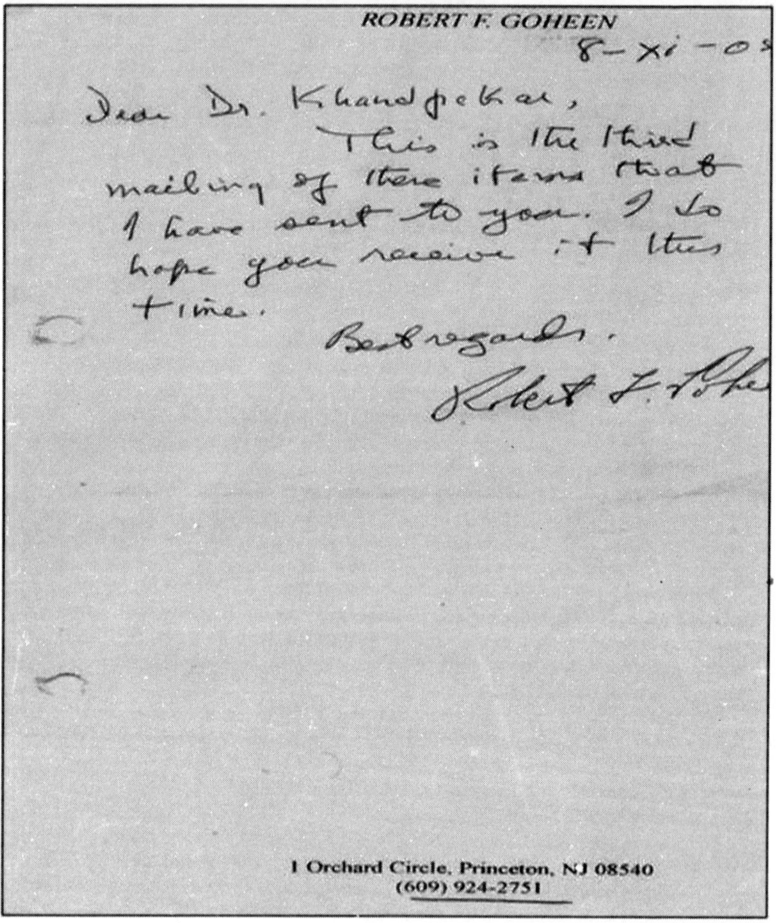

ROBERT F. GOHEEN

8-xi-0

Dear Dr. Khandpekar,

This is the third mailing of these items that I have sent to you. I do hope you receive it this time.

Best regards.

Robert F. Gohe

1 Orchard Circle, Princeton, NJ 08540
(609) 924-2751

Dr. Ronald Seaton's recent recommendation Letter for Ms. Neeta M. Khandpekar

RONALD S. SEATON, M.D.
P. O. Box 523
Penney Farms, FL 32079

Copy

21 January 2009

Research Fellowship Program
Presbyterian Historical Society
425 Lombard Street
Philadelphia, PA 19147-1516

Re: Dr. Mrs. Neeta Khadkpekar

Dear Colleagues:

Dr. Neeta Khandpekar is again applying for a Presbyterian Research Scholarship. Just before the death of Dr. Robert Goheen, former Ambassador to India, Dr. Khandpekar was working with him and with us, collecting whatever historical material we had about Presbyterian mission efforts in Western India.

Dr. Khandpekar has published significant papers on this particular subject that has been a memorable part of our missionary lives. With the help of the Presbyterian Research Scholarship she plans to search out and record more details of this remarkable story of mission work and its impact on Western India.

I highly recommend your consideration of Dr. Khandpekar's application for this scholarship.

Cordially,

Ronald S. Seaton

Ronald S. Seaton, M.D.

Appendix -3

Questionnaire (please use additional sheets if needed)

1. Full and Correct Name of your Institution: ________________
2. Name of the Head of the Institution :____________________
3. Name of the Congregation / Diocese : __________________
4. Educational Qualifications of the Head: __________________
5. A brief History of your Institution: ____________________
6. Chief goals of your Institution: ________________________
7. Factors which motivated you to become a Priest / Religious: ____
8. How many years of religious training have you undergone:____
9. How are Priests / Religious selected for educational work: ____
10. How many years Priests or Religious have been serving in the same Institution: ___________________________________
11. How many Priests / Religious Assistants you have got at this time in your Institution: ____________________________
12. How do the Lay People contribute towards the goals of your institution: ________
13. Is there any provision for the care of sick or aged Priests or Religious Sisters: ________
14. How do you consider your Institution different or better than other Institutions in your area: ____________________ ____
15. Any annual Publication of your Institution: _____________
16. Funding received from various Bodies (optional): __________
17. Any other information is welcome and I'm sure it will be of great help to me.

Place and Date: ______________ Signature: _____________

Outcome of Questionnaire Survey

Institution	*Region/ Area*	*Congregation/ Diocese*	*Chief Goals*	*Motivation to Priests*
St. Xaviers High School	Manickpur, Vasai	Jesuits	To Serve Poor	Love for God and his People
Pushpanjali College of Education	Papady, Vasai	Carmelite Religious	Vasai Girls School	To help miserable and untouchables
Nirmalamata Girls High School	Manickpur, Vasai	Canossian Daughters of Charity	Education for Girl Child and poor.	God's Call, reach out to poor and needy
Society of St. Anthony	Vasai	Sisters of Our Lady of Fatima	Education for poor and marginalized	To love god alone and serve with his love and care
Sanjeevani Foundation: Lourdes Community Centre	Kalyan (w)	Sisters of Mercy of the Holy Cross / Mumbai	Restore Humanity, Dignity, Eco preservation & Communal Harmony	Social Situation
Shanti Bhavan, Home for Aged	Kalyan (w)	Mumbai	Care and Comfort the Aged and Sick	To Serve the Underprivileged
St. Judes School	Kalyan(e)	Mumbai	Character forming, Discipline, Honesty	Inspiration of Priests helping Poor
Our lady of Lourdes Church	Kalyan (w)	Mumbai	Holistic development of Parishioners	Inspiration of Priests, Serve Humanity and God
Our Lady of Lourdes	Kalyan (w)	Mumbai	Education	Service to Humanity
NavJeevan Centre, Tokwada	Kalyan	Mumbai	Rehabilitation of commercial sex workers	Call of Jesus
Mar Thoma Church	Kalyan (w)	Mumbai	Religious work and School for mentally Challenged students	Call of Jesus

Institution	*Region/ Area*	*Congregation/ Diocese*	*Chief Goals*	*Motivation to Priests*
Thomas Baptista High School and Junior College	Vasai	Vasai Diocese	Create honest and good citizens	—
SPJ Sadhana School (Sophia College)	Mumbai	Religious of the Sacred Heart/ Mumbai	Empowering persons with special needs	—
Sophia Shree B K Somani Memorial Polytechnic	Mumbai	Society of the sacred heart	Transformation of the society through the value based education given to students	—

Appendix - 4

Picture: One of the line drawings from New Community (Indianised) Bible showing the women wearing *Bindi* and the nose ring.

Bibiliography

Primary Sources

(A) Bulletins

Western India Notes **(WIN)**, Baisinger Memorial Library, Miraj, Maharashtra (issues)
November 1923
May and September 1924
July 1925
February and June 1927
January, March, June and December 1930
December 1931
December 1932
April, July and December 1933
April 1939
December 1940
February and April 1942
April 1944
April 1949
January 1951
January, April and July 1961
January and July 1962

Oriental Christian Spectator (Edited by John Wilson in 1830), 19th Century issues, Wilson College Library, Mumbai. It covered feedback of readers, society's glance by Missionaries, and evils in Hinduism etc. It was printed at American Mission, Bombay. The January 1831 issue of OCS was 40 pages and on the last page the poetry 'The Peace of God' can be seen.
OCS, December 1831, Vol.VII, January 1856
OCS, August 1856 (Also biographical sketch of Rev. Robert Nesbit of the Free Church of Scotlands Mission in Bombay)
OCS, January-February 1849
OCS, July 1859 OCS (a word for The Bombay Catholic Examiner can be seen), July 1860, August 1861,January 1863, October 1860, November 1860

The Poona Observer was a Triweekly Journal of News, Politics and Literature Published every Tuesday, Thursday and Saturday. In 1861 it was a four page big size paper. (January 14, 1862)

(B) List of Periodicals and News papers

The Calcutta Review January – June 1845

***The Bombay Guardian* (BG) weekly News Paper**
This weekly was established in March 1851- the last issue of this weekly available in Maharashtra State Archives Mumbai is of July 22 1905 with total of 31 issues. Initially it was published every Friday and later every Saturday. It had circulation in India, Europe, America, Australia, China etc.

1851 : April 11
1856 : May 17, May 24, May 31, June 07, June 21, August 16, September 06, September 20, October 11, October 18, November 15
1857 : March 7, April 25, June 13, June 27, August 22
1859 : March 26
1863 : February 7, May 9, May 16
1874 : March 28

1880 : January 31, February 7, February 28, May 28, June 19, July 17, September 04
1881 : February 12, April 23, April 30, July 16
1882 : January 7, January 21, February 11, April 15, September 2, September 11
1883 : April 28, August 26
1884 : April 12, May 04
1885 : July 25, December 26
1886 : March 20, April 17, May issue, July 03, August 28, November 10, December 11
1887 : January 22
1888 : January 21, March 10, May issue, November 10, September 29, December 29
1889 : March 02, March 16, March 23
1890 : September issue
1891 : September issue, October 03
1892 : February 20, June 25, September 17
1893 : June 03, June 17, August 26
1895 : March 02, July 20, November 16
1896 : March 21, April 04, July 18
1897 : January issue, May issue
1898 : January 01, March issue, July 28
1899 : April 15, May 06, May 20, July 08, September 16
1900 : November 10, December 08, December 15
1901 : March 16, September 21, December 14
1902 : May 03
1903 : November 14
1904 : March 05, April 30, May 14, June 18, November 26
1905 : January 21, March 04, July 08

The Bombay Tract and Book Society (BTBS) formed in 1828 supplied Christian vernacular literature and its special supplements were attached with the Bombay Guardian in 1857, 1858 and 1859.

Missionary Herald

More than 50 page monthly which covered news from all over the world of the American Board of Commissioners for Foreign Missions, was the oldest periodical in America. It succeeded The Panapolist (established in 1805) in 1818. It was published from Boston. In Ahmednagar College Library, Maharashtra its issues from 1837 to 1939 can be found.

Dnyanodaya (meaning Rise of Knowledge)

Weekly Newspaper of American Marathi Mission. It was established in 1842, in 1947 it was published every Thursday (April 17, November 13, 1947)

Wilson College Library (Mumbai) and Ahmednagar College Library (Near Pune, Maharashtra).

International Bulletin

Around 95 page Bulletin published twice a year. Vol. 22, No.1 (January 1998)

***The Voice of India* (edited by Malabari Behramji)**

It was a fortnightly magazine published at Bombay containing opinions of the native press of India on important Subjects. It was of around 40 pages with about 9 page advertisements.

The Examiner, Issues available in St. Pius Seminary, Goregaon, Mumbai, 1990, February 1997.

The Catholic News Review (Bombay,1990)

The Telegraph and Courier Newspaper : March 24, April 12 (Bombay, 1847)

Bhartiya Vidya - King Thiba of Burma in India 1885-1916 (supplement, 56 pages), Vol. XXV, 1965

Bamdad

Rev. Dhanjibhai Nawroji edited two Anglo Vernacular magazines-The *Gyan Deepaka* and *Bamdad* in Gujarati (*BG*, December 11, 1886)

April 15 (1882), July 08 (1905), December 14 (1901)

(The *Bamdad* issues of 1858, 1859, 1860, 1861 are available at The K. R., Cama Oriental Institute, Mumbai)

Vainateya

It was a weekly newspaper (every tuesday) published in marathi by M. D. Shirodkar from Sawantwadi (Konkan). In the year 1927-28 it consisted of a eight page supplement and in the year 1951, it was made 12 pages.

(1927) issue, (1928) issue

Times of India
1888: February 8

The Davidsonian - was a weekly News Paper of Davidson College, USA. It was a member of North Carolina Collegiate and Southern Collegiate Presbyterian Association. The digital archives of the College web site contain the issues from 1914 to 2006.

Christian Medical Journal of India
Vol. 20, No. 4, October - December 2005
Vol. 21, No.1, January - March 2006

The Indian Antiquary Journal of Oriental Research

The Indian Antiquary (IA), Journal of Oriental Research from 1872-1933. The volumes of the same can be referred from the Asiatic Society Library and Heras Institute of Indian History and Culture at St. Xavier's College in Mumbai.

(C) Accounts of Travel

James Forbes, *Oriental Memoirs,* (selected and abridged from a series of familiar letters written during the 17th C residence in India) (London, 1813)

John Fryer, *A New Account of East India and Persia in Eight Letters* (London, 1698)

(D) Memoirs and Biographies

Dr. Goheen's recollections of the Missionary History of Vengurla written down in 1962 and published as Golden Jubilee souvenir, 1915-65 entitled "St. Lukes Hospital, Vengurla".

(E) Reports

A Short History of the Elphinstone High School, 1824-1924, Bombay, 1925

Annual Report of the American Board of Commissions for Foreign Missions (1827-71)

Annual Report of the Bombay Auxiliary Scottish Missionary Society (1830, 1831, 1844, 1853, 1855, 1857, 1858, Bombay)

Clark, Alden William Hazen, Clara Bruce, *Centennial Volume of the American Marathi Mission of the American Board of Commissioners for Foreign Missions*, Pune, 1913)

League of National Archives, File No: 29098, 1931

Life and Light for Women, published by Woman's Board of Mission, Vol. xxxi (Boston, 1901)

Paradise on the West Coast - Vengurla, Coloured Pamphlet issued by the Lions Club of Vengurla, undated.

Renovation of the cathedral Church of Bombay 1864', in *Bombay Pamphlets*, Vol. 6, Education Society's Press, Byculla, 1864

Report of the American Marathi Mission for the year (1890-1900, 1901-1910, 1911-1920)

Report of the *Commission on Christian Higher Education in India*, 1931, OUP, London

Rev. B. H. Badley, *Indian Missionary Directory and Memorial Volume* (1876)

Robert F. Goheen Papers, 1939-2008 (bulk 1939-2000): Finding Aid, Princeton University, Department of Rare Books and Special Collections retrieved from http://www.princeton.edu/~mudd * on 14th September 2008

Scottish Missionary and Philanthropic Register, Vol. VII, No. 10, October 1825

St. Lukes Hospital Vengurla Golden Jubilee Volume (1915-1965)

St. Xavier's College (Annual Magazine) Mumbai, 1999

The Origin and History of Missions, Vol. 2 (Boston, 1837)

(F) Private Communication (Appendix 2)

Correspondence Letters of Late Dr. R. F. Goheen (son of Dr. R. H. H. Goheen) and former ambassador to India, Princeton, USA

Edith and Dr. Ronald Seaton, American Presbyterian Western India Missionary presently in USA.

Dr. Lester Servid, American Presbyterian Western India Missionary presently in USA.

(G) Others

Readers Digest, *Universal Dictionary* (reprint) (RD Association Ltd., UK, 1988)

R. J. Unstead's *Dictionary of History* (Wardlock Publication, New York, 1976)

Secondary Sources

(A) Gazeteers

Gazetteer of Bombay City and Island, Vol. I-III (Bombay, 1909)

Gazetteer of Bombay Presidency Ratnagiri and Sawantwadi District, Vol. X (Mumbai, 1996)

J. M. Campbell, *Gazetteer of Bombay Presidency, Kolaba and Janjira, reprint* (Bombay, 1986)

Maharashtra State Gazetteer: Ratnagiri District, revised (Bombay, 1962)

The Imperial Gazetter of India, Vol. VIII (Oxford,1908)

(B) Books and Monographs

Acharya Kala and others (ed.) *A Dialogue -Hindu-Christian Cosmology and Religion,* (Mumbai 1999)

Albuquerque T., *Urbs Prima in Indis,* An epoch in History of Bombay, 1840-1865 (South Asia Books, New Delhi, 1985)

Albuquerque T., *To Love is to Serve: Catholics of Bombay* (Heras Institute, Bombay, 1986)

Avel Evelyn, *The Anglo Indian Community - Survival in India* (Chankya Pub, New Delhi, 1988)

Bagal J. C., *Womens Education in Western India* : the first phase (World Press Private Ltd.,Calcutta, 1956)

Baldock John, *The Elements of Christian Symbolism* (Element Books Ltd, USA, 1990)

Bearce G. D., *British Attitudes towards India 1784-1858* (OUP, London, 1961)

Bhagwat V., *Stree Prasnanchi Vatchal* (M) (Pratima Prakashan, Pune, 2004)

Bhattacharya Srinibas, *Guidance in Education* (Asia Pub, New York, 1963)

Bhattacharya S. K., *Christian Missionaries and Indian Societies,* (Mohit Publications, New Delhi, 1999)

Billington Mary Frances, *Woman in India* (Chapman & Hall, London, 1895)

Borges Charles, *The Economics of the Goa Jesuits 1542-1759 An explanation of Their Rise and Fall* (Concept, New Delhi, 1994)

Breuilly E. and Palmer M. (ed), *Christianity and Ecology* (Cassell Publishers, Ltd., New York, 1992)

Brown Ashley, *On the Bombay Coast and Deccan* (SPCK, London, 1937)

Butterfield Kenyon L. -*The Christian Mission in rural India* (OUP, London, 1930)

Buzacott A. *Mission Life in the Islands of the Pacific* (John Snow and Co., London, 1966)

Carre Abbe, *The Travels of Abbe Carre in India and the Near East 1672-1674*, Vol. III (AES, New Delhi, 1990)

Chakravarti U, *Rewriting History: The Life and Times of Pandita Ramabai* (Zubaan, New Delhi, 1998)

Chakravarti Uma and Gill Preeti (Eds.) *Shadow Lives; Writings on Widowhood* (Zubaan, New Delhi, 2001)

Chakravarti Uma, *Gendering Caste through a Feminist Lens* (Stree Pub, Calcutta, 2003)

Chappeli Jennie, *Pandita Ramabai – A Great Life in Indian Missions* (Basingstoke: Pickering & Inglis, Great Britain, 1968)

Chatterjee Rimi, *Empires of the Mind, The History of OUP in India under the Raj* (OUP, New Delhi, 2006)

Chicherov A I, *Indian Economic Development in the 16th-18th Centuries* (International Publication, Moscow, 1971)

Choondal Chummar, "*The Missionaries and Malayalam Journalism*" (Minerva Books, Kerala,1975)

Correa Francis, *Samvadi Bolibhasha Loksahitya* (M) (Saptarshi Praskashan, Mumbai 1992)

Costa Cosme Josa, *A Missiological Conflict Between Padroado and Propaganda in the East* (Pilar, Goa, 1997)

Cottineau Denis L. de Loguen "*A Historical Sketch of Goa: The Metropolis of the Portuguese Settlements in India*" (reprint B. R. Publishing Co, New Delhi, 2006)

Cunha Gerson Da, *Notes on the Hisory and the Antiqities of Chaul and Bassein (Reprint),* (Asian Education Services, New Delhi, 1993)

Dabre T., *The God-experience of Tukaram: A study in Religious Symbolism* (Jnana Deepa Vidyapeeth, Pune, 1987)

Dandekar A., (ed.) *Mythos and Logos of the Warlis: A Tribal Worldview* (Concept, New Delhi, 1998) David M. D. (ed), *Asia and Christianity* (Himalaya Pub, Mumbai, 1985)

David M. D., *John Wilson and his Institution* (Wilson Education Society, Bombay, 1975)

David M. D., Missions : *Cross Cultural Encounter and Change in Western India* (Manohar, New Delhi, 2001)

David M. D., *How much can we do for others: A Brief History of the YMCA* (Ebenezer Printing House, Mumbai 2005)

D'Costa Antony, *The Call of the Orient, A Response by Jesuits in the Sixteenth Century* (Heras Institute, Mumbai, 1999)

Dhingra Saroj, 'Missionary Contribution to the Health Services Development in India' in *St. Francis Xavier His Times and Legacy* ed. Carlo Mata and Kala Acharya, Mumbai, 2007

Downs Frederick S, *History of Christianity in India* Vol. V Part 5 (CHAI, Bangalore, 1992)

D'Silva Regin, *India's only canonized Saint Gonsalo Garcia of Bassein* (St. Gonsala Garcia Pub, Vasai, 2003)

D'Souza Eunice and Pereira Lindsay, *Womens Voices* (OUP, New Delhi, 2002)

De Souza Teotonio R., "The Christian Missions in the Aftermath of Discoveries" in De Souza T. R. (ed.) *Discoveries Missionary Expansion and Asian Cultures,* (Concept, New Delhi, 1994)

Drego P. A., *The Charism of Karuna - Life Story of Sister Karuna Mary Braganza,* (Alfreruby Publishers, Mumbai, 2011)

Dsouza D., *Capucin Missions in India* (Sage Pub, Mangalore, 2000)

Dwivedi Sharada, *Premchand Roychand* (Eminince Designs Pvt. Ltd., Mumbai, 2006)

Eyre Chatterton D. D., *A History of the Church of England in India since the early days of the East India Company* (SPCK, London, 1924)

Gandhi Anjali, *School Social Work* (Common Wealth Pub, New Delhi, 1990)

Gandhi M. K., *Christian Missions: Their Place in India* (Navjeevan Publishing House, Ahmedabad, 1941)

Ghose Indira, *Women Travellers in Colonial India* (OUP, Delhi, 1998)

Farooqui Amar, *Opium City: The Making of early Victorian Bombay* (Three Essays Press, New Delhi, 2006)

Forbes Geraldine 'Education for Women' in *Women and Social Reform in* Sumit Sarkar and Tanika Sarkar (eds), *Modern India* (CUP, New Delhi, 2007)

Foster William (ed.), *Early Travels in India 1583-1619* (OUP, London, 1921)

Frere Bartle, *Indian Missions* (G.C.S.I & Co., London, 1873)

Goel Sita Ram, *Papacy, Its Doctrine and History* (Voice of India, New Delhi, 1986)

Haig Elizabeth, *The Floral Symbolism of the Great Masters* (K. Paul, Trench, Trubner & Co. Ltd., London, 1913)

Hambye E. R., *History of Christianity in India, 18th Century*, Vol.3 (CHAI, Bangalore, 1997)

Hayes Carlton J. H., *Christianity and Western Civilisation* (OUP, London, 1954)

Hewat E. H. K., *Christ and Western India* (Asia Publishing House, Bombay, 1950)

Hew Arthur May, *Christianity and the Government of India* (Faber and Gwyer, London, 1929)

Hull Ernest, *Bombay Mission History*, Vol. II, (Examiner Press, Bombay, 1927-30)

Ifeka Caroline, 'The Image of Goa' in T. R. De Souza (ed) *Indo-Portuguese History Old Issues New Questions* (Concept, New Delhi, 1985)

Ingham K., *Reformers in India*, 1793- 1833 (CUP, Cambridge, 1936)

Jeyakumar Arthur, *History of Christianity in India* (ISPCK, Delhi, 2002)

Karhade Veena, *Mahatma Jyotiba Phule* (Marathi), Lok Vanghmaya Graha, (Lok Vanghmaya Graha, Mumbai, 2003)

Karhadkar K. S., *Baba Padmanji: Kal Va Kartutva* (Marathi) (Maharashtra Rajya Sahitya ane Sanskriti Mandal, Mumbai,1979)

Karlekar Malavika, Voices from Within: Early Personal Narratives of Bengali Women (OUP, New Delhi 1991)

Karlekar Shrikant, 'Geo Morphology of the Konkan Coast', in Diddee J., Joag S., Kale V. S. and Datye V. S. (ed) *Geography of Maharashtra* (Rawat Pub, New Delhi, 2002)

Keller Nalini, *Women under the Cross changing Gender Roles in Christian families* (Cosmo, New Delhi, 1997)

Khobrekar V. G., *History of Konkan (1630-1818)* (Snehavardhan Publishers, Bombay, 1985)

Kinikar Roy (ed) *International Women Years Book* (Yashodhara Publishers, Bombay, 1975)

Knoll Mark A. and others (ed), E*erdmans Handbook to Christianity in America*, (Grand Rapids, Michigan,1980)

Kosambi Meera, *At the intersection of Gender Reform and Religious Belief. Pandita Ramabai's contribution and the Age of consent controversy* (S.N.D.T. Women's University, Research Centre for Women's Studies, Mumbai, 1993)

Kosambi Meera (ed) of RCWS Gender Series "*Pandita Ramabai's feminist and Christian Conversion*" (Research Centre for Women's Studies, S.N.D.T. Women's University, Bombay, 1995)

Kulkarni A. R., The Proselytisation and Purification movement in Konkan and Goa in *Discoveries, Missionary expansion and Asian Cultures* edited by Teotonio R. D'Souza (Concept, New Delhi, 1994)

Kulkarni A. R., *Medieval Maratha Country* (Books & Books, New Delhi, 1996)

Lach Donald F., *India in the Eyes of Europe* (Univ. of Chicago Press, USA, 1968)

Lederle M., *Philiosophical trends in modern Maharashtra* (Popular Prakashan, Bombay, 1976)

Lokuge Chandani (ed), *Krupabai Satthianadhan -Saguna., The first autobiographical novel in English by an Indian Women,* (OUP. Delhi, 1998)

Longmate Norman *The Water Drinkers: A History of Temperance,* (Hamilton, Great Britain, 1968)

Machwe P., *Keshavsut* (Makers of Indian Literature Series) (Sahitya Akademy, Delhi,1982)

Mathur Y. B., *Womens Education in India 1813-1966* (Asia Pub House, New Delhi, 1973)

Mantri Shriram, *Fakan Gajli Vengurleche* (Indraneel Prakshan, Mumbai, 2003)

Masani R. P., *Dadabhai Naoroji* (George Allen & Unwin Ltd, New Delhi,1975)

Meersman Achilles, *The Friars Minor or Franciscans in India* (Rotti Press, Karachi, 1943)

Mehrotra S. R., *The Emergence of the Indian National Congress* (Rupa & Co., New Delhi, 2004)

Mhamai S. K. (ed), *Goa: Educational Institutions through the Ages* (Panaji: Directorate of Archives and Archaeology, Govt. of Goa, Goa, 2002)

Moffett S. H., *A History of Christianity in* Asia: Beginnings to 1500 (Harper, San Francisco, 1992)

Moraes G. M., *A History of Christianity in India from early times to St. Francis Xavier A. D. 52-1542* (Kannada Sahitya Parishad, Bangalore, 1983)

M. Mitchell (ed), *Baba Padmanji, An autobiography* (Madras, 1892), *In Western India: Recollections of my early Missionary life* (David Douglas, Edinburgh, 1899),

Murray Peter and Linda, The Oxford Companion to Christian Art and Architecture (OUP, New Delhi, 1996)

Nair Jessie H., *Bunglows in Heaven: A Story of Pandita Ramabai* (Pandita Radhakrishna Meena, Missionaries and Myth Making: Salvation Army and Itinerant Communities in Madras Presidency, (Teen Murti, New Delhi, 1997)

Newell H. A., *Bombay: The Gate of India* (Raghubir Singh Books, Bombay, 1924)

Ramabai Mukti Mission, Kedgaon, Pune, 1993)

Ramabai Pandita, *The High Caste Hindoo Women*, reprint (Maharashtra State Board for Literature and Culture, 1981, Mumbai)

Ramabai Pandita, A *Testimony of our inexhaustible Treasure*, (Pandita Ramabai Mukti Mission, Pune, 2001)

Ramanna Mriduala, *Western Medicine and Public Health in Colonial Bombay* (Orient Longman, New Delhi, 2002)

Ratus Leslie J. and Rozario Errol (ed), Catholic Directory of the Archdiocese of Bombay, 3rd Edition, Ahura Printing Press, Bombay, 1982.

Nairne Alexander, *The History of Konkan*, Reprint (Asian Education Services, New Delhi, 1988)

Oddie G. A., *Social Protest in India British Protestant Missionaries and Social Reforms 1850-1900* (Manohar, New Delhi, 1979)

Padmanji Baba, *Arunodaya* (M) (Anglo Vernacular Press, Mumbai, 1955)

Parulekar R. V., *Survey of Indigenous Education in the Province of Bombay: 1820-1830* (Asia Publishing House, Bombay, 1951)

Pereira L. and D'Souza E (ed) *Women's Voices Selections from Nineteenth and Early Twentieth Century Indian Writing in English* (OUP, 2002)

Pollock, J. C. Shadows fall Apart, *The Story of the Zenana Bible and Medical Mission* (Hodder, London, 1958)

Priolkar A. K., *The Goa Inquisition* (Bombay Univ. Press, Bombay, 1961)

Robinson R., *Christians of India* (Sage, New Delhi, 2003)

Rodrigues Pia de Menezes, "Interactive relationship between Goa and Bombay Journalism" in P. P. Shirodkar (ed), *Goa's External Relations* (Other India Book Store, Goa, 1992)

Roy A., *Civility and Empire Literature and Culture in British India 1822-1922 (*Routledge, London, 2006)

Saldanha Julian, *Inculturation* (St. Pauls, Mumbai, 1996)

Sathianathan Santhasheela, *Contribution of Saints and Seers* (Kanishka Pub, New Delhi, 1996)

Saldhana Julian S. J., *Mission Themes and Issues* (Claretian Publishers, Bangalore, 2006)

Satthianadhan K. *Saguna* (The First Autobioraphical Novel in English by an Indian Women Ed by Chandani Lokuge) (OUP, Delhi, 1998)

Savelle Max, *A History of World Civilization* (Holt, Rineheart and Winston Publishers, USA, 1960)

Sen S. P. (ed) *Dictionary of National Biography* Vol. II, III (Institute of Historical Studies, Calcutta, 1974)

Sharma R. B., *History of Christian Missions: A North Indian Perspective* (Mittal Publications, New Delhi, 2005)

Sheppard Samuel T, *Bombay* (Times of India Press, Bombay, 1922)

Sherring M. A., *The History of Protestant Missions in India,* 1706-1881 (Religious Tract Society, London, 1884)

Silva Louis D., *The Christian Community and the National Mainstream* (Spicer College Press, Poona, undated)

Smith George, *The Life of John Wilson* (J Murray, London, 1879)

Sundar Clarke, *Let the Indian Church be Indian* (Christian Literature Society, Madras, 1980)

Sunthankar B. R., *Maharashtra 1858-1920* (Manmohan Bhatkal Popular Book Depot, Bombay, 1993)

Suryavanshi S. N., *Physician Extraorinaire - Dr. Sir, Willian James Wanless* (World of Life Publications, Pune, 1991)

Swaro D., *The Christian Missionaries in Orissa Their Impact on Nineteenth Century Society* (Pustak, Calcutta, 1990)

Thakur S. C. *Christian and Hindu Ethics* (Allen and Unwin, London, 1969)

Thomas P., Christians, *Christianity in India and Pakistan* (Allen & Unwin Publishers, London, 1954)

Thomas P., *Churches in India* (Government Publication Division, Faridabad, 1964)

Thomas Stephens, *Christ Puran (Marathi Poetry)* (Popular Prakashan, Mumbai, 1996)

Tilak D. N., *Maharashtrachi Tejaswini: Pandita Ramabai* (M) (Nagrik Prakashan, Nasik,1960)

Tremenheere C. W., *Missions in India: The System of Education in Government and Mission Schools contrasted* (Demy Svo. Sewed, London, 1876)

Vaughan James, *The Religious History of India* (reprint, Vedam books, Delhi, 1999)

Vịshwanathan Gauri, *Masks of Conquest. Literary Study and British Rule in India* (Columbia UP, USA, 1989)

Wilder R. R., *Mission Schools in India of the American Board of Commissioners of Foreign Missions* (Congregational Publishing Society. Boston, 1861)

Welingkar Joseph, *German Jesuits on the West Coast of India 1854-2004* (West Zone Jesuits, Pune, 2004) Wilder R. R., Mission Schools in India (University of Michigan, Boston, 1861)

William John K., *Christianity in India: A Historical Narrative* (Smith Elder and Co., London, 1859)

Wilson K., *The Twice Alienated Culture of Dalit Christians,* (Booklinks, Hyderabad, 1982)

Wittcower Rudolph, *Art and Architecture in Italy 1600*-1750 (Penguin Books, Harmondsworth,1958)

Yesudas R. N., *The History of London Missionary Society in Travancore 1806-1908* (South Indian Social Centre, Trivandrum, 1980)

Zakariah K. C., *The Syrian Christains of Kerala* (Orient Longman, New Delhi, 2006)

(C) Articles in Journals and Proceedings

Aiyangar S., History of The Syrian Church" in *The Quarterly Journal of the Mythic Society* Vol. 3, No. 4, 1912

Bearce George D., "John Stuart Mill and India" *in Journal of the Bombay Branch of the Asiatic Society*, Vol. 29, part 2, (Bombay, 1954)

Catanach I. J. 'The Gendered Terrain of Disaster?', *South Asia: Journal of South Asian Studies* (New Zealand, 2007)

Charier Sreenivasa C. S. "European Pioneer Studies in South Indian Languages" in *Bhartiya Vidya*, Vol. 5, (Bombay 1945)

Claerhout Saraha, J. D. Roover, "The Question of Conversation in India", in EPW, Vol. XL, No. 28, (July 2005)

Costa Benedict 'Much ado about Nuns in *The illustrated Weekly of India* (Bombay,1970)

David M. D., 'Historic Bassein' in *Indica*, Vol. 24, No. 2 (Bombay, September 1987)

Doctor Adhi H., 'Missionary teachings and social reformers in 19th Century India' in Toe Tonia D'Souza (ed), Discoveries, Missionary Expansion and Mission Cultures, (New Delhi, 1994)

Emilsen William W., "The Legacy of John Copley Winslow, in *International Bulletin* Vol. 21 No. 1 (June 1997)

Heras S. J., 'The Decay of the Portuguese power in India', *Journal of Bombay Historical Society*, Vol. I (Bombay,1928)

Iyer T. G. L. 'Everything we want is Beyond the Comfort Zone' in *Bhavan's Journal*, (Chennai, December 2007)

King J. S., The Fate St. mark according to an Arab Historian of the 12th Century, *Indian Antiquary*, (October 1889)

Moraes G. M., 'Contribution of Cunha Rivara to Indian Historiography', *India Past and Present*, Vol. I, No.2 (1984)

Philip Oomman "Christianity in India-Retrospect and Prospect" in *The Indian Review* Vol.46 No.2 (February 1945)

West C. C., 'Missiology: An Ecumenical Introduction- Texts and Contexts of G. A. Grierson, The Early Publications of the Serampore Missionaries, *Indian Antiquary* (June 1903) Global Christianity in *Journal of Ecumenical Studies*, Vol. 34 (1997)

Karl Muller, "Inculturation and Evangelization" in *Indian Missiological Review* Vol. 12 No. 1 (Indore, April 1990)

Khandpekar Neeta, "The Bombay Guardian and Missionaries", *24th State level conference of Maharashtra Itihas Parishad,* (Ambejogai, Maharashtra, January 2005)

Khandpekar Neeta, "Bombay Guardians News Coverage and its Historical Relevance", *13th Conference of Akhil Maharashtra Itihas Parishad* (Ambernath, Mumbai, January 2005)

Khandpekar Neeta,"Missionary Efforts of Narayan Sheshadri", *25th Conference of Marathwada Itihas Parishad*, (Aurangabad, Maharashtra, November 2005)

Khandpekar Neeta, "Notable Christian Converts covered by Bombay Guardian", *14th Conference of Akhil Maharashtra itihas Parishad* (Bhusawal, Maharashtra, January 2006)

Khandpekar Neeta, "Some Medieval Indian Saints and Christianity", *National Conference on Santavaani*, (Mumbai, September 2006)

Khandpekar Neeta, Influence of some Bhakti saints on Christians, *Seminar*, Maniben Nanavati Womens College, 22-23 March 2006

Khandpekar Neeta, A glance of Missionary activities in Konkan, *National Level Seminar*, Dapoli, Feb 2006

Khandpekar Neeta, Impact of Christianity on Socio Economic Life of Konkan- *Church History Association of India (CHAI)* (Goa, October 2005)

Khandpekar Neeta, Trace of Social and Gender issues of Missionaries in the 19th Century, *Third Biennial International Conference* (Gwalior, October 2006)

Khandpekar Neeta , Impact of Christian Missionaries on indigenous people of Konkan, *19th International Conference of the International Association of Historians of Asia (IAHA)* (Manila, 22-25 November 2006)

Neeta Khandpekar, Missionary Activities in North Konkan (16th and 17th Centuries), *Indica*, 42 (Mumbai, 2006)

Khandpekar Neeta, Portuguese Presence in Konkan (16th and 17th Centuries), *Journal of Indian History* (Kerala, 2006)

Khandpekar Neeta, Missionary work in Bombay, Seminar at SNDT College of Arts and SCB College of Commerce and Economics, Mumbai, 28th March 2006.

Khandpekar Neeta, Impact of Christian Missionaries on Indigenous People of Konkan, *The Fifth International Convention of Asia Scholars at Kuala Lumpur*, Malaysia 2-5th Aug 2007

Kulkarni A. R., Appa's work of Social Reconstruction in Konkan (1905-1971) , *State level seminar to Explore Historical Wealth of Konkan* (February 2003)

Kulkarni A. R., " Medieval Maharashtra : A Fusion Of Cultures" in *Indian Historical Review*, Vol. XXVIII, No. 1-2 (January & July 2001) (New Delhi, 2003)

Lenka J. and Malliek Minati Growth of Primary Education in Orissa: Quality VS Quantity in *Southern Economist*, Vol. 46, No.1 (May 2007)

Munshi Rustamji Nasavanji 'The Life story of the old portuguese Bell' in *The Journal of the Bombay Branch of the Original Royal Asiatic Society*, Vol. XXV (No.71-73) 1917-21 reprint (Mumbai,1969)

N. Benjamin, "Great Famine of 1896-97, The Missionary factor" in *Indian Church History Review*, June 2006

Penha H. J. D., "The Past on Prologue: Bandra's History in *Heras Institute Seminar* (Mumbai, 1985)

Pinto J. Prasad "Cultural contribution of the Capucins in India" in *Indian Missiological Review* (July 1990)

Pio Edwina, "Bandra Churches and Shrines", *Heras Institute Seminar on Bandra*- A changing Subarb, (Bombay, 1986)

Pio Edwina 'Conversions in Bassein (1534-1739) A critique' in *Indica*, Vol. 24, No (Bombay, September 1987)

Scottschneider David A., "William Carey, Modern Missions and the Moravian Influence" in *International Bulletin* Vol. 22, No.1 (Jan 1998)

Seth M. J., "The Second Oldest Christian Church in Bengal" in *Bengal Past and Present*, Jan-June 1936

Silva R. D., 'The active Missionary orders in Portuguese Bassein' in *Proceedings of 35th Session of Indian History Congress (IHC)* (Jadhavpur, 1974)

Silva R. D., "Early Phase of Christianity in Bassein " in *Proceedings of 33rd Session of IHC,* (Muzzafarpur, 1973)

Silva R. D.' "Education Finance of Portuguese Bassein" in *Proceedings of 34th Session of IHC,* (Chandigarh, 1973)

Soares A., "Four Centuries of Education" in *The Mission Field* (Bombay, 1925)

Souza Daniel D., "Tibet-Hindustan Mission as the Nucleus of North India Mission" in *Indian Missiological Review* Vol. 12, No. 2 (July 1990)

Temple R. C., The Name " Bassein" in *The Indian Antiquary*, reprint, (New Delhi, January 1893)

Tupper Martin K. 'The Opium Trade" published in *BG*, Oct 11, 1856

(D) Research Dissertations

Bhave Neelima, *Social Change in Early19th century Maharashtra as reflected in contemporary literary output:* Project report of Asiatic Society Fellowship, (Mumbai, Jan-Dec 2000)

Cheema K. S., British policy in Western India with special reference to the Bombay City and the Deccan, 1830-1875, Ph.D Thesis (Bombay, 2001)

Dalvi D. A., *Renaissance in the 19th Century Maharashtra,* 1832-1874, Ph.D Thesis (Bombay, 1990)

Fernandes Austin, *History of Sawantwadi From 1800 to 1948*, Ph.D Thesis (Bombay, 2003)

Joshi Arun R., *Renaissance in Western India 1823-1892,* Part I, Ph.D Thesis, (Mumbai, 1976)

Joshi Sulabha, "An evaluative Study a few selected continuing education programmes for women for weaker section, run by YWCA, Bombay", *Masters Diploma in Adult and Continuing Education of SNDT*, (Mumbai, May 1987)

Krishnamurti Sulochana, *English Education and its Impact*, Ph.D Thesis, (Bombay, 1987)

Mahajan S. G., *History of the Public Library Movement in Western Maharashtra (1805-1921),* Ph.D. Thesis, (Pune 1979)

Mosheni Mehdi, *Economic History of Bombay in the Nineteenth Century*, Ph.D Thesis, (Bombay, 1998)

Narayanan Aruna, *History of Bombay 1885-1905* Ph.D. Thesis (Bombay, 1993)

Nilesh Preeta, 'Law and Social Change', *Four Judicial Cases in 19th Century Bombay*, Ph.D Thesis, (Bombay, December 2000)

Patwardhan Sheela, "*History of Development of Women Education in the Central Division of the Bombay Presidency 1818-1905,* Ph.D. Thesis (Pune, 1990)

Pandya Shubhada S., *Leprosy in the Bombay Presidency, 1840-1897, Perceptions and Approaches to its Control* (Bombay, 2001)

Ramanna Mridulla, *English Education and Social Change in Bombay City 1815-1858*, Ph.D Thesis (Bombay, 1985)

Ranade Rekha, *Sir Bartel Frere and his Times: A Study of its Bombay Years 1862-67*, Ph.D Thesis, (Pune, 1988)

Rodrigues Jenifer, *A History of the Catholic Christian Community in Maharashtra* 1850-1950, Ph.D Thesis (Bombay, 2007)

Shirgaonkar S. R., *Protestant Christ Missionarianche Maharashrtatil Chalwal* (in marathi), Ph.D Thesis, (Bombay, 1972)

Saswadkar P. L., *Brahmendra Swami- His Life and Role in Maratha History*, Ph.D Thesis (Poona,1961)

Sutar A. M., *Christianity in the Western Maharashtra in the 19th Century*, Ph.D Thesis (Kolhapur, 1980)

(E) Newspapers

Amrita Shodhan, "*The Changing face of Bombay*", Mumbai News Line, (Mumbai, 26th June 2000)

DNA January 26 (Mumbai, 2008)

Fr. Francis D' Britto, "*If you have a Thai and a Korean Christ Why not a Indian one*", Times of India (Mumbai, 16th December 2001)

M. S. Naravane, *"Portuguese Churches at Bassein"*, Maritime Heritage Foundation (Quarterly Newsletter), Vol. I, No. 3 (Mumbai, 2001)

Mumbai Mirror, January 4, (Mumbai, 2007)

Puneet N. Yadav *Barefoot Teachers get a taste of history* in *DNA* 12th April (Mumbai, 2007)

(F) Private Communication

Fr. Aubrey Mascrahnes, Heras Institute (Fort, 5th February 2007)

Fr. Bishop Dabre, Vasai Diocese (Vasai, 4th December 2006)

Fr. Julian Saldanha, St. Pius Seminary (Goregaon, 10th October 2006)

Fr. Rudolf Andrade, Uran Church (Uran, 25th August 2005)

Mr. and Mrs. Dhanawade (Vengurla, 10th October 2005)

Index